Reviving the Soul

The Best of Andrew Murray's Devotional Writings

Reviving the Soul

The Best of Andrew Murray's Devotional Writings

Edited and compiled by
Robert Backhouse

Marshall Pickering
An Imprint of HarperCollinsPublishers

Marshall Pickering is an Imprint of
HarperCollins*Religious*
Part of HarperCollins*Publishers*
77–85 Fulham Palace Road, London W6 8JB

First published in Great Britain
in 1995 by Marshall Pickering

1   3   5   7   9   10   8   6   4   2

A catalogue record for this book is
available from the British Library

ISBN 0 551 02909–9

Typeset by Harper Phototypesetters Limited,
Northampton, England
Printed and bound in Great Britain by
HarperCollinsManufacturing Glasgow

Contents

Introduction

Andrew Murray has an abiding influence on Christians today, a hundred years after his prime of life. Three reasons for this can be gleaned from the preface to *Abide in Christ*, where he highlights his distinctively devotional approach. First, he writes, we should seek a living union with Christ:

> If in our orthodox churches, abiding in Christ, living in union with him, to the experience of his daily and hourly presence and keeping, were preached with the same distinctiveness and urgency as his atonement and pardon through his death, I am confident that many would be found to accept with gladness the invitation to such a life. Its influence would be manifest in their experience of the purity and the power, the love and the joy, the fruit-bearing, and all the blessedness which the Saviour linked with abiding in him.

Secondly, we should seek a whole-hearted surrender to Christ:

> I earnestly pray that the Lord would, by whatever means, make tens of thousands of his dear children who are still living divided lives, to see how he claims them wholly for himself, and how the whole-hearted surrender to abide in him alone brings complete

joy. Let each of us who has begun to taste the sweetness of this life, yield himself wholly to be a witness to the grace and power of our Lord to keep us united to himself, and seek by word and walk to win others to follow him fully.

Thirdly, growth takes time:

It needs time to grow into Jeus the Vine: do not expect to abide in him unless you will give him that time. It is not enough to read God's Word, or the meditations offered here, and then to ask God to bless us. No. It needs time, day by day, with Jesus and with God.

Andrew Murray, 1828-1917, was born in Graaff-Reimet, South Africa, son of a Scottish Dutch Reformed Church minister. He grew up in South Africa, but spent seven years as a student in Scotland, studying for his MA degree at Aberdeen University. After this he spent three years in Utrecht, Holland, studying theology.

Murray's time in Scotland was especially formative. He sat at the feet of a number of Presbyterian preachers and scholars, such as M. Cheyne, the Bonar brothers and Chalmers. One man in particular, the Rev. William C. Burns, was responsible for Murray's keen interest in holiness and revival.

Murray returned to South Africa, where he lived the rest of his life. He was ordained in 1848 and became the first permanent Dutch Reformed Church minister north of the Orange River, on the frontier of South Africa. In 1860 Murray went to Cape Colony and a year later a revival movement broke out in his Worcester pastorate. This swept like a prairie fire through South Africa. Murray was quickly labelled a 'revivalist' and became much sought after as a conference speaker. He travelled to Great Britain, continental Europe, America, India, China, Australia, New Zealand and Canada.

One of the main reasons for the abiding worth and excellence of

Murray's writings is that they stress the vital necessity of a fruitful, inner, spiritual life. Ralph G. Turnbull wrote: 'the secret of our author is a sane mysticism, an inner life of the spirit out of which is the radiance of Christlike character and influence.' Murray spoke and wrote about subjects people have a thirst for: holiness, prayer, 'pentecostal' power, and Christlikeness. Murray's most popular books were on personal piety, such as *The New Life, The Holiest of All, With Christ in the School of Prayer* and *Absolute Surrender*. Wherever he went, Murray never tired of emphasizing the importance of these devotional topics. Alexander Whyte summed this up once, in a letter to Andrew Murray: 'Happy man, you have been chosen and ordained of God *to go to the heart of things*.'

Murray also always attempted to expound Scripture and base everything he had to say on the teaching of the Bible, rather than on his or someone else's ideas. Had he lived today he might well have been thought of as a 'charismatic' Christian. Books of his like *The Full Blessing of Pentecost* and *The Second Blessing* have undoubtedly influenced modern-day Pentecostalism. Unlike so many Christian speakers today, Andew Murray would have been welcomed with open arms by a wide variety of Christian conferences – from the Keswick Convention to Spring Harvest. Interdenominational movements such as the Inter-Varsity Fellowship, both in America and England, were also much influenced by Murray's teaching. It is hard to chart exactly how much influence Murray had in China, but his writings made a great impact on the famous Chinese Christian leader Watchman Nee (1903-1972), who spoke and wrote in a very similar vein.

Murray wrote some 250 books and pamphlets in English and Dutch. While most focused on personal holiness, Murray also became immersed in the raging social battles of South Africa, and was a firm opponent of both British imperialism and the Afrikaner nationalist movement.

Murray's unashamed emphasis on the necessity of Christian experience helped the birth of the African independent church movement. Some of the spiritual lessons from this movement are being slowly assimilated by Christians in the West. The African independent church movement has over 12,000 churches, in 34 countries, with over 20,000,000 members. They are now the fourth largest strand of Christianity, alongside the Roman Catholic, Orthodox and Protestant traditions. They emphasize a radical biblicism rather than the fundamentalism of some Christian groups. They do not teach a particular doctrine of the inspiration of the Bible. They are more interested in people discovering the *living* word of the *living* God, and so they emphasize his *living* presence in everyday experience. This is exactly in line with the preaching and writing of Andrew Murray, as the pages of this book will show.

In his outstanding biography of Andrew Murray, *The Life of Andrew Murray of South Africa* (Marshall, Morgan and Scott, 1919), J. Du Plessis gives this glowing testimonial:

> To a greater extent than almost any other religious writer of our age Mr Murray possessed the insight and the authority of one of the prophets of olden time. At critical moments in the history of the church he never failed to raise his voice and to direct attention to the real issues. Those who are intimate with his career in South Africa will agree that there was no man who could rise to a great occasion like Andrew Murray. He possessed the gift of speaking, at the right season, the right and just word, of opening up the larger view and kindling the nobler emotions. This gift he exercised in his writings also.

Robert Backhouse
Norwich, 1994

God: Father, Son and Holy Spirit

Different Roles of the Trinity

Because ye are sons, God sent forth the Spirit of his
Son into your hearts, crying 'Abba, Father'.
(GALATIANS 4:6)

When God had revealed his love in the gift of his Son, his great work was completed. When Christ had died upon the cross, with his 'It is finished', and had been raised up again, and seated upon the throne of God, his work was completed. Then began the dispensation of the Spirit, whose office it was to reveal and impart all that the work of God and of Christ had prepared. This work of the Holy Spirit has not yet been accomplished; it is for this that Christ sits upon the throne, henceforth expecting till all his enemies be made his footstool.

The great difference between the work of the Father and the Son, and the work of the Holy Spirit, is that while the former wrought out their work for and on behalf of men, as a salvation prepared for their acceptance, the office of the Holy Spirit is to impart to them that grace which enables them to accept and to live out what the Father and the Son have provided. The great mark of

1

the operation of the Spirit is that in this dispensation his work and man's work are inextricably linked together, so that whatever the Spirit does he does through man, and whatever is to be done in the Kingdom of God it is man who does it. In the world of men the Holy Spirit can manifest himself in no way than in, and as, the spirit of man. It is the dispensation in which we are to prove what man's part is in the carrying out of God's plan.

[From *Aids to Devotion*]

The Trinity and God's Love

Christ Jesus was born in Bethlehem, and just so I am born again by the Holy Spirit. But Christ Jesus had to be born again the second time. He had to live and be tried, tempted and tested, to be developed and to be perfected, and then he had to give up his life, and out of the grave, when he was in hopeless, helpless, dark death, God raised him up. That is what the Christian must come to. The birth in Bethlehem is the likeness of my new birth when I was converted, but the birth from the grave when Christ became the first-born of the dead is the likeness and promise of that full birth in which the power of the death and life of Christ come into me, and I know what it is to be dead with Christ and risen with him – dead unto self and made alive unto God. Let the one great thing that you do from the morning early when you awake, to the evening when you go to sleep, be this: 'Have trust in God for what he can do in making you partakers of Christ's death as the death to self, and his life as a life to God and in God, a life of perfect love.' Say to God: 'My Father, I trust in thee for what thou alone canst do,' and say to yourself, 'I am going to believe in God, in the mighty power with which he raised Christ from the dead to work in me and in God's children around me.'

'What are we to expect?' We know what we are seeking and we know what we have got to do, but now comes the question, 'What are we to expect?' My answer is, 'Let us expect something beyond all expectation.' We have so often limited God by our thoughts, and we are doing it still. Yet Paul speaks of 'love that passeth knowledge,' and then says further, 'God is able to do above all that we can ask or think.' Now prepare yourself for something that passeth knowledge, for something that is above what you can think, and give God the honour of doing something divine. Then, further, if you ask, 'What must I expect?' I would sum it up in these words: 'Jesus himself.' The work of God the Father is to beget God the Son, and that is the work which goes on through eternity. When we read of the eternal generation, that does not mean that it was a thing in the past. Eternity – what is eternity? Eternity is ever going on. It is an ever-present now, and the one work of God the Father is to beget the Son. What do I expect? I expect God to give to all who are prepared the indwelling Christ in their hearts, in a power they have never known, so that they may get rooted and grounded in love, and know the love that passeth knowledge. That is what we need and what we may expect. God has nothing for us but Jesus. Anything beyond that God cannot give us, but God is willing and able to give this – the living Son born afresh into us. And then he reveals him to us, and when the living Christ dwell in us, he will break open the fountain of love within us. That is what we want. Expect it now. Fix your eye upon Jesus, Jesus himself. He must do it. He has done it. He has taught us on Calvary what it is that he gave up his life for, that in his fellowship with us our old man might be crucified with him. He has done it all for us. We want God to reveal to us what that means, and to make us partakers of it. You may say: 'I have so often tried to believe in Jesus, but there has been so much failure and I am so ignorant.' Paul prayed that God would strengthen believers mightily by the Holy Spirit. It is only the Father who can reveal the Son, and he does it only by the Holy Spirit.

When Jesus dwells in us, then we are filled with love unto all the fullness of God – the Triune God, not only in heaven but in our hearts. Fix your hearts upon this: the Father must do it, and what the Father will do, I must expect – the Father, God Almighty, to give this Jesus into my heart as an indwelling Saviour; what the Father does is to strengthen us with might by the Holy Spirit in the inner man. Expect that. Fix your heart upon God. That is the one way to the Father, and as you go along, step by step, let your heart be filled with this: God is Love. Love is the divine omnipotence. Love is the life and the glory of God. Yes, God is Love. There is the love of the Father, and the love of the Son, and the love of the Spirit. Let us fix our hope in the love of the Father giving the Son into our hearts. Let us rejoice in the Son coming with God's perfect love to dwell within. Let us bow in stillness while the Holy Spirit works mightily within us to shed abroad the love. God will come unto us, and will bring us into his banqueting house, and his banner over us will be love. May God teach the waiting heart to expect this, nothing less than the Perfect Love of God perfected in us.

[From *Love Made Perfect*]

The Trinity's Unity

For this cause I bow my knees unto the Father that he
would grant you that ye may be strengthened with
power through his Spirit in the inward man; that
Christ may dwell in your hearts through faith; to the
end that ye, being rooted and grounded in love, may
be strong to know the love of Christ which passeth
knowledge, that ye may be filled unto all the fullness
of God. Now unto him that is able to do exceeding
abundantly above all that we ask or think, according
to the power that worketh in us [i.e. the Holy
Spirit], *unto him be the glory in Christ Jesus for ever*
and ever. Amen.
(EPHESIANS 3:14-21)

4

These words are remarkable for the way in which they present the truth of the holy Trinity in its bearing on our practical life. Many Christians understand that it is right and needful at different times, in the persuit of the Christian life, to give special attention to the three Persons of the blessed Trinity. They often feel it difficult to combine the various truths into one, and to know how to worship the three in one. Our text reveals the wondrous relationship and the perfect unity. We have the Spirit within us as the power of God, and yet he does not work at our will or his own. It is the Father who, according to the riches of his glory, grants us to be strengthened 'through the Spirit in the inner man.' It is the Father, who does exceeding abundantly above what we ask or think 'according to the power that worketh in us.' So far from the presence of the Spirit within us being to us instead of God, he renders us more absolutely and unceasingly dependent on the Father. The Spirit can only work as the Father works through him. We need to combine the two truths – a deep, reverent, truthful consciousness of the Holy Spirit as indwelling, with a continual and dependent waiting on the Father to work through him.

Even so with Christ. We bow our knees to God as Father in the name of the Son. We ask him to strengthen us through the Spirit with the one object that Christ may dwell in our heart. So the Son leads to the Father and the Father again reveals the Son in us. And then, again, as the Son dwells in the heart, and it is rooted and grounded in love, drawing life out of divine love as its soil, bringing forth fruits and doing works of love, we are led on to be filled with all the fullness of God. The whole heart with the inner and outer life becomes the scene of the blessed interchange of the operation of the holy Three. As our hearts believe this we give glory through Christ to him who is able to do more than we can think by his Holy Spirit.

What a wonderful salvation this of which our heart is the scene; the Father ever breathing his Spirit into us, and by his daily renewing fitting it to be the home of Christ; the Holy Spirit ever revealing and forming Christ within us, so that his very nature, and disposition, and character becomes ours; the Son imparting his life of love, and leading us on to be filled with all the fullness of God.

This is meant to be our everyday religion. Oh! let us worship the three-in-one God in the fullness of faith every day. In whatever direction our Bible study and prayer lead us, let this ever be the centre from which we go out and to which we return. We were created in the image of the three-in-one God. The salvation by which God restores us is an inward salvation; it is nothing to us if it is not wrought in our heart and enjoyed there. The God who saves us can do it in no other way than as the indwelling God, filling us with all his fullness. Let us worship and wait; let us believe and give him glory.

Have you ever noticed in Ephesians how the three Persons of the Trinity are always mentioned together?

1:3   The Father, Jesus Christ, spiritual (i.e. Holy Ghost) blessings.

1:12,13   The Father, to the praise of his glory in Christ, sealed with the Holy Spirit.

1:17   The Father, our Lord Jesus, the Spirit of wisdom.

2:18   Access through Christ, in one Spirit, unto the Father.

2:22   In Christ, a habitation of God, through the Spirit.

3:4-9   The mystery of Christ, hid in God, preached by the grace of God, revealed by the Spirit.

4:4-6   One Spirit, one Lord, one God and Father.

5:18-20   Filled with the Spirit, giving thanks to God, in the name of Christ.

6:10-18   Strong in the Lord, the whole armour of God, the sword of the Spirit, praying in the Spirit.

As you study and compare these passages, and seek to gather up their teaching in some true and humble conception of the glory of our God, notice specially what an intensely practical truth this of the holy Trinity is. Scripture teaches little of its mystery in the divine nature, almost all it has to say has reference to God's work in us, and our faith and experience of his salvation.

A true faith in the Trinity will make us strong, and enable us to become God-possessed Christians. The divine Spirit making himself one with our life and inner being, the blessed Son dwelling in us, as the way to perfect fellowship with God; the Father, through the Spirit and the Son, working out day by day his purpose – that we be filled with all the fullness of God.

Let us bow our knees unto the Father! Then the mystery of the Trinity will be known and experienced.

[From *Prayer's Inner Chamber*]

The Sprinkling of Blood, and the Trinity

> *Peter ... to ... the elect according to the*
> *foreknowledge of God the Father, through*
> *sanctification of the Spirit, unto obedience and*
> *sprinkling of the blood of Jesus Christ: grace unto*
> *you, and peace, be multiplied.*
> (1 PETER 1:1-2)

The Tri-unity of the Godhead is often considered as merely a matter of doctrine, and having no close relationship to the Christian life.

This is not the view of the New Testament, when it describes the work of redemption, or the idea of the life of God. In the epistles the three persons are constantly named together, so that in each activity of grace all three together have a share in it. God is triune; but in everything that he does, and at all times, the three are one. This is in entire agreement with what we see in nature. A trinity is found in everything. There is the hidden, inner nature; the outward form; and the effect. It is not otherwise in the Godhead. The Father is the eternal being – I AM – the hidden foundation of all things, and fountain of all life. The Son is the outward form, the express image, the revelation of God. The Spirit is the executive power of the Godhead. The nature of the hidden unity is revealed and made known in the Son, and that is imparted to us is experienced by us through the agency of the Spirit. In all their activities the three are inseparably one.

Everything is *of* the Father, everything is *in* the Son, everything is *through* the Spirit.

In the words of our text, which Peter writes to believers to whom also he sends his greetings, we find the relationship in which each redeemed one stands to the three persons of the Godhead is clearly set forth.

Foreknowledge
They are elect 'according to the foreknowledge of God' (1 Peter 1:2). The source of our redemption is in the counsel of God.

Sanctification
They are chosen 'through sanctification of the Spirit' (1 Peter 1:2): the entire carrying out of the counsel of God is through the Holy Spirit, and the sanctification and the impartation of divine holiness which he works.

Obedience
They are elect 'unto obedience and sprinkling of the blood of Jesus Christ' (1 Peter 1:2): the final purpose of God is the restoration of man to a state where the will of God will be done on earth, as it is done in heaven, and where everything will resound to the glory of the free grace which has been revealed so gloriously in the death and blood of the Son of God.

The place which 'the sprinkling of blood' takes is most remarkable. It is mentioned last, as the great final end, in which according to the foreknowledge of the Father, the sanctification of the Spirit, and submission to the obedience of Christ, it finds completion.

[From *The Blood of the Cross*]

Channels for the Holy Trinity

1. God is an ever flowing fountain of pure love and blessedness.

2. Christ is the reservoir wherein the fullness of God was made visible as grace, and has been opened for us.

3. The Holy Spirit is the stream of living water that flows from under the throne of God and of the Lamb.

4. The redeemed, God's believing children, are the channels through which the love of the Father, the grace of Christ, and the powerful operation of the Spirit are brought to the earth, there to be imparted to others.

5. What an impression we gain here of the wonderful partnership into which God takes us up, as dispensers of the grace of God! Prayer, when we chiefly pray for ourselves, is but the beginning of the life of prayer. The glory of prayer is that we have power as intercessors to bring the grace of Christ, and the engergizing power of the Spirit, upon those souls which are still in darkness.

6. The more surely the channel is connected with the reservoir, the more certainly will the water flow unhindered through it. The more we are occupied in prayer with the fullness of Christ, and with the Spirit who proceeds from him, and the more firmly we abide in fellowship with him, the more surely will our lives be happy and strong. This, however, is still only a preparation for the reality. The more we give ourselves up to fellowship and converse with the triune God, the sooner shall we receive the courage and ability to pray down blessing on souls, on ministers, and on the Church around us.

7. Are you truly a channel which is always open, so that the water may flow through you to the thirsty ones in the dry land? Have you offered unreservedly to God, to become a bearer of the energizing operations of the Holy Spirit?

8. Is it not, perhaps, because you have thought only of yourself in prayer that you have experienced so little of the power of prayer? Do understand that the new prayer life into which you have entered in the Lord Jesus can be sustained and strengthened only

by the intercession in which you labour for the souls around you, to bring them to know the Lord? Oh, meditate on this – God an ever flowing fountain of love and blessing, and I his child, a living channel through which every day the Spirit and life can be brought to the earth!

[From *The Prayer Life*]

In God's Service

The Will of God, the Salvation of the Perishing

*It is not the will of your Father which is in heaven
that one of these little ones should perish.*
(MATTHEW 18:14)

What inspirations these words have given to God's workers on behalf of orphans, of waifs and strays, of children in India perishing from famine, or in Africa from slavery. What courage to thousands of teachers for the little ones of whom they had charge. What patience and strength it has breathed into the hearts of those who have had to deal with the neglected and the outcast in every land. It was their joy and hope that they knew that they were doing the will of God. Yes more, they knew that the mighty will of God was working itself out through them. These all have experienced how blessed it was at times to look away from their own little and limited interests and duties, and to cast themselves into the mighty stream of God's loving will which is slowly but surely working out his blessed purpose. There they found themselves in fellowship with God's own Son, and with the saints of all ages, whose one glory it had been that they had known and fulfilled the redeeming will of God.

[From *Thy Will Be Done*]

11

Bearing Fruit in every Good Work

*... That ye might walk worthy of the Lord unto all
pleasing, being fruitful in every good work, and
increasing in the knowledge of God; strengthened
with all might, according to his glorious power, unto
all patience and longsuffering with joyfulness.*
(COLOSSIANS 1:10-11).

There is a difference between fruit and work. Fruit is that which
comes spontaneously, without thought or will, the natural and
necessary outcome of a healthy life. Work, on the contrary, is the
product of effort guided by intelligent thought and will. In the
Chrsitian life we have the two elements in combination. All the
true work must be fruit, the growth and product of our inner life,
the operation of God's Spirit within us. And yet all fruit must be
work, the effort of our deliberate purpose and exertion. In the
words, 'bearing fruit in every good work', we have the practical
summing up of the truth taught in some previous chapters.
Because God works by his life in us, the work we do is fruit.
Because, in the faith of his working, we have to will and to work, the
fruit we bear is work. In the harmony between the perfect spon-
taneity that comes from God's life and Spirit animating us, and our
co-operation with him as his intelligent fellow labourers, lies the
secret of all true work.

In the words that precede our text, 'filled with the knowledge of
his will in all wisdom and spiritual understanding', we have the
human side, our need of knowledge and wisdom; in the words that
follow, 'strengthened with all might, according to his glorious
power', we have the divine side. God teaching and strengthening,
man learning to understand and patiently do his will; such is the
double life that will be fruitful in every good work.

It has been said of the Christian life that the natural man must
first become spiritual, and then again the spiritual man must

become natural. As the whole natural life becomes truly spiritual, all our work will partake of the nature of fruit, the outgrowth of the life of God within us. And as the spiritual again becomes perfectly natural to us, a second nature in which we are wholly at home, all the fruit will bear the mark of true work, calling into full exercise every faculty of our being.

'Being fruitful in every good work.' The words suggest again the great thought, that as an apple tree or vine is planted solely for its fruit, so the great purpose of our redemption is that God may have us for his work and service. It has been well said: 'The end of man is an Action and not a Thought, though it were of the noblest.' It is in his work that the nobility of man's nature as ruler of the world is proved. It is for good works that we have been created anew in Christ Jesus: it is when men see our good works that our Father in heaven will be glorified, and have the honour which is his due for his workmanship. In the parable of the vine our Lord insisted on this: 'He that abideth in Me, and I in him, the same beareth much fruit.' 'Herein is My Father glorified, that ye bear much fruit.' Nothing is more to the honour of a gardener than to succeed in raising an abundant crop – much fruit brings glory to God. . . . The call to be fruitful in every good work is for every Christian without exception. The grace that fits for it, of which the prayer, in which our words are found, speaks, is for every one. Every branch fruitful in every good work – this is an essential part of God's Gospel.

'Being fruitful in every good work.' Let us study to get a full impression of the two sides of this divine truth. God's first creation of life was in the vegetable kingdom. There it was a life without anything of will or self-effort, all growth and fruit was simply his own direct work, the spontaneous outcome of his hidden working. In the creation of the animal kingdom there was an advance. A new element was introduced – thought and will and work. In man these two elements were united in perfect harmony. The absolute dependence of the grass and the lily on the God who clothes them with their beauty were to be the groundwork of our relationship – nature has nothing but what it receives from God. Our works are to be fruit, the product of a God-given power. But to this was added the true mark of our God-likeness, the power of will and independent action: all fruit is to be our own work. As we grasp this we shall see how the most absolute acknowledgement of our having nothing in ourselves is consistent with the deepest sense of obligation and the strongest will to exert our powers to the very utmost. We shall learn to study the prayer of our text as those who must seek all their wisdom and strength from God alone. And we shall boldly give ourselves, as those who are responsible for the use of that wisdom and strength, to the diligence and the sacrifice and the effort needed for a life bearing fruit in every good work.

[From *Working for God*]

Greater Works

Verily, verily, I say unto you, he that believeth on me,
the works that I shall do shall he do also; and greater
works than these shall he do; because I go to the
Father. And whatsoever ye shall ask in my name, that
shall I do, that the Father may be glorified in the Son.
If ye shall ask any thing in my name, I will do it.
(JOHN 14:12-14)

In the words (verse 10), 'The Father that dwelleth in me, he doeth the works,' Christ had revealed the secret of his and of all divine service – man yielding himself for God to dwell and to work in him. When Christ now promises, 'he that believeth on me, the works that I do shall he do also,' the law of the divine inworking remains unchanged. In us, as much as in him, one might even say a thousand times more than with him, it must remain: The Father in me doeth the works. With Christ and with us, it is 'the same God who worketh all in all'.

14

How this is to come about we learn from the works, 'he that believeth on me.' That does not only mean for salvation, as a Saviour from sin. It means much more. Christ had just said (verses 10-11), 'Believest thou not that I am in the Father, and the Father in me? . . . the Father that dwelleth in me, he doeth the works.' We need to believe in Christ as the One in and through whom the Father never stops working. To believe in Christ is to receive him into the heart. When we see the Father's working inseparably connected with Christ, we know that to believe in Christ, and receive him into the heart, is to receive the Father dwelling in him and working through him. The works his disciples are to do cannot possibly be done in any other way than his own were done.

This becomes still clearer from what our Lord adds: 'And greater works than these shall he do; because I go unto the Father' (John 14:12). What the greater works are, is evident. The disciples at Pentecost with three thousand baptized, and multitudes added to the Lord; Philip in Samaria, with the whole city filled with joy; the men of Cyprus and Cyrene, and, later on, Barnabas in Antioch, with many people added to the Lord; Paul in his travels, and a countless number of Christ's servants down to our day, have, in the ingathering of souls, done what the Master condescendingly calls greater works than he did in the days of his humiliation and weakness.

The reason why it should be so our Lord makes plain, 'because I go to the Father.' When he entered the glory of the Father, all power in heaven and on earth was given to him as our Redeemer. In a way more glorious than ever the Father was to work through him; and he then to work through his disciples. Even as his own work on earth, in the days of the weakness of the flesh, had been in a power received from the Father in heaven, so his people, in their weakness, would do works like his, and greater works in the same way, through a power received from heaven. The law of the divine working is unchangeable: God's work can only be done by God himself. . . .

The words that follow bring out still more strongly the great truths we have been learning, that it is our Lord himself who will work all in us, even as the Father did in him, and that our posture is to be exactly what his was, one of entire receptivity and dependence. 'Greater works than these shall he do, because I go to the Father. And whatsoever ye shall ask in my name, that will I do.' Christ connects the greater works the believer is to do, with the promise that he will do whatever the believer asks. Prayer in the name of Jesus will be the expression of that dependence that waits on him for his working, to which he gives the promise: 'Whatsoever ye ask, I will do, in you and through you.' And when he adds, 'that the Father may be glorified in the Son', he reminds us how he had glorified the Father, by yielding to him as Father, to work all his work in himself as Son. In heaven Christ would still glorify the Father, by receiving from the Father the power, and working in his disciples what the Father would. The creature, as the Son himself, can give the Father no higher glory than yielding to him to work all. The believer can glorify the Father in no other way than the Son, by an absolute and unceasing dependence on the Son, in whom the Father works, to communicate and work in us all the Father's work. 'If ye shall ask anything in my name, that will I do,' and so you shall do greater works.

Let every believer strive to learn the one blessed lesson. I am to do the works I have seen Christ doing; I may even do greater works as I yield myself to Christ exalted on the throne, in a power he did not have on earth; I may count on him working in me according to that power. My one need is the spirit of dependence and waiting, and prayer and faith, that Christ abiding in me will do the works, even whatsoever I ask.

[From *Working for God*]

The Work of Soul-Saving

Brethren, if any of you do err from the truth, and one convert him; Let him know that he which converteth a sinner from the error of his ways shall save a soul from death, and shall hide a multitude of sins.

(JAMES 5:19–20)

We sometimes hesitate to speak of men being converted and saved by men. Scripture here twice uses the expression of one man converting another, and once of his saving him. Let us not hesitate to accept it as part of our work, of our high prerogative as the sons of God, to convert and to save men. 'For it is God who worketh in us.'

'Shall save a soul from death. . . .' Every workman studies the material in which he works: the carpenter the wood, the goldsmith the gold. 'Our works are wrought in God.' In our good works we deal with souls. Even when we can at first do no more than reach and help their bodies, our aim is the soul. For these Christ came to die. For these God has appointed us to watch and labour. Let us study these. What care a huntsman or a fisherman takes to know the habits of the spoil he seeks. Let us remember that it needs Divine wisdom and training and skill to become winners of souls. The only way to get that training and skill is to begin to work: Christ himself will teach each one who waits on him.

In that training the Church with its ministers has a part to take. The daily experience of ordinary life and teaching prove how often there exist in a man unsuspected powers, which must be called out by training before they are known to be there. When a man thus becomes conscious and master of the power there is in himself he is, as it were, a new creature; the power and enjoyment of life is doubled. Every believer has hidden within himself the power of saving souls. The kingdom of heaven is within us as a seed, and every one of the gifts and graces of the spirit are each also hidden seed. The highest aim of the ministry is to waken the consciousness of this hidden seed of power to save souls. A depressing sense of ignorance or impotence keeps many back. James writes: 'Let him who converts another know that he has saved a soul from death.' Every believer needs to be taught to know and use the wondrous blessed power with which he has been endowed. When God said to Abraham: 'I will bless thee, then shall all the nations of the earth be blessed,' he called him to a faith not only in the blessing that would come to him from above, but in the power of blessing he would be in the world. It is a wonderful moment in the life of a child of God when he sees that the second blessing is as sure as the first.

'He shall save a soul.' Our Lord bears the name of Jesus, Saviour. He is the embodiment of God's saving love. Saving souls is his own great work, is his work alone. As our faith in him grows to know and receive all there is in him, as he lives in us, and dwells in our heart and disposition, saving souls will become the great work to which our life will be given. We shall be the willing and intelligent instrument through whom he will do his mighty work.

'If any err, and one convert him, he which converteth a sinner shall save a soul.' The words suggest personal work. We chiefly think of large gatherings to whom the Gospel is preached; the thought here is of one who has erred and is sought after. We increasingly do our work through associations and organizations. 'If one convert him, he saveth a soul'; it is the love and labour of some individual believer that has won the erring one back. It is this we need in the Church of Christ – every believer who truly follows Jesus Christ looking out for those who are erring from the way, loving them, and labouring to help them back. Not one of us may say, 'Am I my brother's keeper?' We are in the world only and solely that as the members of Christ's body we may continue and carry out his saving work. As saving souls was and is his work, his joy, his glory, let it be ours. . . .

'Know that he which converteth a sinner shall save a soul.' 'If ye know these things, happy are ye if you do them.'. . . . Is there not more than one Christian around me wandering from the way, needing loving help and not unwilling to receive it? Are there not some whom I could take by the hand, and encourage to begin again? Are there not many who have never been in the right way, for some of whom Christ Jesus would use me, if I were truly at his disposal?

If I feel afraid – let me believe that the love of God as a seed dwells within me, not only calling but enabling me actually to do the work. Let me yield myself to the Holy Spirit to fill my heart with that love, and fit me for its service. Jesus the Saviour lives to save; he dwells in me; he will do his saving work through me. 'Know that he which converteth a sinner shall save a soul from death, and cover a multitude of sins.'

[From *Working for God*]

Doing God's Will

The Bond of Union with our Lord Jesus

Whosoever shall do the will of my Father which is in heaven, the same is my brother, and sister, and mother. (MATTHEW 12:50)

The way into the most intimate union with Christ is very simple: doing the will of his Father. Of one who does this he says: the same is my brother and sister and mother.

What does this mean? A brother or sister, or one who is born of the same father, shares the same love, and home, and care; bears in some measure the same likeness in disposition and character; is bound to his other brothers and sisters by these ties in a common love. When Christ calls one of us a brother or sister, it means nothing less. Like him, we are born of God: the Father's life, and love, and likeness are in us, as in him. As the elder brother, he gives to us and shares with us all he has; he pours out on us all the love with which the Father loves him. He is not ashamed to call us brethren. He delights in our relationship to him, in our welfare, in our society. He only lives to find his happiness in us, and in what he can do for us. The one thing he longs for is that we should know and claim our relationship, should come to him and be free with him as no brother or sister ever was.

Let us pray for the quickening of the Holy Spirit to make all this a reality. Just think of what a joy would come into the believer's life if he truly realized this: Jesus loves me as a brother, yes me, just as I am, all unworthy and sinful. He loves me as a brother. No elder brother ever watched over a weak younger brother so tenderly as my elder brother watches over me. He wants me to know it. He gives the command: 'Say to my brethren, I ascend to my Father and your Father.' He wants me to know it; he longs that I should live with him as a brother in the Father's presence: he is able and willing to make the possibility a reality. He invites us to come and say in tender reverence, O my holy elder brother – I dare scarce say, and yet I may and I will – I am thy brother; thou art my brother. He can enable us to realize it and abide in his presence all the day and every day.

[From *Thy Will Be Done*]

Determining God's Will

There is a general will of God for all his children, which we can, in some measure, learn out of the Bible. But there is a special individual application of these commands – God's will concerning each of us personally, which only the Holy Spirit can teach. And he will not teach it except to those who have taken the vow of obedience.

This is the reason why there are so many unanswered prayers for God to make known his will. Jesus said, 'If any man *wills* to do his will, he shall know of the teaching, whether it be of God.' If a man's will is really set on doing God's will, that is, if his heart is given up to do, and he as a consequence does it so far as he knows it, he shall know what God has further to teach him.

It is simply what is true of every scholar with the art he studies, of every apprentice with his trade, of every man in business – doing is the one condition of truly knowing. And so obedience, the doing of God's will so far as we know, and the will and the vow to do it all as he reveals it, is the spiritual organ, the capacity for receiving the true knowledge of what is God's will for each of us.

In connection with this let me press upon you three things:

1.*Seek to have a deep sense of your very great ignorance of God's will, and of your impotence by any effort to know it aright.*

The consciousness of ignorance lies at the root of true teachableness. 'The meek will he guide in the way' – those who humbly confess their need of teaching. Head-knowledge gives only human thoughts without power. God by his Spirit gives a living knowledge that enters the love of the heart, and works effectually.

2. *Cultivate a strong faith that God will make you know wisdom in the hidden part, in the heart.*

You may have known so little of this in your Christian life hitherto that the thought appears strange. Learn that God's working, the place where he gives his life and light, is in the heart, deeper than all out thoughts. Any uncertainty about God's will makes a joyful obedience impossible. Believe most confidently that the Father is willing to make known what he wants you to do. Count upon him for this. Expect it certainly.

3. In view of the darkness and deceitfulness of the flesh and fleshly mind, *ask God very earnestly for the searching and convincing light of the Holy Spirit.*

There may be many things which you have been accustomed to think lawful or allowable, which your Father wants different. To consider it settled that they are the will of God because others and you think so may effectually shut you out from knowing God's will in other things. Bring everything, without reserve, to the judgement of the Word, explained and applied by the Holy Spirit. Wait on God to lead you to know that everything you are and do is pleasing in his sight.

[From *The School of Obedience*]

The Will of God, the Glory of Heaven

The glory and the blessedness of heaven consist in nothing but this, that God's will is done there in and by all. There is nothing to hinder God's working freely and fully all his blessed will in its countless hosts. To all that he wills for them of goodness and blessedness and service their whole being is surrendered in submission and adoration. God lives in them and they in God. They are filled with the fullness of God.

In the Lord's Prayer our Master teaches us to come to the Father with the wonderful petition, that his will may be done on earth, even as in heaven!. . . .

We consider what God's will includes, that we may know aright what our Lord means and what we are to expect, when we pray: Thy will be done!

There is, first, the will of God's holy providence. Everything that happens on earth comes to the child of God as the will of his Father. In his infinite wisdom God so overrules all the evil of men and devils, that in permitting it, he can take it up into his will, and make it work out his purposes. Joseph says of the sin of his brethren: 'Ye thought evil against me, but God meant it unto good.' Jesus said to Pilate: 'Thou couldest have no power against me, except it were given thee from above.' In everything that came on him he saw God's will: it was all the cup the Father gave him. It is when the Christian learns to see God's will in everything that comes to him, grievous or pleasing, great or small, that the prayer, thy will be done, will become the unceasing expression of adoring submission and praise. The whole world, with its dark mysteries, and life, with all its difficulties, will be illumined with the light of God's presence and rule. And the soul will taste the rest and the bliss of knowing that it is every moment encircled and watched over by God's will, that nothing can separate it from the love of which the will is the expression. Happy the Christian who receives everything in Providence as the will of his Father.

There is, next, the will of God's righteous precepts. Every

23

command of our Father in heaven is a ray of the divine will. Radiant to the eye that can see it, with all the perfection of the divine nature. It comes as a proof of the divine condescension, tenderly accommodating itself to our feebleness, as it puts the divine will into human words, suited to our special capacity and circumstances. We all naturally connect the rays of light on earth with the sun from which they come. The more the Christian learns to link every precept with the infinite will of love whence it comes, the more will he see the nobility and the joy of a life of entire obedience, the privilege and the honour of carrying out in human form the perfect will of the Father in heaven. He then learns to say of God's precepts what first appeared too high: They are the rejoicing of my heart. And, thy will be done, as in heaven, becomes the secret inspiration of a glad fulfilment of all God's commands.

Then comes – the will of God's precious promises. We often fail in the power of grasping or holding some promise, of which we fain would have the comfort, because we deal with it as a fragment, and do not connect it with the great whole of God's blessed will for us. Let every believer seek earnestly to realize what God's will in his promises is. It is his determination to do a certain thing. His engagement to do it for or in me, if I will trust him. Behind the promise there is the faithful almighty God waiting to fulfil it. What a strength it would give in prayer, what a confidence in expectation, to be quiet, and trace the promise to the living will, the loving heart, that wills to make it true to every one that yields himself in trust and dependence. As 'thy will be done', in view of God's providence, was the language of a glad submission, in view of his precepts, the surrender to a full obedience, so here, in relation to the promises, it becomes the song of an assured hope. Thy will be done, by thyself in us, O our Father in heaven.

[From *Thy Will Be Done*]

Thy Will Be Done

They will be done in earth as it is in heaven.
(MATTHEW 6:10)

1. The will of God is the living power to which the world owes its existence. Through that will and according to that will it is what it is. It is the expression or manifestation or embodiment of that divine will in its wisdom, power and goodness. It has, in beauty and glory, but what it owes to God, having willed it. As that Will formed it, so it upholds it every day. Creation then does what it was destined for, it shows forth the glory of God. They gave glory to him that liveth for ever and ever, saying, 'Thou art worthy to receive glory, for thou hast created all things, and because of thy will they are, and were created.'

2. This is true of inanimate nature. It is still more true of intelligent creatures. The divine Will undertook the creation of a creature will in its own image and likeness, with the living power to know and accept and co-operate with that Will to which it owed its being. The blessedness of the unfallen angels consists in counting it their highest honour and happiness to be able to will and do exactly what God wills and does. The glory of heaven is that God's will is done there. The sin and misery of fallen angels and men consists simply in their having turned away from, and refused to abide in, and to do, the will of God.

3. Redemption is nothing but the restoration of God's will to its place in the world. To this end Christ came and showed in a human life, how man has but one thing to live for, the doing of God's will. He showed us how there was one way of conquering self-will – by a death to it, in obeying God's will even unto death. So he atoned for our self-will and conquered it for us, and opened a path through death and resurrection, into a life entirely united with, and devoted to , the will of God.

4. God's redeeming will is now able to do in fallen man, what his

25

creating will had wrought and ever works in nature, or in unfallen beings. In Christ and his example, God has revealed the devotion to and the delight in his will, which he asks and expects of us. In Christ and his Spirit he renews and takes possession of our will: works in it, both to will and to do, making us able and willing to do all his will. He himself worketh all things to the purpose of his will. He makes us perfect in every good thing to do his will, working in us that which is pleasing in his sight. As this is revealed by the Holy Spirit and believed and received into the heart, we begin to get an insight into the prayer, 'Thy will be done in earth, as it is in heaven,' and the true desire is awakened for the life it promises.

5. How essential it is to the believer that he realize his relations to God's will, and its claim on him.

Many, many, believers have no conception of what their faith or their feeling ought to be in regard to the will of God. How few who say: My whole thought of blessedness is in nothing but the most complete harmony with the will of God. I feel my one need to be, the ever maintained surrender, not, in the very least thing, ever to do other than what God wills me to do. By God's grace every hour of my life may be a living in the will of God, and doing it as it is done in heaven.

6. It is only as a living faith in the divine Will working out its purpose increasingly in us masters the heart, that we shall have the courage to believe in the answer to the prayer our Lord taught us. It is only as we see that it is through Jesus Christ that this working of God's will in us is carried out, that we shall understand how it is the close union to him that gives the confidence that God will work all in us. And it is only this confidence in God through Jesus Christ that will assure us that we too can do our part, and that our feeble will on earth can truly ever correspond and co-operate with the will of God. Let us but accept our destiny and our obligation as the one thing our heart desires, that in everything the will of God be done in us and by us, as it is done in heaven, that faith will overcome the world.

7. The will may not be disconnected from its living union with

26

the Father here, nor the living presence of the blessed Son. It is only by a divine guidance given through the Holy Spirit, that the will of God in its beauty, in its application to daily life, in its ever growing revelation, can be truly known. This teaching will be given, not to the wise and prudent, but to the babes, the men and women of childlike disposition, who are willing to wait for, and depend on what is given them. The divine guidance will lead in the path of God's will.

8. Our secret communion with God is the place where we repeat and learn the great lessons.

The God whom I worship asks of me perfect union with his will ... My worship means: 'I delight to do thy Will, O God.'

[From *Prayer's Inner Chamber*]

The Father's Will

I can of mine own self do nothing: as I hear, I judge:
and my judgement is just; because I seek not mine
own will, but the will of the Father which hath sent
me. (JOHN 5:30)

The will of God is the power by which the universe exists from moment to moment. It is by the unceasing active exercise of his will that the sun shines, and that every lily is clothed with beauty. There is no goodness, or strength, or beauty, but as he wills it. The glory and blessedness of heaven are nothing but the working of his will. The hosts of heaven live with their wills turned and opened to him, and find their happiness in allowing his will to do its perfect work in them. When the blessed Son became man to lead us in the way to God, he told us that the whole secret of his life was, not doing his own will, but yielding himself so to do the will of the Father, that his will should receive and work out that which the will of the

27

Father worked in him. He said that he had been sent, and that he had delighted to come, for the one purpose, with his human will and his human body, to do not his own will, but the will of the Father. He set us the example of a man, a true man, finding his blessedness and his way to God's glory, in the absolute surrender to God's will. He thus showed us what the duty was for which man was created, and what the new life he was to bring his people. In such entire dependence on God, as to do nothing of himself, and to judge nothing but as he heard from the Father, he was able always to give a righteous judgment. He could count upon God to give him all the wisdom and the strength he needed, to work out his own will perfectly in him. All for the one simple reason: 'Because I seek not mine own will, but the will of him that sent me.'

'Not mine own will, but the will of him that sent me!' But had our Lord Jesus his own will, a will different from the Father's, that he needed to say: Not my will? Had he a will that needed to be denied? Undoubtedly. But was not such a will sin? By no means. This was the glory of the creation of man that he had a self-hood, his own will, a power of self-determination, by which he was to decide what he should be. This was not sin, that man had his own desire and thought and will. Without this he could not be a free creature. He had a will, with which to decide whether he should act according to the will of God or not. Sin only came when man held to his own will as creature in opposition to the will of God. As man, made like unto us in all things, 'in all points tempted like as we are, yet without sin,' Christ had a human will: for instance to eat when he was hungry, or to shrink from suffering, when he saw it coming. We know how in the temptation in the wilderness, he kept the former, in the prospect of his death, the latter, in perfect subjection to the Father's will. (Matthew 4:4; Luke 12:50; John 12:27.) It is just this that gives its infinite worth to his sacrifice; it was the unceasing sacrifice of his human will to the Father. 'I seek not mine own will, but the will of him that sent me.'

These words reveal to us the inmost meaning of Christ's redemption. They teach us what the life is for which we were created, and out of which we fell in paradise. They show us wherein the sinfulness of that fallen state consists out of which Christ came to deliver us: he seeks to free us from our self-will. They reveal to us the true creature life and the true Son – life, perfect oneness of will with God's will. They open to us the secret power of Christ's redeeming work – atoning for our self-will by his loyalty at all costs to God's will; and the true nature of the salvation and the life he gives us – the will and the power to say: I delight to do thy will, O God. Every spirit seeks a form in which to embody itself: these words give the highest revelation of the life in which the spirit that was in Christ embodied itself in him, and embodies itself in all who seek truly and fully to accept his salvation to the uttermost. I seek not my will, but the will of him that sent me, is the keynote of the only life well-pleasing to the Father on earth, and fit for his fellowship in heaven.

How little God's children know the Christ he has given them. And how little the true nature of the salvation Christ came to bring. How many there are who have never been taught that salvation out of self-will into doing God's will is alone true blessedness. And how many who, if they think they know it as a truth, never set themselves to seek this first as the true entrance into the kingdom of God and his righteousness. And yet this is in very deed what Christ revealed, and promised, what he secured on Calvary, and bestowed from heaven in the Holy Spirit. How can we become possessed of this blessed life?

I have pointed out previously how great the difference is between the idea of the law of a state, as contained in a statute book, and the will of a king to whom one stands in a personal relationship. If we would truly, however distantly, follow in Christ's footsteps, we must stand with him in the same close personal relationship to the Father. Without this the most earnest efforts to do the Father's will must prove a failure. When our Lord so often spoke of 'The will of my Father, which is in heaven,' he wanted us to understand that it was the living personality and love that was at once motive and power for the obedience. When he spoke 'of the will of him that sent me,' he showed that it was not only the consciousness of having a work, but the desire of pleasing the one who sent him, that was the mainspring of all he did. We need the sense of the presence and nearness of the God whose will we are to do as much as our Lord did. Separate the thing you have to do from him whose will it is, and it becomes a burden and an impossibility. Live in the faith that he has sent you, that it is his living loving will, over which he watches, which he himself even works out, that you are doing – instead of its being a burden you are to carry, it becomes a power that carries you. The will of the Father is such a beautiful, wise, gently, loving will, that to know it as the breathing out of the heart of God, makes it an infinite attraction and delight.

And how can we enter into this experience of the Father's nearness, and thus be able to do everything as his will? There is only one way. Jesus Christ must work it in us. And that not as from without, strengthening our faculties or assisting our efforts. No, this blessed doing of the Father's will is the mark of his life as Son. He can work it in us, as we yield ourselves wholly and receive him truly to dwell in us. It is right and needful that we should set ourselves with all earnestness and make the attempt. It is only by its failure that we really learn how entirely he must and will do all. . . . It is only when he comes in and manifests himself in the heart and dwells there, that he can work this full salvation in us. 'Blessed are they that hunger and thirst after righteousness, for they shall be filled.'

[From *Thy Will Be Done*]

The Will of God

*If any man willeth to do [God's] will, he shall know
of the teaching, whether it be of God, or whether I
speak from myself.* (JOHN 7:17)

In our text we have both a command and a promise. God and man
are fellow labourers in the working out of God's salvation. *Man
must be willing to do God's will* – that is man's side of the matter. If
man fulfils this condition, *he will have the teaching and promises of
Christ revealed to him in power*. That is God's part.

There are many of us who know God's promises intellectually,
and yet we feel a terrible lack of power. Now Jesus says that if we
will do God's will we shall know and feel that the promises come
from God, and we shall experience them in power.

What is the condition which we must comply with? We see it in
Christ's words, 'If any man willeth to do his will. . . .' Some people
say they cannot do the will of God because they do not know what it
is. Perhaps there is a measure of truth in this, but there is something which we are apt to forget: the cause of our ignorance is our
unwillingness to do God's will. Do you feel that there is a leak in
your life? What is the cause of it? Isn's it that you have never
absolutely and sincerely said, 'I am going to do God's will, whatever it may cost me: my one aim is simply to do the will of God
every moment of my life'? This determination to do nothing but
the will of God is the secret of a holy and healthy Christian life.

God's side of the matter

Why does God say he cannot bless, teach us or lead us while we
continue to do even one little bit of our own will? It is because he
knows that our own will always brings us into trouble. The will of
God is his glory. The will of man is the measure of his wisdom, of
his strength of character, of his righteousness. God's will is the
manifestation of his hidden glory. It shows his nature. He says, 'If

you want to take hold of me, you must embrace my will.' Some people want to take hold of his love, or his gentleness, or his power. But all of these are united in his will. If you refuse to take hold of his will, you cannot take hold of the rest of him.

The will of God is the glory and the blessedness of heaven. Some people's concept of heaven is childish; they think of it in terms of beautiful hymns, angels and brilliant light. But it is the will of God which makes heaven; his will works in the heart of every angel. They give themselves up to the glory of doing the will of God: they find their delight in doing it. So can heaven be any different for us? There is no chance of our ever finding any other glory. The only way to have heaven, to be blessed, is to do the will of God.

Christ is the will of God. If you try to take Christ without the will of God you take a feeble Christ, a half-Christ, a Christ of your own imagination. Christ said that his meat and drink was to do the will of God. He said, 'I delight to do thy will, O God' (Psalm 4:8). He fed on the will of God: his happiness consisted in doing it. One cannot accept such a Christ without longing to do the will of God. And yet many Christians say they really cannot completely give up their will! Such people do not want the real Christ. When he had done the will of God Jesus went to the Garden of Gethsemane and prayed again and again, 'Not my will, but thine be done' (Luke 22:42). In effect he was saying, 'I would sooner anything happened rather than that I should fail to do God's will.' If that is my Christ, can I expect to have a strong, deep and joyful Christian life if I do not give myself up to do the will of God all day and every day?

This is what constitutes the Christian life. Sin is simply the rejection of the will of God. Man refused to do God's will and preferred to go his own way. This is precisely the trouble with every Christian whose life is unsatisfactory. A Christian is someone who says, 'I have nothing to do but the will of God: it is my will and my determination to do what God wishes.'

Man's side of the matter

There are four steps which generally have to be taken before a

Christian can live a satisfactory life. First, *he must accept the truth which Jesus teaches*. Will you say, 'I recognize that it is God's desire that every Christian should live only to do the will of God in every detail of life'? This means that you will deliberately refuse to wilfully do anything which you know to be contrary to that will . . . This means that you will take time to wait on God in order to find out what his will is. It means that you will take pains and trouble to make sure you know what it is that God wishes. Many carelessly say that they are doing the will of God, when they have never really seriously taken the time to find out what God wants; they are mistaking their own wishes and inclinations for the will of God.

Secondly, a Christian *must confess his sins and shortcomings*. Are you willing to really admit your heart-failure to yourself and to God? Most people want to be good, because they know that being good means being happy. For example, many want to be delivered from a bad temper, because it often brings them into disgrace. You may have been willing to be good, but haven't you failed to desire to do the will of God in every moment of your life? Many Christians have no conception of even trying to do this. They do not even aim at such a life. How such people need conviction of sin! They need to admit to God that their root-evil is that they have tried to please themselves rather than do his will.

Thirdly, a Christian must believe that *Jesus is able to change his life*. He can cleanse away the past. Oh, if each Christian could only see that a dark cloud of accumulated sin hangs over his soul, spoiling his joy! You cannot creep out of this cloud, as a snake creeps out of its skin. But Christ can cleanse it away and restore you to God's full favour. He did the will of God while he was on the earth, and he also lives today to do the Father's will in your heart. I hear many people talk about doctrines of grace, but there is one doctrine of grace which I hear very little about, and that is *the doctrine of sufficient grace*. God never asks you to do anything without at the same time giving you the power to do it. Do you believe that? Or do you say, as most Christians do, 'It is impossible for me to do the will of God'? They do not ask what God says on the

33

subject; they just consult themselves and say, 'I do not see any chance of my doing it.'

Fourthly, a Christian must say, '*I surrender*.' Commit yourself and say, 'In the power of Christ I can and will do the will of God.' Do I really need to plead with you to do this? Isn't God's will the most beautiful thing in heaven and earth? Where does the beauty of the sunshine, of the flower, of all nature come from if not from the will of God? Come, then, and let us tell him that we want to live only to do his will. We should remember that our hearts get hardened if, having seen the light, we get accustomed to it or turn away from it. Let us surrender ourselves fully to God.

[From *Christ is All*]

Obeying God's Holy Word

Feeding on the Word

*Thy words were found and I did eat them; and Thy
word was unto me the joy and rejoicing of my heart.*
(JEREMIAH 15:16)

Here you have three things. The findings of God's Word. This only
comes to those who seek diligently for it. Then the eating. This
means the personal appropriation for our own sustenance, the
taking up into our being, the words of God. 'Man shall not live by
bread alone, but by every word that proceedeth out of the mouth of
God.' And then the rejoicing, 'The kingdom of heaven is like unto
treasure hid in a field; the which when a man hath found, he hideth,
and for joy thereof goeth and selleth all that he hath, and buyeth
that field.' There we have the finding, and the appropriating, and
the rejoicing. 'Thy words were found, and I did eat them; and Thy
word was unto me the joy and rejoicing of my heart.'

[From *Prayer's Inner Chamber*]

35

The Heart and the Understanding

*Trust in the Lord with all thine heart, and lean not
unto thine own understanding.*
(PROVERBS 3:5)

The chief object of the Book of Proverbs is to teach knowledge and
discretion, and to guide in the path of wisdom and understanding.
To understand righteousness, to understand the fear of the Lord,
to find good understanding, it is to this the Proverbs offer to guide
us. But it gives the warning – in the pursuit of this, to distinguish
between trusting to our own understanding and intellect, and
seeking spiritual understanding, that which God gives, even an
understanding heart. 'Trust in the Lord with all thine heart, and
lean not unto thine own understanding.' In all our seeking after
knowledge and wisdom, in all our planning our life, or studying the
Word, we have these two powers – the understanding or intellect,
which knows things from without, by nature and the conception
we form – the heart, which knows them by experience as it takes
them up into the will and affection.

I am deeply persuaded that one of the chief reasons why so much
Bible teaching and Bible knowledge is comparatively fruitless, one
of the chief causes of the lack of holiness, and devotion, and power
in the church, is to be found here – the trusting to our own understanding in religion. . .

Trust not, wholly distrust, thy own understanding. It can only
give thee thoughts and conceptions of divine things without the
reality. It will deceive thee with the thought that the truth, if
received into the mind, will somehow surely enter the heart. And
so it will blind thee to the terrible experience which is so universal,
that men daily read, and every Sunday delight to hear God's Word,
and yet are made neither humble, nor holy, nor heavenly minded by
it.

Instead of the understanding come with the heart to the Bible.

Instead of the understanding trust in the Lord, and that with all thy heart. Let not the understanding but the whole heart set upon the living God as the teacher, be the chief thing, when thou enterest thy closet. Then shalt thou find good understanding. God will give thee an understanding heart, a spiritual understanding.

[From *Prayer's Inner Chamber*]

Christ's Use of Scripture

When the Lord Jesus was made man, he became entirely dependent on the Word of God, he submitted himself wholly to it. His mother taught it him. The teachers of Nazareth instructed him in it. In meditation and prayer, in the excercise of obedience and faith, he was led, during his silent years of preparation, to understand and appropriate it. The Word of the Father was to the Son the life of his soul. What he said in the wilderness was spoken from his inmost personal experience: 'Man shall not live by bread alone, but by every word that proceedeth out of the mouth of God.' He felt he could not live but as the Word brought him the life of the Father. His whole life was a life of faith, a depending on the Word of the Father. The Word was to him, not instead of the Father, but the vehicle for the living fellowship with the living God. And he had his whole mind and heart so filled with it that the Holy Spirit could at each moment find within him, all ready for use, the right word to suggest just as he needed it.

Child of God, would you become a man of God, strong in faith, full of blessing, rich in fruit to the glory of God, be full of the Word of God, then, like Christ, make the Word your bread. Let it dwell richly in you. Have your heart full of it. Feed on it. Believe it. Obey it. It is only by believing and obeying that the Word can enter into our inward parts, into our very being. Take it day by day as the Word that proceedeth, not has proceeded, but proceedeth, is proceeding out of the mouth of God, as the Word of the living God,

37

who in it holds living fellowship with his children, and speaks to them in living power. Take your thoughts of God's will, and God's work, and God's purpose with you, and the world, not from the church, not from Christians around you, but from the Word taught you by the Father, and, like Christ, you will be able to fulfil all that is written in the Scripture concerning you.

In Christ's use of Scripture the most remarkable thing is this: *he found himself there; he saw there his own image and likeness.* And he gave himself to the fulfilment of what he found written there. It was this that encouraged him under the bitterest sufferings, and strengthened him for the most difficult work. Everywhere he saw traced by God's own hand the divine waymark: *through suffering to glory.* He had but one thought: to be what the Father had said he should be, to have his life correspond exactly to the image of what he should be as he found it in the Word of God.

Disciple of Jesus, in the Scriptures *thy likeness, too, is to be found,* a picture of what the Father means thee to be. Seek to have a deep and clear impression of what the Father says in his Word that thou shouldest be. If this is once fully understood, it in inconceivable what has been written concerning me in God's book; I have seen the image of what I am called in God's counsel to be: this thought inspires the soul with a faith that conquers the world.

[From *Like Christ*]

The Power of God's Word

The word of God which also worketh in you that believe. (1 THESSALONIANS 2:13)

The value of the words of a man depends upon my knowledge of him who speaks. What a difference when a man gives me the promise! I will give you the half of all I have, whether the speaker be a poor man who owns a shilling, or a millionaire who offers to share his fortune with me. One of the first requisites to fruitful Bible study is the knowledge of God as the omnipotent one, and of the power of his Word.

The power of God's Word is infinite. 'By the word of the Lord were the heavens made. He spake and it was done; He commanded and it stood fast.' In the word of God his omnipotence works: it has creative power and calls into existence the very thing of which it speaks.

As the Word of the living God it is a living Word, and gives life. It can not only call into existence, but make alive again that which is dead. Its quickening power can raise dead bodies, can give eternal life to dead souls. All spiritual life comes through it, for we are born of incorruptible seed by the Word of God that liveth and abideth for ever.

Here there lies hidden from many one of the deepest secrets of the blessing of God's Word – the faith in its creative and quickening energy. The Word will work in me the very disposition or grace which it commands or promises. 'It worketh effectually in them that believe.' Nothing can resist its power when received into the heart through the Holy Spirit. 'It worketh effectually in them that believe.' 'The voice of the Lord is power.' Everything depends upon learning the art of receiving that Word into the heart. And in learning this art the first step is – faith in its loving, its omnipotent, its creative power. By his Word 'God calleth the things that are not, as though they were.'

As true as this is of all God's mighty deeds from creation on to the resurrection of the dead, it is true too of every word spoken to us in his holy book. Two things keep us from believing this as we should. The one is the terrible experience in all around, and perhaps in ourselves too, of the Word being made of none effect by human wisdom or unbelief or worldliness. The other is the neglect of the teaching of Scripture that the Word is a seed. Seeds are small, seeds may be long dormant, seeds have to be hidden, and when they sprout are of slow growth. Because the action of God's word is hidden and unobserved, slow and apparently feeble, we do not believe in its omnipotence. Let us make it one of our first lessons. The Word I study then is the power of God unto salvation: it will work in me all I need, all the Father asks.

What a prospect this faith would open up for our spiritual life! We should see all the treasures and blessings of God's grace to be within our reach. The Word has power to enlighten our darkness: in our hearts it will bring the light of God, the sense of his love, and the knowledge of his will. The Word can fill us with strength and courage to conquer every enemy, and do whatever God asks us to do. The Word would cleanse, and sanctify, would work in us faith and obedience, would become in us the seed of every trait in the likeness of our Lord. Through the Word the Spirit would lead us into all truth, that is, make all that is in the Word true in us, and so prepare our heart to be the habitation of the Father and the Son.

[From *Prayer's Inner Chamber*]

Prayer and the Word

The expression of a convert from heathenism has often been quoted: I pray, I speak to God; I read in the Bible, God speaks to me. There is a verse in the history of Moses in which this thought is beautifully brought out. We read (Numbers 7:89), 'When Moses was gone into the tabernacle of the congregation to speak with God, then he heard the voice of one speaking unto him from off the mercy seat. . . . and God spake unto him.' When he went in to pray for himself or his people, and to wait for instructions, he found One waiting for him. What a lesson for our morning watch. A prayerful spirit is the spirit to which God will speak. A prayerful spirit will be a listening spirit waiting to hear what God says. In the fellowship with God his presence and the part he takes must be as real as my own. We want to ask what is needed that our Scripture reading and praying may be such true fellowship with God.

1. *Get into the right place*

'Moses went into the tabernacle to speak with God.' He separated himself from the people, and went where he could be with God alone. He went to the place where God was to be found. Jesus has told us where that place is. He calls us to enter into our closet, and shut the door, and pray to our Father which seeth in secret. Anywhere where we really are alone with God may be to us the secret of his presence. To speak with God needs separation from all else. It needs a heart intently set upon and in full expectation of meeting God personally, and having direct dealings with him. Those who go there to speak to God, will hear the Voice of One speaking to them.

2. *Get into the right position*

He heard the Voice of One speaking from off the mercy seat. Bow before the mercy seat. There the consciousness of your unworthiness will not hinder you, but be a real help in trusting God. There you may have the assured confidence that your upward look will be met by his eye, that your prayer can be heard, that his loving answer will be given. Bow before the mercy seat, and be sure that the God of mercy will see and bless you.

3. *Get into the right disposition – the listening attitude*

Many are so occupied with the much or the little they have to say in their prayers, that the Voice of One speaking off the mercy seat is never heard, because it is not expected or waited for. 'Thus saith the Lord, The heaven is my throne, and the earth is my footstool . . . to this man will I look, even to him that is poor and of a contrite spirit, and trembleth at my word.' Let us enter the closet, and set ourselves to pray, with a heart that humbly waits to hear God speak; in the Word we read, we shall indeed hear the Voice of One speaking to us. The highest blessedness of prayer will be our ceasing to pray, to let God speak.

Prayer and the Word are inseparably linked together: power in the use of either depends upon the presence of the other. The

Word gives me matter for prayer, telling me what God will do for me. It shows me the path of prayer, telling me how God would have me come. It gives me the power for prayers, the courage of the assurance I will be heard. And it brings me the answer to prayer, as it teaches what God will do for me. And so, on the other hand, prayer prepares the heart for receiving the Word from God himself, for the teaching of the Spirit to give the spiritual understanding of it, for the faith that is made partaker of the mighty working.

[From *Prayer's Inner Chamber*]

God's Thoughts and Our Thoughts

As the heavens are higher than the earth so are my
thoughts higher than your thoughts.
(ISAIAH 55:9)

On earth the words of a wise man often mean something different from what a hearer understands of them. How natural then that the words of God, as he understands them, mean something infinitely higher than we at once apprehend.

There is very great need for remembering this. Doing so will lead us continually from resting content with our knowledge and thoughts of the Word, to wonder and wait what may be its full blessing as God has meant it. It will give our prayer for the Holy Spirit's teaching new point and urgency, even to shew us what has not yet entered into our heart to conceive. It will give confidence to the hope that there is for us, even in this life, a fulfilment beyond our highest thoughts.

God's Word thus has two meanings. The one is that which it has in the mind of God, making the human words actually the bearer of all the glory of divine wisdom, and power, and love. The other is our feeble, partial, defective apprehension of it. Even after grace and experience have made such words as the love of God, the grace of God, the power of God, or any one of the many promises connected with these verities very true and real to us, there is still an infinite fullness in the Word we have not yet known.

How strikingly this is put in our text from Isaiah. 'As the heavens are higher than the earth.' Our faith in the fact is so simple and clear that no one would dream of trying with his little arm to reach the sun or the stars. To climb the highest mountain would not avail. We do with our whole heart believe it. And now God says, even so, 'my thoughts are higher than your thoughts.' Even when the Word has spoken out God's thoughts, and our thoughts have sought to take them in, they still remain, as high above our thoughts as the heavens are higher than the earth. All the infinities of God and the eternal world dwell in the Word as the seed of eternal life. And as the full-grown oak is so mysteriously greater than the acorn from which it springs, so God's words are but seeds from which God's mighty wonders of grace can grow up.

Faith in this Word would teach us two lessons, the one of ignorance, the other of expectation. We should learn to come to the Word as little children. Jesus said, 'Thou hast hid these things from the wise and prudent, and hast revealed them unto babes.' The prudent and the wise are not necessarily hypocrites or enemies. There are many of God's own dear children, who, by neglecting to cultivate continually a childlike spirit, unconsciously resting on the scripturalness of their creed, or the honesty of their Scripture study, have spiritual truth hidden from them, and never become spiritual men. Who among men knoweth the things of a man, save the spirit of the man, which is in him? Even so the things of God none knoweth, save the Spirit of God. But we received the Spirit of God, that we might know! Let a deep sense of our ignorance, a deep distrust of our own power of understanding the things of God even, mark our Bible study.

The deeper our despair of entering aright into the thoughts of God, the greater the confidence of expectancy may be. God wants to make his Word true in us. 'Thy children shall be taught of God.' The Holy Spirit is already in us to reveal the things of God. In answer to our humble believing prayer God will, through him, give an evergrowing insight into the mystery of God – our wonderful union and likeness to Christ, his living in us, and our being as he was in this world.

[From *Prayer's Inner Chamber*]

The Bible Student

Blessed is the man whose delight is in the law of the Lord; and in his law doth he meditate day and night.
(PSALM 1:1-2)

Let us look at the principle underlying the demand for more Bible study, and in faithfulness to which alone, it can be truly carried out.

1. God's Word is the only authentic revelation of God's will. All human statements of divine truth, however correct, are defective and carry a measure of human authority. In the Word, the voice of God speaks to us directly. Every child of God is called to direct communion with the Father, through the Word. As God reveals all his heart and grace in it, his child can, if he receives it from God, get all the life and power there is in the Word into his own heart and being. We know how few second-hand reports of messages or events can be fully trusted. Very few men report accurately what they have heard. Every believer has the right and calling, to stand in direct communication with God. It is in the Word God has revealed, it is in the Word he still reveals himself to each individual.

2. This Word of God is a living Word. It carries a divine quickening power in it. The human expression of the truth is often a mere conception or image of the truth, appealing to the mind and

having little or no effect. The faith of its being God's own Word and of the presence and power in it, makes it effectual. All life or spirit creates for itself a form in which it is made manifest. The words in which God has chosen to clothe his own divine thoughts are God-breathed and the life of God dwells in them. God is not the God of the dead but of the living. The Word was not only inspired when first given: the Spirit of God still breathes in it. God is still in and with his Word. Christians and teachers need to believe this. It will lead them to give the simple divine Word a confidence that no human teaching may have.

3. God himself can alone, and most surely will, be the interpreter of his own Word. Divine truth needs a divine teacher. Spiritual apprehension of spiritual things can only come of the Holy Spirit. The deeper the conviction of the unique character of the Word, essentially different from, and infinitely exalted above, all mere human apprehension, the more urgently will the need be felt of a supernatural, a directly divine teaching. The soul will be brought to seek God himself, and it will be led to find him in the Holy Spirit who dwells in the heart. As the Spirit, in whom God, so wonderfully, has entered our very life and indentified himself within, is waited on and trusted, he will make us know wisdom in the hidden part, in the heart and disposition. The word prayerfully read and cherished in the heart in this faith, will, through the Spirit, be both light and life within us.

4. The Word then brings us into the closest and most intimate fellowship with God – unity of will and life. In the Word God has revealed his whole heart and all his will: in his law and precepts what he wills us to do: in his redemption and his promises what he wills to do for us. As we accept that will in the Word as from God himself, and yield ourselves to its working, we learn to know God in his will, in the power of which he works in us, and in which his condescending love is known. And the Word works out his richest purpose as it fills us with the reverence and dependence that comes from the divine presence and nearness. Nothing less than this must be our aim, may be our experience, in all our Bible study. Let us

now take these four thoughts over again and make the practical application.

In holy Scripture we have the very words in which the holy God has spoken and in which he speaks to us. These words are, today, full of the life of God. God is in them, and makes his presence and power known to them who seek him in them.

[From *Prayer's Inner Chamber*]

The Seed is the Word

I think it may be confidently said that in all nature there is no other illustration of what the Word of God is, so true, so full of meaning, as that of the seed. To have a full spiritual insight into it is a wonderful means of grace.

The points of resemblance are easily stated. There is the apparent insignificance of the seed – a little thing as compared with the tree that springs from it. There is the life, enclosed and dormant within a husk. There is the need of a suitable soil, without which growth is impossible. There is the slow growth with its length of time calling for the long patience of the husbandman. And there is the fruit, in which the seed reproduces and multiplies itself. In all these respects, the seed teaches us most precious lessons as to our use of God's Word.

1. *The lesson of faith*
Faith does not look at appearances. As far as we can judge, it looks most improbable that a Word of God should give life in the soul, should work in us the very grace of which it speaks, should transform our whole character, should fill us with strength. And yet so it is. When once we have learned to believe that the Word can work effectually the very truth of which it is the expression, we have found one of the chief secrets of our Bible study. We shall then receive each word as the pledge and the power of a divine working.

2. *The lesson of labour*

The seed needs to be gathered, and kept, and put into the prepared soil. And so the mind has to gather from Scripture and understand and pass on to the heart, as the only soil in which this heavenly seed can grow, the words which meet our need. We cannot give the life or the growth. Nor do we need to; it is there. But what we can do is to hide the Word in our hearts, and keep it there, waiting for the sunshine that comes from above.

3. *The lesson of patience*

The effect of the Word on the heart is in most cases not immediate. It needs time to strike root, and grow up: Christ's words must abide in us. We must not only day by day increase our store of Bible knowledge – this is only like gathering the grain in a barn – but watch over these words of command or promise that we have specially taken, and allow them room in our heart to spread both root and branches. We need to know what seed we have put in, and to cultivate a watchful but patient expectancy. In due time we shall reap, if we faint not.

4. *The lesson of fruitfulness*

However insignificant that little seed of a Word of God appear, however feeble its life may seem, however deep hidden the very thought of what it speaks may be, and however trying the slowness of its growth may be to our patience – be sure the fruit will come. The very truth and life and power of God, of which the Word contained the thought, will grow and ripen within you. And just as a seed bears a fruit, containing the same seed for new reproduction, so the Word will not only bring you the fruit it promised, but that fruit will each time become a seed which you carry to others to give life and blessing.

Not only the Word, but 'The kingdom of heaven is like a seed.' And all the grace of it comes in no other way than as a hidden seed in the heart of the regenerate. Christ is a seed. The Holy Spirit is a seed. The love of God shed abroad in the heart is a seed. The exceeding greatness of the power that worketh in us is a seed. The hidden life is there in the heart, but not at once or always felt in its power. The divine glory is there, but often without form or comeliness, to be known only by faith, to be counted and acted on even when not felt, to be waited for in its springing forth and its growth.

As this central truth each time is firmly grasped and held, as the law of all the heavenly life on earth, the study of God's Word becomes an act of faith, and surrender and dependence upon the living God. I believe humbly, almost tremblingly, in the divine seed that there is in the Word, and the power of God's Spirit to make it true in my life and experience.

[From *Prayer's Inner Chamber*]

Meditation

Blessed is the man whose delight is in the law of the Lord; and in his law doeth he meditate day and night. (PSALM 1:1-2; JOSHUA 1:8;
PSALM 119:15, 23, 48, 78, 97, 99, 148;
1 TIMOTHY 4:15)

Let the words of my mouth and the meditation of my heart be acceptable in thy sight, O Lord.
(PSALM 19:14 and 49:3)

In meditation the heart holds and appropriates the Word. Just as in reflection the understanding grasps all the meaning and bearings of a truth, so in meditation the heart assimilates it and makes it a part of its own life. We need continual reminding that the heart means the will and the affection. The meditation of the heart implies desire, acceptance, surrender, love. Out of the heart are the issues of life; what the heart truly believes, that it receives with love and joy, and allows to master and rule the life. The intellect gathers and prepares the food on which we are to feed. In meditation the heart takes it in and feeds on it.

The art of meditation needs to be cultivated. Just as a man needs to be trained to concentrate his mental powers so as to think clearly and accurately, so a Christian needs carefully to consider and meditate, until the holy habit has been formed of yielding up the whole heart to every word of God.

Sometimes it is asked how this power of meditation can be cultivated. The very first thing is to present ourselves before God. It is his Word; that Word has no power of blessing apart from him. It is into his presence and fellowship that the word is meant to bring us. Practise his presence, and take the Word as from himself in the assurance that he will make it work effectually in the heart. In Psalm 119 you have the word seven times, but each time as part of a prayer addressed to God. 'I will meditate in *thy* precepts.' 'Thy servant did meditate in *thy* statutes.' 'O how I love *thy* law, it is my meditation all the day.' Meditation is the heart turning towards God with his own Word, seeking to take it up into the affection and will, into its very life.

Another element of true meditation is quiet restfulness. In our study of Scripture, in our endeavour to grasp an argument, or to master a difficulty, our intellect often needs to put forth its utmost efforts. The habit of soul required in meditation is different. Here we turn with some truth we have found, or some mystery in which we are waiting for divine teaching to hide the word we are engaged with in the depth of the heart, and believe that, by the Holy Spirit, its meaning and power will be revealed in our inner life. 'Thou desirest truth in inward parts; and in the hidden part thou shalt make me to know wisdom.' In the description of our Lord's mother we are told: 'Mary kept all these things and pondered them in her heart.' In his mother keeping all these sayings in her heart we have the image of a soul that has begun to know Christ and is on the sure way to know him better.

It is hardly necessary to say further that in meditation the personal application takes a prominent place. This is all too little the case with our intellectual study of the Bible. Its object is to know and understand. In meditation the chief object is to appropriate and experience. A readiness to believe every promise implicitly, to obey every command unhesitatingly, to 'stand perfect and complete in all the will of God', is the only true spirit of Bible study. It is in quiet meditation that this faith is exercised, that this allegiance is rendered, that the full surrender to all God's will is made, and that assurance is received of grace to perform our vows.

And then meditation must lead to prayer. It provides matter for prayer. It must lead on to prayer, to ask and receive definitely what it has seen in the Word or accepted in the Word. Its value is that it is the preparation for prayer, deliberate and wholehearted supplication for what the heart has felt that the Word has revealed as needful or possible. That means the rest of faith, that looks upward in the assurance that the Word will open up and prove its power in the soul that meekly and patiently gives itself away to it.

The reward of resting for a time from intellectual effort, and cultivating the habit of holy meditation, will be that in course of time the two will be brought into harmony, and all our study be animated by the spirit of a quiet waiting on God and yielding up of the heart and life to the Word.

Our fellowship with God is meant for all the day. The blessing of securing a habit of true meditation in the morning watch will be that we shall be brought nearer the blessedness of the man of the first Psalm: 'Blessed is the man whose delight is in the law of the Lord; and in his law doth he meditate day and night.'

Let all workers and leaders of God's people remember that they need this more than others if they are to train them to it, and keep up their own communication unbroken with the only source of strength and blessing.

[From *The Inner Chamber and the Inner Life*]

Psalm 119 and its Teaching

Oh how I love thy law! it is my meditation all the day. (PSALM 119:97)

Consider how I love thy precepts.
(PSALM 119:159)

I love them exceedingly. (PSALM 119:167)

In holy Scripture there is one portion wholly devoted to teaching us the place which God's Word is meant to have in our esteem, and the way we can secure its blessing. It is the longest chapter in the Bible, and, with hardly an exception, in every one of its 176 verses, we have under different names mention made of the Word. Anyone who really wants to know how to study his Bible according to God's will ought to make a careful study of this Psalm. There ought to come a time in his life when he resolves to study its teaching and carry it out into practice. How can we wonder that our Bible study does not bring more spiritual profit and strength, if we neglect the divine directory it offers us for that study? It is possible you have never read it once through as a whole. If you have not time, find time, some free Sunday hour – or why not some free week-day hour? – in which you read it through and try to take in its chief thought, or at least to catch its spirit. If you find it difficult to do this by reading it once, read it more than once. This will make you feel the need of giving it more careful thought. The following hints may help you in its study.

First, note all the different names under which God's Word is spoken of.

Second, note all the different verbs expressing what we ought to feel and do in regard to the Word. Let this lead us to consider what the place is that God's Word claims in your heart and life, and how every faculty of your being – desire, love, joy, trust, obedience, action – is called out by it.

Third, count and note how many times the writer speaks in the past tense of his having kept, observed, stuck to, delighted in God's testimonies. How many times he expresses in the present tense how he rejoices in, loves, and esteems God's law. And then how in the future tense he promises and vows to observe God's precepts to the end. Put all these together and see how more than a hundred times he presents his soul before God as one who honours and keeps his law. Study this especially as these expressions are connected with his prayers to God, until you have a clear image of the righteous man whose fervent, effectual prayer availeth much.

Fourth, study the prayers themselves and note down the different requests he makes with regard to the Word, whether for the teaching to understand and the power to keep them, or for the blessing promised in the Word, and to be found in keeping them. Note especially prayers like 'Teach me thy statutes.' 'Give me understanding.' Also there where the plea is 'according to thy Word'.

Fifth, count the verses in which there is any allusion to affliction, whether from his own state or from his enemies, or the sins of the wicked or God delaying 'to help him'; and learn how it is in the time of trouble that we need God's Word specially, and that this alone can bring comfort to us.

Sixth, then comes one of the most important things. Mark how often the little pronoun, thou, thine, thee, occurs, and how often it is understood in every petition: 'Teach thou me.' 'Quicken thou me' and you will see how the whole psalm is a prayer spoken to God. All the Psalmist has to say about the Word of God, whether with regard to his own attachment to it, or his need of God's teaching and quickening, is spoken upwards into the face of God. He believes that it is pleasing to God and good for his own soul to connect his meditation and thoughts on the Word as continually and as closely as possible, by prayer, with the living God himself. Every thought of God's Word instead of drawing him off from God leads him to fellowship with God. The Word of God becomes to him the rich and inexhaustible material for holding communion with the God whose it is and to whom it is meant to lead. As we gradually get an insight into these truths from the single verses we shall get a new meaning. And when, from time to time, we take a whole paragraph with its eight verses we shall find how they help to lift us up with, and through, the Word into God's presence, and into that life of obedience and joy which says 'I have sworn, and will perform it, that I will keep thy righteous judgement.' 'Oh how I love thy law! it is my meditation all the day.'

Let us seek by the grace of the Holy Spirit to have the devotional life which the Psalm reveals wrought into our morning watch. Let God's Word every day and before everything else lead us to God. Let every blessing in it be a matter of prayer, very specially our need of divine teaching. Let our intense attachment to it be our childlike plea and confidence that the father will help us. Let our prayers be followed by the vow that as God quickens and blesses us, we shall run the way of his commandments, and let all that God's Word brings ourselves make us the more earnest in longing that all men should know and serve him.

[From *Prayer's Inner Chamber*]

The Example of Jesus

Suffering

For so is the will of God, that with well doing ye may put to silence the ignorance of foolish men . . . if when ye do well, and suffer for it, ye take it patiently, this is acceptable with God . . . because Christ also suffered for us, leaving us an example, that ye should follow his steps. (1 PETER 2:15, 20-21)

It is better, if the will of God be so, that ye suffer for well doing, than for evil doing. For Christ also hath once suffered for sins. (1 PETER 3:17-18)

But rejoice, inasmuch as ye are partakers of Christ's sufferings . . . Wherefore let them that suffer according to the will of God commit the keeping of their souls to him in well doing, as unto a faithful Creator. (1 PETER 4:13, 19)

Before Peter had received the Holy Spirit, he could not understand that suffering had to be borne as God's will. When Christ spoke of

54

his suffering he reproved him, and had to bear the rebuke: 'Get thee behind me, Satan.' When his discipleship brought him into danger and suffering, he denied his Lord. He could not see that suffering was God's will. With Pentecost everything was changed. He knew no fear. He rejoiced that he was counted worthy to suffer for his name. In his epistle he connects Christ's suffering for our sins with his example, calling us to suffer like him. Through suffering to glory is the keynote of his exhortation to the saints. Let us listen to what he teaches us of the will of God in suffering.

The first lesson is: To regard all suffering as the will of God for us. 'If the will of God be so, that ye suffer for well doing', 'them that suffer according to the will of God.' He is speaking of the suffering of injustice at the hands of our fellow men. Very many, who think they are ready to endure trial that comes direct from God, find it very hard to bear unkind, or hard, or unjust treatment from men. And yet it is just here that Christ's teaching and example, and all scriptural instruction, call upon us to accept and bow to the will of God. Whether it be in the most flagrant injustice, and the most terrible suffering – such as our Lord endured at the hands of Caiaphas and Pilate – or the smaller vexations that we meet with in daily life from enemies or friends, all suffering must be to us the will of God. Nothing can come to us without the will of God. What is done may be most contrary to the will of God, and the doer most guilty in his sight – that it is done to us, that we suffer by it, is God's will. And the first duty of the child of God is – not to look at the man who does it, to seek to be avenged of him, or delivered from his hands, but to recognize and bow beneath it as the Father's will. That one thought – it is the Father's will – changes our feelings towards it, enables us to accept it as a blessing, changes it from an evil into a good. In all suffering let the first thought be, to see the Father's hand, and count on the Father's help. Then no circumstance whatever can for one moment take us out of the blessed will of God.

The second lesson is: Always suffer with well-doing. In all the three texts the word 'well-doing' occurs. If we suffer when we do wrong, and take it patiently, this is no glory. But if we suffer when we do well, and take it patiently, this is acceptable with God – that so by well-doing we put to silence the ignorance of foolish men. For it is better, if the will of God be so, that ye suffer for well-doing than for evil-doing. And it is in well-doing we can commit our souls unto a faithful Creator. The one thing we are to care for is that, if we suffer, it is not to be for wrong-doing, but for well-doing. And also with well-doing, not allowing the suffering to call forth anything that is sinful. That must be our one desire in suffering. It is caused by sin, it is meant to take away sin – how terrible if I make it the occasion of more sin, and turn it to the very opposite of what God means it to be. Men may learn from us what the power of grace is, to soften and to strengthen; what the reality is of the heavenly life and the joy that enables us to bear all loss; and what the blessing is of the service of the divine Master, who can make his own path of suffering so attractive and so blessed to his followers.

Here is the third lesson: In suffering to commit our souls to God's faithful keeping. What a precious privilege! Amid all the temptation suffering brings, God himself offers to take charge of the keeping of our souls. Going down into the darkness of death, our Lord Jesus said: 'Father, into thy hands I commend my spirit.' Into every dark cloud of suffering into which we enter, we may say this too. From all the strife of tongues and the pride of man, from all that there is in ourselves of the tendency to impatience or anger, to quick judgements or unloving dispositions, the faithful Creator can keep the soul committed to him. He who sends the suffering as his will, has beforehand provided a place of safety, where the blessing of the suffering will assuredly be given. Let us say: 'I know whom I have believed, and am persuaded that he is able to keep that which I have committed unto him.'

Then comes the last lesson: In all our suffering according to the will of God, Christ is our pattern and our strength. In all the three chapters Christ's suffering for our sake is connected with our suffering for his sake. 'Christ also suffered for us, leaving us an example – that ye should follow in his steps' (2:21). 'It is better. . . .

that ye suffer for well doing, than for evil doing. For Christ also hath once suffered for sins, the just for the unjust' (3:17-18). 'Forasmuch as Christ hath suffered for us in the flesh, arm yourselves likewise with the same mind . . . But rejoice, inasmuch as ye are partakers of Christ's sufferings . . . for the spirit of glory and of God resteth upon you' (4:1, 13-14). The sufferings of believers are as indispensable as are those of Christ. They are to be borne in the same spirit. They are the means of fellowship with him, and conformity to his image. Christ Jesus accepted and bore all suffering, of whatever nature, great or small, whether coming in the ordinary course of events or specially devised against himself, as the will of God. He endured it, as the necessary result of sin, in submission to the will of the Father who sent it, as the school in which he was to prove that his will was one with the Father's and that the Father's will was over all.

Christ is our pattern, because he is our life. In time of suffering proof is given that the spirit of glory and the spirit of God rests upon us. Oh, that all believers, who desire to live wholly to the will of God, might understand how much depends upon their recognizing God's will in all suffering, and bearing all according to the will of God! And might understand, too, how impossible it is to disconnect Christ's sufferings for us from ours for him. He suffered for us as our head, in whom we are made alive. We can only suffer for him as he lives in us. The attempt to do or bear the will of God aright, as long as we are living on a different level from that on which Christ lived, must be failure. It is only where the whole-hearted surrender, to live and die for the will of God as he did, possesses the soul that the mighty power of his love and grace and Spirit can do their wonders in the life.

[From *Thy Will Be Done*]

Christ, Our Life

Christ, who is our life. (COLOSSIANS 3:4)

This is a truth of infinite depth and richness. It lies at the very root of the Christian life, and leads into all its fullness and blessing. To understand it we must study it in three stages: Christ's life in the flesh on earth; Christ's life by the Spirit in the heart: and Christ's life in heaven working through us for the world.

The Christ-life in the flesh on earth

Before we can fully accept the Christ-life we must know what to expect from it – what it offers us, what its spirit and character is. We can only discover this from the life of Christ on earth. He lived in the flesh in order to make visible to us what the divine life is, to show us how a man ought to live with his God, how we will live when we have Christ as our life in us. It will help us if we study the divine life of Christ in the light of its root virtue – that is, *humility*.

He is the Lamb of God, meek and gentle and patient. It was a divine humility in heaven which moved him to come into the world as a servant: 'Being in the form of God. . . . [he] emptied himself, taking the form of a servant' (Philippians 2:6-7, RV). In true human humility he gave himself up to death on the cross: 'Being found in fashion as a man, he humbled himself, becoming obedient even unto death' (verse 8). He said of himself, 'Learn of me; for I am meek and lowly in heart' (Matthew 11:29, RV). In him was fulfilled Zechariah's prophecy: 'Behold, thy king cometh unto thee. . . lowly, and riding upon an ass' (9:9, RV). In everything he said about his Father he always spoke of his own entire dependence upon him. He could do nothing by himself (John 5:19, 30; 6:38; 7:16, 28, 40, 42; 8:28, 54; 12:49; 14:10, 24).

In all his dealings with men, in his bearing of reproach, injustice and suffering, in his readiness to help and serve, in his self-abasement and compassion, he always thought of himself as of no account. He did everything with the meekness, sweetness and gentleness of the Lamb of God. Humility is the root of his perfect character and atonement, and of the perfect life which he gives us.

Why does this have to be so? Because pride was the one root of all sin, the cause of man's fall and of all disobedience. Pride had been the fall of the devil. In Paradise he breathed his poison into our first parents. Pride of knowledge, pride of will, pride of power, pride of life – it became the source of all rebellion against God, all selfishness and hatred amongst men, all darkness and discontent in the heart. Christ came to restore to us our right relation to God and to man. The only way he could do this was by his humility atoning for our pride, by giving us his humility instead of our pride, so that we might once again take our right place before God.

We can see this pride very clearly in his disciples – it was the root of their unbelief (John 5:44). How frequently Christ found it necessary to speak to them about humility (Matthew 18:1-4; 20:27; 23:11-12; Luke 14:11; 17:10; 18:14; 22:24, 26; John 13:16). Without this humility in Christ and in us, there is no salvation.

All Christians should look at their lives and compare them with Christ's humility. Let each one of us examine himself, and see how much of that humility he has attained. Before we can receive and desire and display that Christ-life we must appreciate our need of it. A deep humbling of our pride is the essential first step towards receiving the humility of Christ as a permanent trait of our lives (Romans 12:3, 1 Corinthians 13:4; Galatians 5:26; Ephesians 4:2; Philippians 2:3; Colossians 3:12; James 4:6; 1 Peter 5:6).

The Christ-life by the Spirit in our hearts

Once we know and hate and confess our own life and its pride, it must then be crucified and killed. The new life of humility must expel the old. Christ the Stronger must cast out Pride the Strong. May God reveal to us how much self has been in our religion, and how nothing but the death to self in the death of Christ can deliver us (Romans 6:1-11; Galatians 2:20; 6:14; Colossians 2:20; 3:3). It is

God's own work to do this; our place is to wait before him in help-lessness and humility.

Then comes the claiming by faith of what Christ is, the claiming of his life as ours. God's way is always from the Outward to the Inward. All we have seen of Jesus as One who is outside of us, we may ask to be made ours within us – not as something which he gives us out of himself, but as something which he himself will be in us. Jesus is the Second Adam. Just as deeply, inwardly and essentially as Adam and his sin has corrupted our nature and dwelt and worked in us, Jesus the Second Adam and his life can become ours. By faith we can have the Son of God in his meekness dwelling in our hearts (Galatians 2:20; 4:19; Ephesians 1:20; 3:17).

Once we have by faith claimed this Christ-life as our own, we wait on the Holy Spirit for the daily revelation and renewal of what there is in the life of Christ for us. As one need after another is discovered, one grace after another is imparted.

In the case of the disciples, we see that even three years of training and instruction in Christ's School did little to teach them humility. Even at the Last Supper there was an argument about who was the greatest among them. The day of Pentecost changed all that. The Holy Spirit brought down the Heavenly Life in power, brought down the glorified Jesus into their hearts, and their selfish-ness was changed into love.

Let us yield ourselves to the death of self, let us by faith claim Christ as our life, and live that life out in the power of the Holy Spirit. At the footstool of the throne of the exalted Jesus, the Holy Spirit comes to his waiting people (Acts 1:1-14; 2:1-4; 1 Corinthians 6:19-20; Galatians 4:6; Romans 8:2; 10:9).

The Christ-life in heaven working through us for the world
The Christ-life on earth had just one object: to glorify the Father by the salvation of the world. In heaven he works out that plan through everyone into whom his life enters. Look at the world now in the light of Christ's claims, promises, power and love. The power of the life of Christ is working in our churches and

missions, in Christian school and social work, in the great Christian societies and in personal evangelism.

You have claimed the Christ-life and you are rejoicing in it or longing for it. Learn to see yourself as a consecrated bearer of the life that is the life of the world. Humility is the end of self – it is the willingness to seek nothing for yourself, to let God use you as he will. Look at the needs of the world, of the people you know, and commit yourself to a life of service. You have asked for the Spirit of the meek and gentle Lamb of God – be like him, a sacrifice.

God will teach each one of us how to let the Christ-life sustain and use us. May our hearts cry with intense desire, 'What is there, Lord, that I can do, so that you may be better known and loved?' And may we have faith that the Lamb of God will dwell in our hearts, breathing his own Spirit into us.

[From *The Reign of Love*]

'And Ye Shall Find Rest to Your Souls'

Come unto me, and I will give you rest. Take my yoke upon you, and learn of me; and ye shall find rest to your souls.
(MATTHEW 11:28-19)

Rest for the soul: such was the first promise with which the Saviour sought to win the heavy-laden sinner. Simple though it appears, the promise is indeed as large and comprehensive as can be found. Rest for the soul – does it not imply deliverance from every fear, the supply of every want, the fulfilment of every desire? And now nothing less than this is the prize with which the Saviour woos back the wandering one – who is mourning that the rest has not been so abiding or so full as it had hoped – to come back and abide in him.

61

Nothing but this was the reason that the rest has either not been found, or, if found, has been disturbed or lost again: you did not abide with, you did not abide in him.

Have you ever noticed how, in the original invitation of the Saviour to come to him, the promise of rest was repeated twice, with such a variation in the conditions as might have suggested that abiding rest could only be found in abiding nearness? First the Saviour says, 'Come unto me, and I will give you rest'; the very moment you come, and believe, I will give you rest – the rest of pardon and acceptance – the rest in my love. But we know that all that God bestows needs time to become fully our own; it must be held fast, and appropriated, and assimilated into our inmost being; without this not even Christ's giving can make it our very own, in full experience and enjoyment. And so the Saviour repeats his promise, in words which clearly speak not so much of the initial rest with which he welcomes the weary one who comes, but of the deeper and personally appropriated rest of the soul that abides with him. He now not only says, 'Come unto me,' but 'Take my yoke upon you and learn of me'; become my scholars, yield yourselves to my training, submit in all things to my will, let your whole life be one with mine – in other words, Abide in me. And then he adds, not only, 'I will give', but 'ye shall *find* rest to your souls'. The rest he gave at coming will become something you have really found and made your very own – the deeper the abiding rest which comes from longer acquaintance and closer friendship, from entire surrender and deeper sympathy. 'Take my yoke, and learn of me,' 'Abide in me' – this is the path to abiding rest.

Do not these words of the Saviour discover what you have perhaps often sought in vain to know, how it is that the rest you at times enjoy is so often lost? It must have been this: you had not understood how *entire surrender to Jesus is the secret of perfect rest*. Giving up one's whole life to him, for him alone to rule and order it; taking up his yoke, and submitting to be led and taught, to learn of him; abiding in him, to be and do only what he wills – these are the conditions of discipleship without which there can be no

62

thought of maintaining the rest that was bestowed on first coming to Christ. The rest is in Christ, and not something he gives apart from himself, and so it is only in having him that the rest can really be kept and enjoyed.

[From *Abide in Christ*]

Christ's Dependence on the Father

Verily, verily I say unto you, The Son can do nothing of himself, but what he seeth the Father doing: for what things soever he doeth, these the Son also doeth in like manner. For the Father loveth the Son, and sheweth him all things that himself doeth: and greater works than these will he show him, that ye may marvel (JOHN 5:19-20)

I know mine own, and mine own know me, even as the Father knoweth me, and I know the Father.
(JOHN 10:14-15, RV)

Our relation to Jesus is the exact counterpart of his to the Father. And so the words in which he sets forth his fellowship with the Father have their truth in us too. And as the words of Jesus in John 5 describe the natural relation between every father and son, whether on earth or in heaven, they are applicable not only to the Only-begotten, but to every one who in and like Jesus is called a son of God.

We cannot better catch the simple truth and force of the illustration than by thinking of Jesus with his earthly father in the carpenter's shop learning his trade. The first thing you notice is the entire *dependence*: 'The son can do nothing of himself, but what he seeth the father doing.' Then you are struck by the implicit *obedience* that just seeks to imitate the father: 'for whatsoever things the father doeth, these doeth the son in like manner'. You then notice the loving *intimacy* to which the father admits him, keeping back none of his secrets: 'for the Father loveth the Son, and showeth him all things that himself doeth'. And in this dependent obedience on his son's part, and the loving teacher on the father's part, you have the pledge of an evergrowing *advance* to greater works: step by step, the son will be led up to all that the father himself can do: 'Greater works than these will he show him, that ye may marvel.'

In this picture we have the reflection of the relationship between God the Father and the Son in his blessed humanity. If his human nature is to be something real and true, and if we are to understand how Christ is in very deed to be our example, we must believe fully in what our blessed Lord here reveals to us of the secrets of his inner life. The words he speaks are literal truth. His dependence on the Father for each moment of his life was absolutely and intensely real: 'The Son can do nothing of himself, but what he seeth the Father doing.' He counted it no humiliation to wait on his Father for his commands: he rather considered it his highest blessedness to say and do only what the Father showed him: 'What things soever the Father doeth, these the Son also doeth in like manner.'

[From *Like Christ*]

Christ's Love

*A new commandment I give unto you, that ye love
one another; even as I have loved you, that ye also
love one another.* (JOHN 13:34)

*This is my commandment, that ye love one another,
even as I have loved you.* (JOHN 15:12)

'*Even as*' – we begin to understand somewhat of the blessedness of those little words. It is not the command of a law which only convinces of sin and impotence; it is a new command under a new covenant that is established on better promises. It is the command from him who asks nothing that he has not provided and now offers to bestow. It is the assurance that he expects nothing from us that he does not work in us: Even as I have loved you, and every moment am pouring out that love on you through the Holy Spirit, even so do ye love one another. The measure, the strength, and the work of your love you will find in my love to you.

Even as I have loved you: those words give us the *measure* of the love wherewith we must love each other. True love knows no measure: it gives itself entirely. It may take into consideration the time and measure of showing it; but love itself is ever whole and undivided. This is the greatest glory of divine love that we have, that of the Father and Son, two persons, who in love remain One Being, each losing himself in the other. This is the glory of the love of Jesus, who is the image of God, that he loves us even as the Father loves him. And this is the glory of brotherly love, that it will know of no law other than to love even as God and Christ.

He who would be like Christ must unhesitatingly accept this as his rule of life. He knows how difficult, how impossible it often is thus to love brethren in whom there is so much that is offensive or unamiable. Before going out to meet them in circumstances where his love may be tried, he goes in secret to the Lord, and with his eye fixed on his own sin and unworthiness asks: How much owest thou thy Lord? He goes to the cross and seeks there to fathom the love wherewith the Lord has loved him. He lets the light of the immeasurable love of him who is in heaven, his Head and his Brother, shine in on his soul, until he learns to feel divine love has but one law: love seeks not its own, love gives itself wholly. And he lays himself on the altar before his Lord: even as thou hast loved me, so will I love the brethren. In virtue of my union with Jesus, and in Jesus with them, there can be no question of anything less: I love them as Christ did. Oh that Christians would close their ears to all the reasonings of their own hearts, and fix their eyes only on the law which he who loves them has promulgated in his own example; they would realise that there is nothing for them to do but this – to accept his commands and to obey them.

[From *Like Christ*]

The 'Process' of Jesus Christ

In the gospel story we find five great points of special importance: the birth, the life on earth, the death, the resurrection, and the ascension. In these we have what an old writer has called 'the process of Jesus Christ', the process by which he became what he is today – our glorified King, and our life. In all this life process we must be made like unto him. Look at the first. What have we to say about his birth? This: He received his life *from God*. What about his life upon earth? He lived that life in dependence *upon God*. About his death? He gave up his life *to God*. About his resurrection? He was raised from the dead *by God*. And about his ascension? He lives his life in glory *with God*.

1. *Christ received his life from God*

And why is it of consequence that we should look to that? Because Christ Jesus had in that the starting point of his whole life. He said: 'The Father sent me'; 'The Father hath given to the Son all things'; 'The Father hath given the Son to have life in himself.' Christ received it as his own life, just as God has his life in himself. And yet, all the time it was a life given and received. 'Because the Father almighty has given this life unto me, the Son of man on earth, I can count upon God to maintain it and to carry me through all.'

And that is the first lesson we need. We need often to meditate on it, and to pray, and to think, and to wait before God, until our hearts open to the wonderful consciousness that the everlasting God has a divine life within us which cannot exist but through him. I believe God has given his life; it roots in him. I shall feel it must be maintained by him. We often think that God has given us a life which is now our own, a spiritual life, and that we are to take charge; and then we complain that we cannot keep it right. No wonder. We must learn to live, learn to live as Jesus did. I have to live as Jesus did. I have a God-given treasure in this earthen vessel. I have the light of the knowledge of the glory of God in the face of Christ. I have the life of God's Son within me given me by God himself, and it can be maintained by God himself only as I live in fellowship with him.

2. Christ lived in dependence on God

How did Christ live out his life during the thirty-three years in which he walked here upon earth? He lived it in dependence on God. You know how continually he says: 'The Son can do nothing of himself. The words that I speak, I speak not of myself.' He waited unceasingly for the teaching, and the commands, and the guidance of the Father. He prayed for power from the Father. Whatever he did, he did in the name of the Father. He, the Son of God, felt the need of much prayer, of persevering prayer, of bringing down from heaven and maintaining the life of fellowship with God in prayer. We hear a great deal about trusting God. Most blessed! And we may say: 'Ah, that is what I want,' and we may forget what is the very secret of all – that God, in Christ, must work all in us. I not only need God as an object of trust, but I must have Christ within as the power to trust; he must live his own life of trust in me. Look at it in that wonderful story of Paul the Apostle, the beloved servant of God. He is in danger of self-confidence, and God in heaven sends that terrible trial in Asia to bring him down, lest he trust in himself and not in the living God. God watched over his servant that he should be kept trusting. Remember that other story about the thorn in the flesh, in 2 Corinthians 12, and think what that means. He was in danger of exalting himself, and the blessed Master came to humble him, and to teach him: 'I keep thee weak, that thou mayest learn to trust not in thyself, but in me.' If we are to enter into the rest of faith, and to abide there; if we are to live the life of vicory in the land of Canaan, it must begin here. We must be broken down from all self-confidence and learn like Christ to depend absolutely and unceasingly upon God. There is a greater work to be done in that than perhaps we know. We must be broken down, and the habit of our souls must be unceasingly: 'I am nothing; God is all. I cannot walk before God for one hour as I should, unless God keep the life he has given me.' What a blessed solution God gives, then, to all our questions and our difficulties, when he says: 'My child, Christ has gone through it all for thee. Christ hath wrought out a new nature that can trust God; and Christ the Living One in heaven will live in thee, and enable thee to live that life of trust.' That is why Paul said: 'Such confidence have we toward God, through Christ.' What does that mean? Does it mean only through Christ as the mediator, or intercessor? Verily, no. It means much more; through Christ living in and enabling us to trust God as he trusted him.

3. *Christ gave up his life to God*

Then comes the death of Christ. What does that teach us of Christ's relation to the Father? It opens up to us one of the deepest and most solemn lessons of Christ's life, one which the Church of Christ understands all too little. We know what the death of Christ means as an atonement, and we never can emphasize too much that blessed substitution and bloodshedding, by which redemption was won for us. But let us remember, that is only half the meaning of his death. The other half is this: just as much as Christ was my substitute, who died for me, just so much he is my head, in whom, and with whom, I die; and just as he lives for me, to intercede, he lives in me, to carry out and to perfect his life. And if I want to know what that life is which he will live in me, I must look at his death. By his death he proved that he possessed life only to hold it, and to spend it, for God. To the very uttermost, without the shadow of a moment's exception, he lived for God – every moment, everywhere, he held life only for his God. And so, if one wants to live a life of perfect trust, there must be the perfect surrender of his life, and his will, even unto the very death. He must be willing to go all lengths with Jesus, even to Calvary. When a boy of twelve years of age Jesus said: 'Wist ye not that I must be about my Father's business?' and again when he came to Jordan to be baptized: 'It becometh us to fulfil all righteousness.' So on through all his life, he ever said: 'It is my meat and drink to do the will of my Father. I come not to do my own will, but the will of him that sent me.' 'Lo, I am come to do thy will, O God.' And in the agony of Gethsemane, his words were: 'Not my will, but thine, be done.'. . . .

Christ owes everything to his death and his grave. And we, too, owe everything to that grave of Jesus. Oh, let us lie every day rooted in the death of Jesus. Be not afraid, but say: 'To my own will I will die; to human wisdom, and human strength, and to the world I will die; for it is in the grave of my Lord that life has its beginning, and its strength and its glory.'

This brings us to our next thought.

4. *Christ was raised from the dead by God*

Christ received his life back again, raised by the Father, by the power of the glory of the Father. Oh, the deep meaning of the resurrection of Christ! What did Christ do when he died? He went down into the darkness and absolute helplesness of death. He gave up a life that was without sin, a life that was God-given, a life that was beautiful and precious; and he said, 'I will give it into the hands of my Father if he asks it,' and he did; and he was there in the grave, waiting on God to do his will; and because he honoured God to the uttermost in his helplessness, God lifted him up to the very uttermost of glory and power. Christ lost nothing by giving up his life in death to the Father. And so, if you want the glory and the life of God to come on you, it is in the grave of utter helplessness that that life of glory will be born. Jesus was raised from the dead, and that resurrection power, by the grace of God, can and will work in us. Let no one expect to live a right life until he lives a full resurrection life in the power of Jesus. Let me state in a different way what this resurrection means.

Christ had a perfect life, given by God. The Father said: 'Will you give up that life to me? Will you part with it at my command?' And Jesus parted with it, but God gave it back to him in a second life ten thousand times more glorious than that earthly life. So God will do to every one of us who willingly consents to part with his life. Have you ever understood it? Jesus was born twice. The first time he was born in Bethlehem. That was a birth into a life of weakness. But the second time he was born from the grave; he is the 'first-born from the dead'. Because he gave up the life that he had by his first birth, God gave him the life of the second birth, in the glory of heaven and the throne of God. Christians, that is exactly what we need to do. A man may be an earnest Christian; a man may be a successful worker; he may be a Christian who has had a measure of growth and advance; but if he has not entered this fullness of blessing, then he needs to come to a second and deeper experience of God's saving power; he needs, just as God brought him out of Egypt, through the Red Sea, to come to a point where God brings him through Jordan into Canaan. Beloved, we have been baptized into the death of Christ. It is as we say: 'I have had a very blessed life, and I have had many blessed experiences, and God has done many things for me; but I am conscious there is something wrong still; I am conscious that this life of rest and victory is not really mine.' Before Christ got his life of rest and victory on the throne, he had to die and give up all. Do you it, too, and you shall share his victory and glory. It is as we follow Jesus in his death that his resurrection, power, and joy will be ours.

5. *Christ lives his life in glory with God*
The fifth step in his wondrous path was: He was lifted up to be forever with the Father. Because he humbled himself, therefore God highly exalted him. Wherein cometh the beauty and blessedness of that exaltation of Jesus? For himself perfect fellowship with the Father; for others participation in the power of God's omnipotence. Yes, that was the fruit of his death. Scripture promises not only that God will, in the resurrection life, give us joy, and peace

that passeth understanding, victory over sin, and rest in God, but he will baptize us with the Holy Ghost; or, in other words, will fill us with the Holy Ghost. Jesus was lifted to the throne of heaven that he might there receive from the Father the Spirit in his new, divine manifestation, to be poured out in his fullness. And as we come to the resurrection life, the life in the faith of him who is one with us, and sits on the throne – as we come to that, we too may be partakers of the fellowship with Christ Jesus as he ever dwells in God's presence, and the Holy Spirit will fill us, to work in us, and out of us, in a way that we have never known.

Jesus got this divine life by depending absolutely on the Father all his life long, depending on him even down into death. Jesus got that life in the full glory of the Spirit to be poured out, by giving himself up in obedience and surrender to God alone, and leaving God even in the grave to work out his mighty power; and that very Christ will live out his life in you and me. Oh, the mystery! Oh, the glory! And, oh, the divine certainty! Jesus Christ means to live out that life in you and me.

[From *The Master's Indwelling*]

Our Lord's Prayer

If I want to find out the nature of perfect love I must look up to God's love to Christ. John 17:26 says: 'Father, that the love where-with thou hast loved me may be in them.' This is Christ's conclusion of his whole prayer. It is the whole object of his work, and that object is this: That the love that I have tasted, that the love which rested on me, and dwells in me, may now pass on to them. And so, if you want to know what the life of perfect love is, you must rise up to heaven itself and see what the love of God to Christ is.

And if you ask: How can I know what this perfect love in the Godhead is? I can answer only, The Father gave his own life to the Son; the Son was begotten of the Father, out of his bosom; in the depths of the Godhead Christ came forth from the Father. If God had not been love, if God had been anything that we could call selfish, he would have been content to be God alone. But he would not be alone. From eternity he set his Son before him as his image and his glory. He gave birth to the Son. When a man gives out his own life to another, that is love; and the love of God is that he gave his life to his only begotten Son, and he said that, to all eternity, he never would live without his Son.

[From *Love Made Perfect*]

The Power and Holiness of Prayer

The connection between the prayer life and the Spirit life is close and indissoluble. It is not merely that we receive the Spirit through prayer, but the Spirit life requires, as an indispensable thing, a continuous prayer life. I can led continually by the Spirit only as I continually give myself to prayer.

This was very evident in the life of our Lord. A study of his life will give us a wonderful view of the power and holiness of prayer.

Consider his baptism. It was when he was baptized and prayed that heaven was opened and the Holy Spirit came down upon him. God desired to crown Christ's surrender of himself to the sinner's baptism in Jordan (which was also a surrender of himself to the sinner's death), with the gift of the Spirit for the work that he must accomplish. *But this could not have taken place had he not prayed*. In the fellowship of worship the Spirit was bestowed on him to lead him out into the desert to spend forty days there in prayer and fasting. Turn to Mark 1:32–35: 'And at even, when the sun did set, they brought unto him all that were diseased, and them that were possessed with devils. And all the city was gathered together at the door . . . And in the morning, rising up a great while before day, he went out, and departed into a solitary place, and there prayed.'

The work of the day and evening had exhausted him. In his healing of the sick and casting out of devils, power had gone out of him. While others still slept, he went away to pray and *to renew his strength in communion with his Father*. He had need of this, otherwise he would not have been ready for the new day. The holy work of delivering souls demands constant renewal through fellowship with God.

Think again of the calling of the apostles as given in Luke 6:12-13: 'And it came to pass in those days, that he went out into a mountain to pray, and *continued all night in prayer to God*. And when it was day, he called unto him his disciples: and of them he chose twelve, whom also he named apostles.' Is it not clear that if anyone wishes to do God's work, *he must take time for fellowship with him, to receive his wisdom and power?* The dependence and helplessness of which this is an evidence, open the way and give God the opportunity of revealing his power. How great was the importance of the choosing of the apostles for Christ's own work, for the early Church, and for all time! It had God's blessing and seal; the stamp of prayer was on it.

Read Luke 9:18, 20: 'And it came to pass, as he was *alone praying*, his disciples were with him: and he asked them saying, Whom say the people that I am?. . . . Peter answering said, The Christ of God.' The Lord had prayed that the Father might reveal to them who he was. It was in answer to prayer that 'he chose twelve, whom also he named apostles'. And when Peter said: 'The Christ of God' the Lord said to him, 'Flesh and blood hath not revealed it unto thee, but my Father which is in heaven' (Matthew 16:17). This great confession was the fruit of prayer.

Read further Luke 9:28-35: 'He took Peter and John and James, and *went up into a mountain to pray*. And *as he prayed*, the fashion of his countenance was altered. . . . And there came a voice out of the cloud, saying, This is my beloved Son: hear him.' Christ had desired that, for the strengthening of their faith, God might give them an assurance from heaven that he was the Son of God. Prayer obtained for our Lord Jesus himself, as well as for his disciples, what happened on the Mount of Transfiguration.

Does it not become still more clear that *what God wills to accom-*

plish on earth needs prayer as its indispensable condition? And there is but one way for Christ and believers. A heart and mouth open toward heaven in believing prayer will certainly not be put to shame.

Read Luke 11:1-13: 'As he was *praying* in a certain plain, when he ceased, one of his disciples said unto him, Lord, *teach us to pray.* . . .' And then he gave them that inexhaustible prayer: 'Our Father who are in heaven.' In this he showed what was going on in his heart, when he prayed that God's name might be hallowed, and his kingdom come, and his will be done, and all of this 'on earth as it is in heaven'. How will this ever come to pass? Through prayer. This prayer has been uttered through the ages by countless millions, to their unspeakable comfort. But forget not this – it was born out of the prayer of our Lord Jesus. He had been praying, and therefore was able to give that glorious answer.

Read John 14:16: 'I will *pray* the Father, and he shall give you another Comforter.' The entire dispensation of the New Testament, with the wonderful outpouring of the Holy Spirit, is the outcome of the prayer of the Lord Jesus. It is as though God had impressed on the gift of the Holy Spirit this seal – in answer to the prayer of the Lord Jesus, and later of his disciples, the Holy Spirit will surely come. But it will be in answer to prayer like that of our Lord, *in which he took time to be alone with God and in that prayer offered himself wholly to God.*

Read John 17, the high priestly, most holy prayer! Here the Son prays first for himself, that the Father will glorify him by giving him power for the cross, by raising him from the dead, by setting him at his right hand. These great things could not take place save through prayer. Prayer had power to obtain them.

Afterward he prayed for his disciples, that the Father might preserve them from the evil one, might keep them from the world, and might sanctify them. And then, further, he prayed for all those who through their word might believe on him, that all might be one in love, even as the Father and the Son were one. This prayer gives us a glimpse into the wonderful relationship between the Father and the Son, and teaches us, that all the blessings of heaven come continually through the prayer of him who is at God's right hand and ever prays for us. But it teaches us, also, that all these blessings must in the same manner be desired and asked for by us. The whole nature and glory of God's blessings consist in this – they must be obtained *in answer to prayer*, by hearts entirely surrendered to him, and hearts that believe in the power of prayer.

Now we come to the most remarkable instance of all. In Gethsemane we see that our Lord, according to his constant habit, consulted and arranged with the Father the work he had to do on earth. First he besought him in agony and bloody sweat to let the cup pass from him; when he understood that this could not be, then he prayed for strength to drink it, and surrendered himself with the words: 'Thy will be done.' He was able to meet the enemy full of courage and in the power of God gave himself over to the death of the cross. *He had prayed*.

Oh, why is it that God's children have so little faith in the glory of prayer, as the great power for subjecting our own wills to that of God, as well as for the confident carrying out of the work of God in spite of our great weakness? Would that we might learn from our Lord Jesus how impossible it is to walk with God, to obtain God's blessing or leading, or to do his work joyously and fruitfully, apart from close unbroken fellowship with him who is ever a living fountain of spiritual life and power!

Let every Christian think over this simple study of the prayer life of our Lord Jesus and endeavour from God's word, with prayer for the leading of the Holy Spirit, *to learn what the life is which the Lord Jesus Christ bestows upon him and supports in him*. It is nothing else than a life of daily prayer. Let each minister especially recognize how entirely vain it is to attempt to do the work of our Lord in any other way than that in which he did it. Let us, as workers, begin to believe that we are set free from the ordinary business of the world, that we may, above everything, have time, in our Saviour's name, and with his Spirit, and in oneness with him, to *ask for and obtain blessing for the world*.

[From *The Prayer Life*]

Christ's Death on the Cross

What the Scriptures Teach About the Blood

Not without blood. (HEBREWS 9:7, 18)

What the Old Testament teaches
Its record about the blood begins at the gates of Eden.

Into the unrevealed mysteries of Eden I do not enter.

But in connection with the sacrifice of Abel all is plain. He brought of 'the firstlings of his flock' to the Lord as a sacrifice, and there, in connection with the first act of worship recorded in the Bible, blood was shed. We learn from Hebrews 11:4 that it was 'by faith' Abel offered an acceptable sacrifice, and his name stands first in the record of those whom the Bible calls 'believers'. He had this witness borne to him that 'he pleased God'. His faith, and God's good pleasure in him, are closely connected with the sacrificial blood.

In the light of later revelation, this testimony, given at the very beginning of human history, is of deep significance. It shows that there can be no approach to God – no fellowship with him by faith – no enjoyment of his favour – apart from the blood.

Scripture gives but short notice of the following sixteen

centuries. Then came the Flood, which was God's judgement on sin, by the destruction of the world of mankind.

But God brought forth a new earth from that awful baptism of water.

Notice, however, that the new earth must be baptized also with blood, and the first recorded act of Noah, after he had left the ark, was the offering of a burnt sacrifice to God. As with Abel, so with Noah at a new beginning, it was 'not without blood'.

Sin once again prevailed, and God laid an entirely new foundation for the establishment of his kingdom on earth.

By the divine call of Abraham, and the miraculous birth of Isaac, God undertook the formation of a people to serve him. But this purpose was not accomplished apart from the shedding of the blood. This is apparent in the most solemn hour of Abraham's life.

God had already entered into covenant relationship with Abraham, and his faith had already been severely tried, and had stood the test. It was reckoned, or counted to him, for righteousness. Yet he must learn that Isaac, the son of promise, who belonged wholly to God, can be truly surrendered to God only by death.

Isaac must die. For Abraham, as well as for Isaac, only by death could freedom from the self-life be obtained.

Abraham must offer Isaac on the altar.

That was not an arbitrary command of God. It was the revelation of a divine truth that it is only through death that a life truly consecrated to God is possible. But it was impossible for Isaac to die and rise again from the dead; for on account of sin, death would hold him fast. But see, his life was spared, and a ram was offered in his place. Through the blood that then flowed on Mount Moriah his life was spared. He, and the people which sprang from him, live before God 'not without blood'. By that blood, however, he was in a figure raised again from the dead. The great lesson of substitution is here clearly taught.

Four hundred years pass, and Isaac has become, in Egypt, the people of Israel. Through her deliverance from Egyptian bondage Israel was to be recognized as God's first-born among the nations.

Here, also, it is 'not without blood'. Neither the electing grace of God, nor his covenant with Abraham, nor the exercise of his omnipotence, which could so easily have destroyed their oppressors, could dispense with the necessity of the blood.

What the blood accomplished on Mount Moriah for one person, who was the Father of the nation, must now be experienced by that nation. By the sprinkling of the door frames of the Israelites with the blood of the Paschal lamb; by the institution of the Passover as an enduring ordinance with the words, 'When I see the blood I will pass over you,' the people were taught that life can be obtained only by the death of a substitute. Life was possible for them only through the blood of a life given in their place, and appropriated by 'the sprinkling of that blood'.

Fifty days later this lesson was enforced in a striking manner. Israel had reached Sinai. God had given his Law as the foundation of his covenant. That covenant must now be established, but as it is expressly stated in Hebrews 9:7, '*not without blood*'. The sacrificial blood must be sprinkled, first on the altar, and then on the book of the Covenant, representing God's side of that Covenant; then on the people, with the declaration, 'This is the blood of the Covenant' (Exodus 24).

It was in that blood the Covenant had its foundation and power. It is by the blood alone that God and man can be brought into covenant fellowship. That which had been foreshadowed at the Gate of Eden, on Mount Ararat, on Moriah, and in Egypt was now confirmed at the foot of Sinai, in a most solemn manner. Without blood there could be no access by sinful man to a Holy God.

There is, however, a marked difference between the manner of applying the blood in the former cases as compared with the latter. On Moriah the life was redeemed by the shedding of the blood. In Egypt it was sprinkled on the door posts of the houses; but at Sinai it was sprinkled on the *persons themselves*. The contact was closer, the application more powerful.

Immediately after the establishment of the covenant the command was given, 'Let them make me a sanctuary that I may dwell among them' (Exodus 25:8). They were to enjoy the full blessedness of having the God of the Covenant abiding among them. Through his grace they may find him, and serve him in his house.

He himself gave, with the minutest care, directions for the arrangement and service of that house. But notice that the blood is the centre and reason of all this. Draw near to the vestibule of the earthly temple of the Heavenly King, and the first thing visible is the altar of burnt offering, where the sprinkling of blood continues, without ceasing, from morning till evening. Enter the Holy Place, and the most conspicuous thing is the golden altar of incense, which also, together with the veil, is constantly sprinkled with the blood. Ask what lies beyond the Holy Place, and you will be told that it is the Most Holy Place where God dwells. If you ask how he dwells there, and how he is approached, you will be told '*not without blood*'. The golden throne where his glory shines is itself sprinkled with *the blood*, once every year, when the high priest alone enters to bring in *the blood*, and to worship God. The highest act in that worship is the sprinkling of *the blood*.

If you inquire further, you will be told that always, and for everything, *the blood* is the one thing needful. At the consecration of the house, or of the priests; at the birth of a child; in the deepest penitence on account of sin; in the highest festival; always, and in everything, the way to fellowship with God is through *the blood* alone.

This continued for fifteen hundred years. At Sinai, in the desert, at Shiloh, in the Temple on Mount Moriah it continued – till our Lord came to make an end of all shadows by bringing in the substance, and by establishing a fellowship with the Holy One, in spirit and truth.

What our Lord Jesus himself teaches
With his coming old things passed away, all things became new. He came from the Father in heaven, and can tell us in divine words the way to the Father.

It is sometimes said that the words '*not without blood*' belong to the Old Testament. But what does our Lord Jesus Christ say? Notice, first, that when John the Baptist announced his coming, he spoke of him as filling a dual office, as '*the Lamb of God* that taketh away the sin of the world'; and then as 'the One who would baptize with the Holy Spirit'. The outpouring of the blood of the Lamb of God must take place before the outpouring of the Spirit could be bestowed. Only when all that the Old Testament taught about the blood has been fulfilled can the dispensation of the Spirit begin.

The Lord Jesus Christ himself plainly declared that his death on the Cross was the purpose for which he came into the world; that it was the necessary condition of the redemption and life which he came to bring. He clearly states that in connection with his death *the shedding of his blood* was necessary.

In the synagogue at Capernaum he spoke of himself as 'the Bread of Life'; of his flesh, 'that he would give it for the life of the world'. Four times over he said most emphatically, 'Except ye . . . drink his *blood* ye have no life in you.' 'He that drinketh my *blood* hath everlasting life.' 'My *blood* is drink indeed.' 'He that drinketh my *blood* dwelleth in me and I in him' (John 6). Our Lord thus declared the fundamental fact that he himself, as the Son of the Father, who came to restore to us our lost life, can do this in no other way than by dying for us; by shedding his blood for us; and then making us partakers of its power.

Our Lord confirmed the teaching of the Old Testament Offerings – that man can live only through the death of another, and thus obtain a life that through Resurrection has become eternal.

But Christ himself cannot make us partakers of that eternal life which he has procured for us, save by the shedding of his blood, and causing us to drink it. Marvellous fact! *'Not without blood'* can eternal life be ours.

Equally striking is our Lord's declaration of the same truth on the last night of his earthly life. Before he completed the great work of his life by giving it 'as a ransom for many', he instituted the Holy Supper, saying – 'This cup is the New Testament in *my blood* that is shed for you and for many for the remission of sins. Drink ye all of it' (Matthew 26:28). 'Without shedding of blood there is no remission of sins.' Without remission of sins there is no life. But by the shedding of his blood he has obtained a new life for us. By what he calls 'the drinking of his blood' he shares his life with us. The blood shed in the Atonement, which frees us from *the guilt* of sin: and from death, *the punishment* of sin; the blood, which by faith we drink, bestows on us his life. The blood he shed was, in the first place *for* us, and is then given *to* us.

The teaching of the apostles under the inspiration of the Holy Spirit
After his resurrection and ascension, our Lord is not any longer known by the apostles 'after the flesh'. Now, all that was symbolic has passed away, and the deep spiritual truths expressed by symbol are unveiled.

But there is no veiling of the blood. It still occupies a prominent place.

Turn first to the Epistle to the Hebrews, which was written purposely to show that the Temple service had become unprofitable, and was intended by God to pass away, now that Christ had come.

Here, if anywhere, it might be expected that the Holy Spirit would emphasize the true spirituality of God's purpose, yet it is just here that the blood of Jesus is spoken of in a manner that imparts a new value to the phrase.

We read concerning our Lord that 'by his own blood he entered in the holy place' (Hebrews 9:12).

'The blood of Christ ... shall purge your conscience' (9:14).

'Having therefore, brethren, boldness to enter into the holiest by the blood of Jesus' (10:19).

'Ye are come ... to Jesus the Mediator of the New Covenant, and to the blood of sprinkling' (12:24).

'Jesus also, that he might sanctify the people with his own blood suffered without the gate' (13:12–13).

'God ... brought again from the dead our Lord Jesus – through the blood of the everlasting covenant' (13:20).

By such words the Holy Spirit teaches us that the blood is really the central power of our entire redemption. '*Not without blood*' is as valid in the New Testament as in the Old.

Nothing but the blood of Jesus, shed in his death for sin, can cover sin on God's side, or remove it on ours.

We find the same teaching in the writings of the apostles. Paul writes of 'being justified freely by his grace through the redemption that is in Christ Jesus . . . through faith in his blood' (Romans 3:24–25), of 'being now justified by his blood' (5:9).

To the Corinthians he declares that the 'cup of blessing which we bless is the communion of the blood of Christ' (1 Corinthians 10:16).

In the Epistle to the Galatians he uses the word '*cross*' to convey the same meaning, while in Colossians he unites the two words and speaks of 'the blood of his cross' (Galatians 6:14; Colossians 1:20).

He reminds the Ephesians that 'We have redemption through his blood' and that we 'are made nigh by the blood of Christ' (Ephesians 1:7 and 2:13).

Peter reminds his readers that they were 'Elect ... unto obedience and sprinkling of the blood of Jesus' (1 Peter 1:2), that they were redeemed by 'the precious blood of Christ' (2:19).

See how John assures his 'little children' that 'The blood of Jesus Christ his Son cleanseth us from all sin' (1 John 1:7). The Son is he 'who came not by water only but by water and blood' (2:6).

All of them agree together in mentioning the blood, and in glorying in it, as the power by which eternal redemption through Christ is fully accomplished and is then applied by the Holy Spirit.

But perhaps this is merely earthly language. What has heaven to say?

What the book of Revelation teaches concerning the future glory and the blood

It is of the greatest importance to notice that in the revelation which God has given in this book, of the glory of his throne and the blessedness of those who surround it, the blood still retains its remarkably prominent place.

On the throne John saw 'A Lamb as it had been slain' (Revelation 5:6). As the Elders fell down before the Lamb they sang a new song saying, 'Thou art worthy ... for thou wast slain and hast redeemed us to God by thy blood' (5:8-9).

Later on when he saw the great company which no man could number, he was told in reply to his question as to who they were, 'They have washed their robes, and made them white in the blood of the Lamb.'

Then again, when he heard the song of victory over the defeat of Satan, its strain was, 'They overcame him by the blood of the Lamb' (12:11).

In the glory of heaven, as seen by John, there was no phrase by which the great purposes of God, the wondrous love of the Son of God, the power of his redemption, and the joy and thanksgiving of the redeemed can be gathered up and expressed save this – '*the blood of the Lamb*'. From the beginning to the end of Scripture, from the closing of the gates of Eden to the opening of the gates of the heavenly Zion, there runs through Scripture a golden thread. It is 'the blood' that unites the beginning and the end, that gloriously restores what sin had destroyed.

[From *The Power of the Blood of Jesus*]

Reconciliation through the blood

Being justified freely by his grace through the redemption that is in Christ Jesus, whom God hath set forth as a propitiation through faith in his blood.
(ROMANS 3:24-25)

In our Lord's work of redemption, reconciliation naturally comes first. It stands first also among the things the sinner has to do, who desires to have a share in redemption. Through it, a participation in the other blessings of redemption is made possible.

Sin, which made reconciliation necessary

In all the work of Christ, and above all in reconciliation, God's object is the removal and destruction of sin. Knowledge of sin is necessary for the knowledge of reconciliation.

We want to understand what there is in sin that needs reconciliation, and how reconciliation renders sin powerless. Then faith will have something to take hold of, and the experience of that blessing is made possible.

Sin has had a twofold effect. It has had *an effect on God*, as well as *on man*. We emphasize generally its effect on man. But the effect it has exercised on God is more terrible and serious. It is because of its effect on God that sin has its power over us. God, as Lord of all, could not overlook sin. It is his unalterable law that sin must bring forth sorrow and death. When man fell into sin, he, by that law of God, was brought under the power of sin. So it is *with the law of God* that redemption must begin, for if sin is powerless against God, and the law of God gives sin no authority over us, then its power over us is destroyed. The knowledge that sin is speechless before God assures us that it has no longer authority over us.

What then was the effect of sin upon God? In his divine nature, he ever remains unchanged and unchangeable, but in his relationship and bearing towards man, an entire change has taken place. Sin is disobedience, a contempt of the authority of God; it seeks to rob God of his honour, as God and Lord. Sin is determined opposition to a holy God. It not only can, but must, awaken his wrath.

While it was God's desire to continue in love and friendship with man, sin has compelled him to become an opponent. Although the love of God towards man remains unchanged, sin made it impossible for him to admit man to fellowship with himself. It has compelled him to pour out upon man his wrath, and curse, and punishment, instead of his love. The change which sin has caused in God's relationship to man is awful.

Man is guilty before God. Guilt is debt. We know what debt is. It is something that one person can demand from another, a claim which must be met and settled.

When sin is committed its after-effects may not be noticed, but its guilt remains. The sinner is guilty. God cannot disregard his own demand that sin must be punished; and his glory, which has been dishonoured, must be upheld. As long as the debt is not discharged, or the guilt expiated, it is, in the nature of the case, impossible for a holy God to allow the sinner to come into his presence.

We often think that the great question for us is, how we can be delivered from the indwelling power of sin; but that is a question of less importance than how we can be delivered from *the guilt* which is heaped up *before God*. Can the guilt of sin be removed? Can the effect of sin *upon God*, in awakening his wrath, be removed? Can sin be blotted out *before God*? If these things can be done, the power of sin will be broken in us also. It is only through *reconciliation* that the guilt of sin can be removed.

The word translated 'reconciliation' means actually 'to cover'. Even heathen people had an idea of this. But in Israel God revealed a *reconciliation* which could so truly cover and remove the guilt of sin that the original relationship between God and man can be entirely restored. This is what true *reconciliation* must do. It must so remove the guilt of sin, that is, *the effect of sin on God*, that man can draw near to God, in the blessed assurance that there is not any longer the least guilt resting on him to keep him away from God.

The blood that wrought out the reconciliation
Reconciliation must be the satisfaction of the demands of God's holy law.

The Lord Jesus accomplished that. By a willing and perfect obedience, he fulfilled the law under which he had placed himself. In the same spirit of complete surrender to the will of the Father, he bore the curse which the law had pronounced against sin. He rendered, in fullest measure of obedience or punishment, all that the law of God could ever ask or desire. The law was perfectly satisfied by him. But how can his fulfilling the demands of the law be reconciliation for the sins of others? Because, both in Creation and in the holy covenant of grace that the Father had made with him, he was recognized as the head of the human race. Because of this, he was able, by becoming flesh, to become a second Adam. When he, the Word, became flesh, he placed himself in a real fellowship with our flesh which was under the power of sin, and he assumed the responsibility for all that sin had done in the flesh against God. His obedience and perfection was not merely that of one man among others, but that of him who had taken their sin upon himself.

As Head of mankind through Creation, as their representative in the covenant, he became their surety. As a perfect satisfaction of the demands of the law was accomplished by the shedding of his blood, this was the reconciliation, the covering of our sin.

Above all, we must never forget that he was God. This bestowed a divine power on him, to unite himself with his creatures, and *to take them up into himself*. It bestowed on his sufferings a virtue of infinite holiness and power. It made the merit of his blood-shedding more than sufficient to deal with all the guilt of human sin. It made his blood such a real *reconciliation*, such a perfect covering of sin, that the holiness of God no longer beholds it. It has been, in truth, blotted out. The blood of Jesus, God's Son, has procured a real, perfect and eternal reconciliation.

What does that mean?

We have spoken of the awful effect of sin on God, of the terrible change which took place in heaven, through sin. Instead of favour, and friendship, and blessing, and the life of God, from heaven, man had nothing to look for except wrath, and curse, and death, and perdition. He could think of God only with fear and terror; without hope, and without love. Sin never ceased to call for vengeance, guilt must be dealt with in full.

But see: the blood of Jesus, God's Son, has been shed! Atonement for sin has been made. Peace is restored. A change has taken place again, as real and widespread as that which sin had brought about. For those who receive the reconciliation, sin has been brought to naught. The wrath of God turns round and hides itself in the depth of divine love.

The righteousness of God no longer terrifies man. It meets him as a friend, with an offer of complete justification. God's countenance beams with pleasure and approval as the penitent sinner draws near to him, and he invites him to intimate fellowship. He opens for him treasure of blessing. There is nothing now that can separate him from God.

The reconciliation through the blood of Jesus has covered his sins; they appear no longer in God's sight. He no longer imputes sin. Reconciliation has wrought out a perfect and eternal redemption.

Oh, who can tell the worth of that precious blood?

It is no wonder that for ever mention will be made of that blood in the song of the redeemed, and through all eternity, as long as heaven lasts, the praise of the blood will resound. 'Thou wast slain and hast redeemed us unto God by thy blood.'

But here is the wonder, that the redeemed on earth do not more heartily join in that song, and that they are not abounding in praise for the reconciliation that the power of the blood has accomplished.

[From *The Power of the Blood of Jesus*]

Crucified with Christ

I have been crucified with Christ; yet I live; and yet no longer I, but Christ liveth in me.
(GALATIANS 2:20)

As in Adam we died out of the life and the will of God into sin and corruption, so in Christ we are made partakers of a new spiritual death, a death to sin and into the will and the life of God. Such was

87

the death Christ died; such is the death we are made partakers of in him. To Paul this was such a reality that he was able to say: 'I have been crucified with Christ; yet I live; and yet no longer I, but Christ liveth in me.' The death with Christ had had such power that he no longer lived his own life; Christ lived his life in him. He had indeed died to the old nature and to sin, and been raised up into the power of the living Christ dwelling in him.

Christ's death on the cross was his highest exhibition of his holiness and victory over sin. And the believer who receives Christ is made partaker of all the power and blessing that the crucified Lord has won. As the believer learns to accept of this by faith, he yields himself as now crucified to the world and dead to its pleasure and pride, its lusts and self-pleasing. He learns that the mystery of the cross, as the crucified Lord reveals its power in him, opens the entrance into the fullest fellowship with Christ and the conformity to his sufferings. And so he learns, in the full depth of its meaning, what the Word has said: 'Christ crucified, the power of God and the wisdom of God.' He grows into a fuller apprehension of the blessedness of daring to say: 'I am crucified with Christ; I live no more; Christ the crucified liveth in me.'

[From *The Secret of the Faith Life*]

The Disposition of our Lord

Let us fix our attention on the disposition of our Lord from which the cross derived its power. We are so accustomed, in speaking about the cross of Christ, to think only of the work that was done there for us, that we take too little notice of that from which that work derives its value – the inner disposition of our Lord of which the cross was only the outward expression. Scripture does not place in the foreground, as most important, the weighty and bitter sufferings of the Lord, which are often emphasized for the purpose of awakening religious feelings, but the inner disposition of the

Lord, which led him to the cross, and inspired him while on it – this, Scripture does emphasize. Neither does Scripture direct attention only to the work which the Lord accomplished for us on the cross; it directs special attention to the work that the cross accomplished in him, and which through him must yet be accomplished in us also.

This appears not only from our Lord's words which he spoke from the cross, but from what he said when on three different occasions he had previously told his disciples that they must take up their cross and follow him. More than once he spoke thus when foretelling his own crucifixion. The thought he wished specially to impress upon them in connection with the cross was that of fellowship with, of conformity to, him. And that this did not consist in merely outward sufferings and persecutions, but in an inward disposition, appears from what he often added, 'deny yourselves and take up the cross'. This is what he desires them to do. Our Lord further teaches us, that neither for him nor for his disciples does the bearing of the cross begin when a material cross is laid upon the shoulders. No! He carried the cross all through his life; what became visible on Golgotha was a manifestation of the disposition which inspired his whole life.

What then did the bearing of the cross mean for the Lord Jesus? And what end could it serve for him? We know that the evil of sin appears in the change it brought about both in the disposition of man towards God, as well as in that of God towards man. With man it resulted in his fall from God, or enmity against God; with God it resulted in his turning away from man, or his wrath. In the first we see the terribleness of its tyranny over man; in the second, the terribleness of the guilt of sin, demanding the judgement of God on man.

The Lord Jesus, who came to deliver man from sin as a whole, had to deal with the power of sin as well as with its guilt; first the one, and then the other. For although we separate these two things, for the sake of making truth clear, sin is ever a unity. Therefore we need to understand not only that our Lord by his atonement on the cross removed the guilt of sin, but that this was made possible by the victory he had first won over the power of sin. It is the glory of the cross that it was the divine means by which both these objects were accomplished.

The Lord Jesus had to bring to naught the power of sin. He could do this only in his own person. Therefore he came in the closest possible likeness of sinful flesh; in the weakness of flesh; with the fullest capacity to be tempted as we are. From his baptism with the Holy Spirit, and the temptation of Satan which followed, up to the fearful soul agony in Gethsemane, and the offering of himself on the cross, his life was a ceaseless strife against self-will and self-honour; against the temptations of the flesh, and of the world, to reach his goal – the setting up of his kingdom – by fleshly or worldly means. Every day he had to take up and carry his cross, that is, to lose his own life and will, by going out of himself and doing and speaking nothing save what he had seen or heard from the Father. That which took place in the temptation in the wilderness, and in the agony of Gethsemane – at the beginning and end of his public ministry – is only a peculiarly clear manifestation of the disposition which characterized his whole life. He was tempted to the sin of self-assertion but he overcame the temptation to satisfy lawful desires – from the first temptation, to obtain bread to satisfy his hunger, till the last, that he might not have to drink the bitter cup of death – that he might be subject to the will of the Father.

So he offered up himself and his life; he denied himself, and took up his cross; he learned obedience and became perfect; in his own person he gained a complete victory over the power of sin, till he was able to testify that the evil one, 'the prince of this world cometh, and hath nothing in me' (John 14:30).

His death on the cross was the last and most glorious achievement in his personal victory over the power of sin; from this the atoning death of the cross derived its value. For a reconciliation was necessary, if guilt was to be removed. No one can contend with sin without at the same time coming into conflict with the wrath of God. These two cannot be separated from one another. The Lord

Jesus desired to deliver man from his sin. He could not do this save by suffering the curse of God's wrath against sin, and bearing it away. But his supreme power to remove guilt and the curse did not lie merely in the fact that he endured so much pain and suffering of death, but that he endured it all *in willing obedience to the Father*, for the maintenance and glorification of his righteousness. It was this disposition of self-sacrifice, of bearing of the cross willingly, which bestowed on the cross its power.

So the Scripture says: 'He humbled himself, and became obedient unto death, even the death of the cross. Wherefore God also hath highly exalted him, and given him a name which is above every name' (Philippians 2:8, 9).

And again: 'Though he were a Son, yet learned he obedience by the things which he suffered; and being made perfect, he became the author of eternal salvation unto all them that obey him' (Hebrews 5:8, 9). It is because Jesus broke down and conquered the power of sin first in his personal life that he can remove from us the guilt of sin, and thus deliver us from both its power and guilt. The cross is the divine sign, proclaiming to us that the way, the only way to the life of God, is through the yielding up in sacrifice of the self-life.

Now this spirit of obedience, this sacrifice of self, which bestowed on the cross its infinite value, bestowed that value also on the blood of the cross. Here again God reveals to us the secret of the power of that blood. That blood is the proof of obedience unto death of the Beloved Son; of that disposition which chose to offer it (the blood), to shed it, to lose his own life rather than commit the sin of pleasing himself; of the sacrifice of everything, even life itself, to glorify the Father. The life which dwelt in that blood – the heart from which it flowed – glowing with love and devotion to God and his will, was one of entire obedience and consecration to him.

And, now, what do you think? If that blood, living and powerful through the Holy Spirit, comes into contact with our hearts, and if we rightly understand what the blood of the cross means, is it possible that the blood should not impart its holy nature to us? But as the blood could not have been shed apart from the sacrifice of 'self' on the cross, so it cannot be received or enjoyed apart from a similar sacrifice of 'self'. That blood will bring to us a 'self' sacrificing disposition, and in our work there will be a conformity to, and an imitation of, the crucified One, making self-sacrifice the highest and most blessed law of our lives. The blood is a living, spiritual, heavenly power. It will bring the soul that is entirely surrendered to it to see and know by experience that there is no entrance into the full life of God, save by the self-sacrifice of the cross.

[From *The Blood of the Cross*]

'Take Up Your Cross'

Keeping Christ's Commandments

If ye know these things, blessed are ye if ye do them.
(JOHN 13:17)

The blessedness and the blessing of God's Word is only to be known by doing it.

The subject is of such supreme importance to the Christian and therefore in our Bible study, that I must ask you to return to it once more. And let us this time just take the one experience. Keeping the Word, or keeping the commandments.

Let us take it first in the farewell discourse. You may be familiar with the passages, but it will be of use to look at them together.

'If ye love me, ye will keep my commandments and the Father shall give you another Comforter' (John 14:15-16).

'He that hath my commandments, and keepeth them, he it is that loveth me: and he that loveth me shall be loved of my Father' (verse 21).

'If a man love me, he will keep my word: and my Father will love him' (verse 23).

'If ye abide in me, and my words abide in you, ask whatsoever ye will, and it shall be done unto you' (15:7).

'If ye keep my commandments, ye shall abide in my love' (15:10).

'Ye are my friends, if ye do whatsoever I command you' (15:14).

Study and compare these passages, until the words enter the heart and work the deep conviction that keeping Christ's commandments is an indispensable condition of all true spiritual blessing.

[From *Prayer's Inner Chamber*]

Learning of Christ

Take my yoke upon you, and learn of me; for I am meek and lowly in heart: and ye shall find rest unto your souls. (MATTHEW 11:29)

All Bible study is learning. All Bible study to be fruitful should be learning of Christ. The Bible is the school book, Christ is the teacher. It is he who opens the understanding, and opens the heart, and opens the seals (Luke 24:45; Acts 16:14; Revelation 5:9). Christ is the living eternal Word of which the written words are the human expression. Christ's presence and teaching are the secret of all true Bible study. The written Word is powerless except as it helps us to the living Word. No one has ever thought of accusing our Lord of not honouring the Old Testament. In his own life he proved that he loved it as coming out of the mouth of God. He ever pointed the Jews to it as the revelation of God and the witness to himself. But with the disciples it is remarkable how he always spoke of his own teaching as what they most needed, and had to obey. It was only after his resurrection, when the union with himself had been effected, and they had already received the first breathings of the Spirit (John 20:22) that we find him expounding the Scriptures. The Jews had their self-made interpretation of the

94

Word: they made it the greatest barrier between themselves and him of whom it spoke. It is often so with Christians too; our human apprehension of Scripture, fortified as it may be by the authority of the Church, or our own circle, becomes the greatest hindrance in the way of Christ's teachings. Christ the living Word seeks first to find his place in our heart and life, to be our only teacher: thus shall we learn of him to honour and understand Scripture.

[From *Prayer's Inner Chamber*]

Unlearning

Unlearning is often the most important part of learning: wrong impressions, prejudices and prepossessions are insuperable obstacles in the way of learning. Until these have been removed the teacher labours in vain. The knowledge he communicates only touches the surface: deep under the surface the pupil is guided by that which has become a second nature to him. The first work of the teacher is to discover, to make the pupil see, to remove, these hindrances.

There can be no true and fruitful learning of Christ where we are not ready to unlearn. By heredity, by education, by tradition, we have our thoughts about religion and God's Word, which are often the greater hindrance in proportion to our assurance that they are indeed the truth. To learn of Christ needs a willingness to subject every truth we hold to his inspection for criticism and correction.

[From *Prayer's Inner Chamber*]

I am Crucified with Christ

I am crucified with Christ. (GALATIANS 2:20)

'I through the law am dead,' says Paul, for 'I am crucified with Christ.' When it pleased God to reveal Christ Jesus in him, he saw how it was the crucified one who as the risen Lord had said unto him: 'I am Jesus.' In that vision he learnt to know Christ as the God-Man, who as the head of his body had been on the Cross the representative of all his people. He learnt that in Christ Jesus he had shared all the power of his death and resurrection. His whole life now consisted in the cultivation of the blessed consciousness: 'I have been crucified with Christ.' There my death to sin and the law is complete; there I receive the spirit and the power to live like Christ.

How many hearts have longed to understand and to experience fully what Paul meant with these words. And what vain struggles these have often been because we did not know how it is only the power of God by the Holy Spirit which can reveal this mystery. Let us in deep reverence bow before that Spirit to guide our thoughts into some spiritual apprehension of this blessed truth. Let us look at it in its divine reality, in its believing apprehension, in its actual experience.

We start with the divine reality of the believer's union with Christ crucified. We all admit that when God in nature gave a seed the property of containing all the stem and branches and fruit that were to grow from it, it was his power which gave each of them its existence. We understand even so that when God made Adam the father of the human race, each one of his children was contained in him, and shared with him the nature in which he sinned and the death he died. It is not different with Christ Jesus. As the second Adam all his seed was contained in him. When on the cross in the awful three hours of darkness he plunged into the sea of wrath to rescue there all whom the Father had given him, he did indeed carry them in his arms through death and resurrection to be seated with him at the right hand of God. They were there so incorporated into Christ Jesus that each of them was crucified with him, died in his death, and rose in his resurrection. When Paul writes: 'Of God ye are in Christ Jesus'; 'God quickened us together with him and raised us up with him', he speaks of a spiritual, but most real and actual union.

It is only when we learn to look at what is a fact with God, a divine living reality, that we shall understand how it is possible for us to say, 'I am crucified with Christ.' To reckon ourselves indeed dead unto sin, and alive unto God in Christ Jesus, means nothing less than this, that not only because God sees it and says it, but because what God sees and says has actually taken place and must be accepted by us as a simple fact. It is our duty to count ourselves as dead with Christ and living in him, too.

Think now of the believing apprehension of this truth. Faith must always be co-extensive with its object, the faith in Christ crucified must take in all that he is, all that he has done for us, all that God has made us in him. This faith is to be like the breath in our body, the divine inspiration by which Jesus Christ maintains his life in us, and by which we confidently rest in the assurance that he keeps our life safe and strong.

In faith there are ever two sides. On the one hand it implies our utter impotence and helplessness, our inability to grasp spiritual truth or spiritual blessing, our absolute dependence for everything on the work of another whom we trust. Then there is the other side, the willingness to yield ourselves fully and unreservedly to him to whom we look for aid. This is one of the deepest lessons in the death of Christ. He went down to the grave in utter weakness, looking to God alone to raise him up: just because he did this he sacrificed all and gave up his life, with all it implied, to the Father's keeping. 'Christ liveth in me' – to say this means an insight into how he lived and died in the faith of God, and how we in like faith may attain to a fellowship in his life and death, and especially in his crucifixion, which to man is utterly impossible.

Man's faith must always rest on God's fact. What God did in uniting us with Christ in his death and resurrection must, day by day, stand out before us as the divine assurance of what God will every hour work within us by his Holy Spirit, to a faith daily renewed in us by the Spirit. As we look to Christ we shall know the divine secret: 'I am crucified with Christ.'

The truth then becomes one of actual experience. We see this in Paul when he says, 'God forbid that I should glory, save in the cross of our Lord Jesus Christ, by whom the world is crucified unto me, and I unto the world.' We see that his whole relation and conduct towards the world was marked by it. When he writes 'As dying, and, behold, we live' (2 Corinthians 6:9); 'I bear in my body the marks of the Lord Jesus'; 'Death worketh in us, but life in you'; 'Christ was crucified in weakness, but liveth by the power of God, even so we are weak in him, but live through the power of God towards you', he speaks of his sufferings, of distress and persecutions, and of all the burden and care he had for souls as a fellowship with Christ in his weakness and his crucifixion.

Let us beware of seeking for the power of confession, 'I am crucified with Christ,' as a high spiritual attainment, without it being a fellowship with his sufferings and conformity to his death in winning men to God. If we are to say, 'I am crucified with Christ,' it must be proved before God and man by a life in the Spirit and the power of the crucified One.

In Christ the cross was the manifestation of a disposition, 'Let this mind be in you, which was also in Christ Jesus . . . who made himself of no reputation, and took upon him the form of a servant . . . and humbled himself, and became obedient unto death, even the death of the cross.' It is in this Christ-like disposition that our crucifixion with Christ can be realized as actual experience and power.

[From *The Apostle Paul's Inner Life*]

Able to Save Completely

*Wherefore also he is able to save to the uttermost
them that draw near unto God through him, seeing he
ever liveth to make intercession for them.*
(HEBREWS 7:25, RV)

The translation, 'able to save to the uttermost' is one which perfectly expresses the sense of the original. However, its meaning is often misunderstood. 'To the uttermost' does not refer to time, to the end of all things. Nor does it refer to the depths from which Christ saves, to his ability to save even the vilest and those farthest away from God. The true meaning is to do with the thorough working out of salvation in those who have already been saved. The verse means, 'Christ is able to save in every way, in all respects, *unto the uttermost*; so that every want and need, in all its breadth and depth is utterly done away' (Delitzsch). He is able to save completely.

This power to save is connected with his always living to pray as our eternal High Priest. There are two elements in the concept of the eternal life of Christ. One is that of unbroken continuity, the other is that of infinite power. The heavenly life of Christ knows no break or change, no fading or failing for one single moment, and its every present instant is filled with the life of the eternal Now. And he sits at the right hand of the Majesty on high, with all the limitless power of God. The words, 'he ever liveth to make intercession' teach us that the eternal life which he lives is just one unceasing, uninterrupted prayer for us and an unceasing, uninterrupted receiving from the Father of the answers to his prayers. He carries out his priestly intercession in 'the power of an endless life' (7:16). Here lies his power to save completely. Just as there ascends from him moment by moment a continuous, all-availing intercession, so there returns from the Father to him, in an unbroken stream, the Spirit and the life and the grace which his praying always secures;

and from him all these blessings descend to us. It was an eternal salvation of which he became the author; it was an eternal redemption which he obtained for us; it is an everlasting priesthood which he ministers in the heavenly sanctuary; it is in unbroken continuity that Jesus is able to save. This is what Scripture means when it says he is able to save completely, because he always lives to pray. His prayer is unceasing, and so is his salvation.

Believer, Jesus lives in ceaseless intercession for you, without one moment's break, so that your faith will not fail, so that you may have uninterrupted communion with God. Do you enjoy such a communion?

[From *The Promise of the Spirit*]

Jesus, the Perfecter of Our Faith

*Let us . . . lay aside every weight, and the sin which
doth so easily beset us, and let us run with patience
the race that is set before us, looking unto Jesus, the
author and perfecter of our faith.*
(HEBREWS 12:1-2, RV)

The practical and the contemplative aspects of the Christian life are often spoken of as being at odds with each other. But these words from Hebrews express them in their perfect unity. 'Let us lay aside every weight, and the sin which doth so easily beset us, and let us run': here we have expressed the active side of Christian life. We are encouraged to leave all hindrances behind, pursue sanctification and with all the energy we possess press on in the race. 'Looking unto Jesus': this is the inner life of meditation, waiting and worship. As we gaze upon the Lord and his glory, we will be changed into his likeness. So we are to run, and yet to look to Jesus at the same time.

100

Faith is the eye of the heart: as our spiritual vision beholds Jesus and remains fixed on him, then our feet will tread swiftly and surely in his footsteps. A deeper knowledge of Jesus, an eye never for a moment taken off him, is the secret of Christian progress. And why is this? Because Jesus is the Leader and Perfecter of our faith. Both of these terms have been used before in this Epistle. In chapter 2 Jesus was called the Leader of our salvation: 'It became him [God] . . . in bringing [or leading] many sons unto glory, to make the captain [or leader] of their salvation perfect through sufferings' (verse 10). In chapter 6 he was spoken of as the 'Fore-runner', entering within the veil to open the way for us (verse 20). In chapter 10 he is depicted as the Leader of our faith. It was he who opened up for us a fresh and living way to God, the way of self-sacrifice in which he himself walked, and in which we are to walk too. He led in the way of faith. It was by faith that he lived his life. He is not only our Example in the life of faith, but our Leader and Forerunner in it too, and as such he helps us and draws us on. The Old Testament saints had given us examples of faith, but theirs was a faith which did not inherit all the promises. But Jesus is the Leader of *our faith*, a faith which passes through death into resurrection life, which enters the Holiest of all and ministers in the power of an endless life.

Looking unto such a Leader, we run the race with patience, because he is also the Perfecter of our faith. One of the great truths of this Epistle is that Christ's perfection is the secret of the Christian's perfection. He is the Perfecter of faith: he perfected it in his own person by acting it out to its fullest possibility when in death he entrusted his spirit to his Father's hands. By his faith he was himself perfected, and proved that perfect faith is the highest perfection, because it gives God room to be all. He, the Perfect One, who has perfected us in himself, is now the perfect object of our faith: he gives himself to us as the highest consummation of all that faith can ask or receive. He is the Perfecter of faith, because he lives and works in us in the power of his endless life and so perfects the faith which is in us. Our going on to perfection is now no hopeless task. It is possible for us to have the same perfect faith which he had, a faith which trusts God for everything. The faith which looks to Jesus, the Perfect One and the Perfecter, is the secret of Christian perfection. Let us run, looking unto Jesus, who in his life on earth was our Leader in faith, and who in his glory on the throne is now the Perfecter of our faith.

Jesus, 'for the joy that was set before him endured the cross, despising shame, and hath sat down at the right hand of the throne of God' (Hebrews 12:2, RV). We need to gaze lengthily upon him there, crowned with honour and glory, our High Priest at the right hand of the Majesty on high. We need to let every thought of him on the throne remind us of the path which brought him there, and which brings us there too. It is the path of faith, obedience, self-sacrifice and suffering – the path of the cross. There is no way into the Holiest of all but the one which Jesus has opened and dedicated. And we also need to let every thought of him in that path of faith and trial lift our hearts once again to the throne, where he reigns in divine authority as the Perfected One and the Perfecter, communicating to us the power of his death and victory – the power of his complete and eternal salvation.

Yes, let us run the race, looking unto Jesus, the Perfecter of our faith.

[From *The Promise of the Spirit*]

Taking Up the Cross

When the Lord told his disciples that they must take up the cross to follow him, they could have little understanding of his meaning. He wished to rouse them to earnest thought and so prepare them for the time when they should see him carrying his cross. From the Jordan, where he had presented himself to be baptized and reckoned among sinners, onward, he carried the cross always in his heart. That is to say, he was always conscious that the sentence of

102

death, because of sin, rested on him, and that he must bear it to the uttermost. As the disciples thought on this and wondered what he meant by it, one thing only helped them – it was the thought of a man who was sentenced to death, and carried his cross to the appointed place.

Christ had said at the same time: 'He that loseth his life for my sake shall find it' (Matthew 10:39). He taught them that they must hate their own life. Their nature was so sinful that nothing less than death could meet their need; it deserved nothing less than death. So the conviction gradually dawned upon them that the taking up of the cross meant: 'I am to feel that my life is under sentence of death, and that under the consciousness of this sentence I must constantly surrender my flesh, my sinful nature, to death.' So they were slowly prepared to see later on that the cross which Christ had carried was the one power to deliver truly from sin, and that they must first receive from him the true cross spirit. They must learn from him what self-humiliation in their weakness and unworthiness was to mean; what the obedience was which crucified their own will in all things, in the greatest as well as in the least; what the self-denial was which did not seek to please the flesh or the world. 'Take thy cross and follow me' (see Matthew 16:24; Mark 8:34; 10:21; Luke 9:23) – that was the word with which Jesus prepared his disciples for the great thought that his mind and disposition might become theirs, that his cross might in very deed become their own.

[From *The Prayer Life*]

Living as Christ's Follower

Walking in God's Statutes

Listen to God's word in Ezekiel in regard to one of the terms of his covenant of peace, his everlasting covenant: 'I will put my Spirit within you, and *cause you to walk in my statutes*, and *ye shall keep my judgements*, and do them' (Ezekiel 34:25; 36:27; 37:26). In the Old Covenant we have nothing of this sort. You have, on the contrary, from the story of the golden calf and the breaking of the Tables of the Covenant onward, the sad fact of continual departure from God. We find God longing for what he would so fain have seen, but was not to be found. 'O that there were such an heart in them, that they would fear me, and keep all my commandments always' (Deuteronomy 5:29). We find throughout the book of Deuteronomy a thing without parallel in the history of any religion or religious lawgiver, that Moses most distinctly prophesies their forsaking of God, with the terrible curses and dispersion that would come upon them. It is only at the close of his threatenings (Deuteronomy 30:6, 8) that he gives the promise of the new time that would come: 'The Lord thy God will circumcise thine heart, to love the Lord thy God with all thine heart, and with all thy soul, and *thou shalt obey* the voice of the Lord thy God.' The whole Old Covenant was dependent on man's faithfulness: 'The Lord thy

God *keepeth covenant* with them *that keep* his commandments.'
God's keeping the covenant availed little if man did not keep it.
Nothing could help man until the '*if ye diligently keep*' of the law
was replaced by the word of promise, 'I will put my Spirit in you,
and *ye shall keep* my judgements, and do them.' The one supreme
difference of the New Covenant, the one thing for which the
Mediator, and the blood, and the Spirit were given; the one fruit
God sought and himself engaged to bring forth was this: a heart
filled with his fear and love, a heart to cleave unto him and not
depart from him, a heart in which his Spirit and his law dwell, a
heart that delights to do his will.

Here is the inmost secret of the New Covenant. It deals with the
heart of man in a way of divine power. It not only appeals to the
heart by every motive of fear or love, of duty or gratitude. That the
law also did. But it also reveals God himself cleansing our heart and
making it new, changing it entirely from a stony heart into a tender,
living, loving heart, putting his Spirit within it, and so, by his
almighty power and love, breathing and working in it, making the
promise true, '*I will cause you* to walk in my statutes, and *ye shall
keep* my judgements.' A heart in perfect harmony with himself, a
life and walk in his way – God has engaged in a covenant to work
this in us. He undertakes for our part in the covenant as much as for
his own.

This is nothing but the restoration of the original relation
between God and the man he had made in his likeness. Man was on
earth to be the very image of God, because God was to live and to
work all in him, and he to find his glory and blessedness in thus
owing all to God. This is the exceeding glory of the New Covenant,
of the Pentecostal dispensation, that by the Holy Spirit God could
now again be the indwelling life of his people, and so make the
promise a reality: 'I will cause you to walk in my statutes.'

[From *The Two Covenants*]

The Joy of Forgiving Others

Beloved followers of Jesus, called to manifest his likeness to the world, learn that as forgiveness of your sins was one of the first things Jesus did for you, forgiveness of others is one of the first that you can do for him. And remember that to the new heart there is a joy even sweeter than that of being forgiven, even the joy of forgiving others. The joy of being forgiven is only that of a sinner and of earth: the joy of forgiving is Christ's own joy, the joy of heaven. Oh, come and see that it is nothing less than the work that Christ himself does, and the joy with which he himself is satisfied, that thou art called to participate in.

It is thus that thou canst bless the world. It is as the forgiving One that Jesus conquers his enemies, and binds his friends to himself. It is as the forgiving One that Jesus has set up his kingdom and continually extends it. It is through the same forgiving love, not only preached but *shown in the life of his disciples*, that the Church will convince the world of God's love. If the world sees men and women loving and forgiving just as Jesus did, it will be compelled to confess that God is with them of a truth.

[From *Like Christ*]

Christ Our Life

'How can I live that life of perfect trust in God?' Many do not know the right answer, or the full answer. It is this: 'Christ must live it in me.' That is what he became man for, as a man to live a life of trust in God, and so to show to us how we ought to live. When he had done that upon earth, he went to heaven, that he might do more than show us, might give us, and live in us that life of trust. It is as we understand what the life of Christ is and how it becomes ours that we shall be prepared to desire and to ask of him that he would live it himself in us. When first we have seen what the life is, then

106

we shall understand how it is that he can actually take possession, and make us like himself. I want especially to direct attention to that first question. I wish to set before you the life of Christ as he lived it, that we may understand what it is that he has for us and that we can expect from him. Christ Jesus lived a life upon earth that he expects us literally to imitate. We often say that we long to be like Christ. We study the traits of his character, mark his footsteps, and pray for grace to be like him, and yet, somehow, we succeed but very little. And why? Because we are wanting to pluck the fruit while the root is absent. If we want really to understand what the imitation of Christ means, we must go to that which constituted the very root of his life before God. It was a life of absolute dependence, absolute trust, absolute surrender, and until we are one with him in what is the principle of his life, it is in vain to seek here or there to copy the graces of that life.

[From *The Master's Indwelling*]

The Presence of Jesus

I want to speak about the presence of Jesus as it is set before us in that blessed story of Christ's walking on the sea (Matthew 14:27). Come and look with me at some points that are suggested to us.

1. Think, first, of the presence of Christ *lost*. You know the disciples loved Christ, clung to him, and with all their failings they delighted in him. But what happened? The Master went up into the mountain to pray, and sent them across the sea all alone without him; there came a storm, and they toiled, rowed, and laboured, but the wind was against them, they made no progress, they were in danger of perishing, and how their hearts said, 'Oh, if only the Master were here!' But his presence was gone. They missed him. Once before, they had been in a storm, and Christ had said, 'Peace, be still,' and all was well; but here they are in darkness, danger, and

terrible trouble, and no Christ to help them. Ah, isn't that the life of many a believer at times? I get into darkness, I have committed sin, the cloud is on me, I miss the face of Jesus; and for days and days I work, worry, and labour; but it is all in vain, for I miss the presence of Christ. Oh, beloved, let us write that down – the presence of Jesus lost is the cause of all our wretchedness and failure.

2. Look at the second step – the presence of Jesus *dreaded*. They were longing for the presence of Christ, and Christ came after midnight: he came walking on the water amid the waves; but they didn't recognize him, and they cried out for fear, 'It is a spirit!' Their beloved Lord was coming nigh, and they knew him not. They dreaded his approach. And, ah, how often have I seen a believer dreading the approach of Christ, crying out for him, longing for him, and yet dreading his coming. And why? Because Christ came in a fashion that they expected not.

3. Then comes the third thought – the presence of Christ *revealed*. Bless God! When Christ heard how they cried, he said, 'Be of good cheer; it is I; be not afraid.' Ah, what gladness those words brought to those hearts! There is Jesus; that dark object appears – that dreaded form. It is our blessed Lord himself. And, dear friends, the Master's object, whether it be by affliction or otherwise, is to prepare for receiving the presence of Christ, and through it all Jesus speaks, 'It is I; be not afraid.' The presence of Christ revealed! I want to tell you that the Son of God, oh, believer, is longing to reveal himself to you. Listen! *Listen!* LISTEN! Is there any longing heart? Jesus says, 'Be of good cheer; it is I; be not afraid.'

4. And now comes the fourth thought; the presence of Jesus *desired*. What happened? Peter heard the Lord, and he was content. He was in the boat, and yonder was Jesus, some thirty, forty, fifty yards distant, and he made as though he would have passed them; and Peter – showing what terrible failure and carnality there was in him; but, bless the Lord, Peter's heart was right with Christ, and he wanted to claim his presence – Peter said, 'Lord, if it be thou, bid me come upon the water to thee.' Yes, Peter could not rest; he

wanted to be as near to Christ as possible. He saw Christ walking on the water; he remembered Christ had said, 'Follow me'; he remembered how Christ, with the miraculous draught of fishes, had proved that he was Master of the sea, and he remembered how Christ had stilled the storm; and, without argument or reflection, all at once he said, 'There is my Lord manifesting himself in a new way; there is my Lord exercising a new and supernatural power, and I can go to my Lord; he is able to make me walk where he walks.' He wanted to walk like Christ, he wanted to walk near Christ. He didn't say, 'Lord, let me walk around the sea here,' but said, 'Lord, let me come to thee.'

5. Then comes the next thought: the presence of Christ *trusted*. The Lord Jesus said, 'Come,' and what did Peter do? He stepped out of the boat. How did he dare to do it against all the laws of nature? How did he dare to do it? He sought Christ, he heard Christ's voice, he trusted Christ's presence and power, and in the faith of Christ he said, 'I can walk on the water,' and he stepped out of the boat. Here is the turning point; here is the crisis. Peter saw Christ in the manifestation of a supernatural power, and Peter believed that supernatural power could work in him, and he could live a supernatural life. He believed this applied to walking on the sea, and herein lies the whole secret of the life of faith. Christ had supernatural power – the power of heaven, the power of holiness, the power of fellowship with God – and Christ can give me grace to live as he lived. If I will but, like Peter, look at Christ and say to Christ, 'Lord, speak the word, and I will come,' and if I will listen to Christ saying, 'Come,' I, too, shall have power to walk upon the waves.

Have you ever seen a more beautiful and more instructive symbol of the Christian life? I once preached on it many years ago, and the thought that filled my heart then was this, the Christian life compared with Peter walking on the waves: nothing so difficult and impossible without Christ, nothing so blessed and safe with Christ. That is the Christian life – impossible without Christ's nearness, most safe and blessed, however difficult, if I only have the presence of Christ. Believers, we have tried to call you to a better life, to a spiritual life, to a holy life, a life in the Spirit, to a life in the fellowship with God. There is only one thing can enable you to live it – you must have the Lord Jesus hold your hand every minute of the day.

6. The presence of Christ *forgotten*. Peter got out of the boat and began to walk toward the Lord Jesus with his eye fixed upon him. The presence of Christ was trusted by him, and he walked boldly over the waves; but all at once he took his eye off Jesus, and he began at once to sink, and there was Peter, his walk of faith at an end, all drenched and drowning and crying, 'Lord, help me!' There are some of you saying in your hearts, I know, 'Ah, that's what will come of your higher-life Christians.' There are people who say, 'You never can live that life; do not talk of it; you must always be failing.' Peter always failed before Pentecost. It was because the Holy Spirit had not yet come, and therefore his experience goes to teach us that while Peter was still in the life of the flesh he must fail, somehow or other.

7. And then comes my last thought: the presence of Jesus *restored*. Yes, Christ stretched out his hand to save Peter. Possibly – for Peter was a very proud, self-confident man – possibly he had to sink there to teach him that it was not his faith that could save him, but the power of Christ. God wants us to learn the lesson that when we fall, then we can cry to Jesus, and at once he reaches out his hand. Remember, Peter walked back to the boat without sinking again. Why? Because Christ was very near him. Remember, it is quite possible, if you use your failure rightly, to be far nearer Christ after it than before. Use it rightly, I say. That is, come and acknowledge, 'In me there is nothing, but I am going to trust my Lord unboundedly.' Let every failure teach you to cling afresh to Christ, and he will prove himself a mighty and a loving Helper. The presence of Jesus restored! Yes, Christ took Peter by the hand and helped him, and I don't know whether they walked hand in hand those forty or fifty yards back to the boat, or whether Christ allowed Peter to walk beside him; but this I know, they were very

110

near to each other, and it was the nearness to his Lord that strengthened Peter.

Remember what has taken place since that happened to Peter. The cross has been erected, the blood has been shed, the grave has been opened, the resurrection has been accomplished, heaven has been opened, and the Spirit of the Exalted One has come down. Do believe that it is possible for the presence of Jesus to be with us every day and all the way. Your God has given you Christ, and he wants to give you Christ into your heart in such a way that his presence will be with you every moment of your life.

Who is willing to lift up his eyes and his heart and to exclaim, 'I want to live according to God's standard'? Who is willing? Who is willing to cast himself into the arms of Jesus and to live a life of faith victorious over the winds and the waves, over the circumstances and difficulties? Who is willing to say this, 'Lord, bid me come to thee upon the water'? Are you willing? Listen! Jesus says, 'Come.' Will you step out at this moment? Yonder is the boat, the old life that Peter had been leading; he had been familiar with the sea from his boyhood, and that boat was a very sacred place; Christ had sat beside him there; Christ had preached from that boat; from that boat of Peter's Christ had given the wonderful draught of fishes. It was a very sacred boat, but Peter left it to come to a place more sacred still – walking with Jesus on the water, a new and divine experience. Your Christian life may be a very sacred thing; you may say, 'Christ life saved me by his blood, he has given me many an experience of grace; God has proved his grace in my heart.' But you confess, 'I haven't got the real life of abiding fellowship; the winds and the waves often terrify me, and I sink.' Oh, come out of the boat of past experiences at once; come out of the boat of external circumstances; come out of the boat, and step out on the word of Christ, and believe, 'With Jesus I can walk upon the water.' When Peter was in the boat, what had he between him and the bottom of the sea? A couple of planks; but when he stepped out upon the water what had he between him and the sea? Not a plank, but the word of the almighty Jesus. Will you come, and without any experience, will you rest upon the word of Jesus, 'Lo, I am with you alway'? Will you rest upon his word, 'Be of good cheer; fear not; it is I'? Every moment Jesus lives in heaven, every moment by his Spirit Jesus whispers that word, and every moment he lives to make it true. Accept it now, accept it now! My Lord Jesus is equal to every emergency. My Lord Jesus can meet the wants of every soul. My whole heart says, 'He *can*, he *can* do it; he *will*, he *will* do it!' Oh, come, believers, and let us claim most deliberately, most quietly, most restfully – let us claim, claim it, *claim it*, CLAIM IT.

[From *The Deeper Christian Life*]

Christ and Money

Jesus beheld how the people cast money into the treasury: and many that were rich cast in much. And a certain poor widow came, and cast in a farthing. Jesus called his disciples, and saith unto them, This poor widow hath cast more in than all: for all they did cast in of their abundance; but she of her want did cast in all that she had, even all her living.

(MARK 12:41-44)

Giving money is a part of our religious life, is watched over by Christ, and must be regulated by his word. Let us try to discover what the Scriptures have to teach us.

1. Money giving a sure test of character

In the world money is the standard of value. It is difficult to express all that money means. It is the symbol of labour and enterprise and cleverness. It is often the token of God's blessing on diligent effort. It is the equivalent of all that it can procure of the service of mind or body, of property or comfort or luxury, of influence and power. No wonder that the world loves it, seeks it above everything, and often worships it. No wonder that it is the standard of value, not only for material things, but for man himself, and that a man is too often valued according to his money.

It is, however, not only thus in the kingdom of this world, but in the kingdom of heaven too, that a man is judged by his money, and yet on a different principle. The world asks, *What* does a man own? Christ, *How* does he use it? The world thinks more about the money getting, Christ about the money giving. And when a man gives, the world still asks, *What* does he give? Christ asks, *How* does he give? The world looks at the money and its amount, Christ at the man and his motive. See this in the story of the poor widow. Many that were rich cast in *much*, but it was out of their abundance; there was no real sacrifice in it; their life was as full and comfortable as ever, it cost them nothing. There was no special love or devotion to God in it; it was part of an easy and traditional religion. The widow cast in *a farthing*. Out of her want she cast in all that she had, even all her living. She gave all to God without reserve, without holding back anything; she gave all.

How different our standard and Christ's. We ask how much a man *gives*. Christ asks how much he *keeps*. We look at the gift. Christ asks whether the gift was a sacrifice. The widow kept nothing over, she gave all; the gift won Christ's heart and approval, for it was in the spirit of his own self-sacrifice, who, being rich, became poor for our sakes. They – out of their abundance – cast in much: she – out of her want – all that she had.

But if our Lord wanted us to do as she did, why did he not leave a clear command? How gladly then would we do it. Ah, there you have it! You want a command to make you do it: that would just be the spirit of the world in the Church looking at *what* we give, at our giving all. And that is just what Christ does not wish and will not have. He wants the generous love that does it unbidden. He wants every gift to be a gift warm and bright with love, a true free-will offering. If you want the Master's approval as the poor widow has it, remember one thing: you must put all at his feet, hold all at his disposal. And that, as the spontaneous expression of a love that, like Mary's, cannot help giving, just because it loves.

All my money giving – what a test of character! Lord Jesus! Oh, give me grace to love thee intently, that I may know how to give.

2. Money giving a great means of grace

Christ called his disciples to come and listen while he talked to them about the giving he saw there. It was to guide their giving and ours. Our giving, if we listen to Christ with the real desire to learn, will have more influence on our growth in grace than we know.

The spirit of the world, 'the lust of the flesh, the lust of the eye, and the pride of life'. Money is the great means the world has for gratifying its desires. Christ has said of his people, 'They are not of the world, as I am not of the world.' They are to show in their disposal of money that they act on unworldly principle, that the spirit of heaven teaches them how to use it. And what does that spirit suggest? Use it for spiritual purposes, for what will last for eternity, for what is pleasing to God. 'They that are Christ's have crucified the flesh and its lusts.' One of the ways of manifesting and maintaining the crucifixion of the flesh is never to use money to gratify it. And the way to conquer every temptation to do so is to have the heart filled with large thoughts of the spiritual power of money. If you would learn to keep the flesh crucified, refuse to spend a penny on its gratification. As much as money spent on self may nourish and strengthen and comfort self, so money sacrificed to God may help the soul in the victory that overcometh the world and the flesh.

3. Money giving a wonderful power for God

What a wonderful religion Christianity is. It takes money, the very embodiment of the power of sense of this world, with its self-interest, it covetousness, and its pride, and it changes money into an instrument for God's service and glory.

Think of the poor. What help and happiness are brought to tens of thousands of helpless ones by the timely gift of a little money

114

from the hand of love. God has allowed the difference of rich and poor for this very purpose – that just as in the interchange of buying and selling mutual dependence upon each other is maintained among men, so in the giving and receiving of charity there should be abundant scope for the blessedness of doing and receiving good. Christ said, 'It is more blessed to give than to receive.' What a Godlike privilege and blessedness to have the power of relieving the needy and making glad the heart of the poor by gold or silver! What a blessed religion that makes the money we give away a source of greater pleasure than that which we spend on ourselves! The latter is mostly spent on what is temporal and carnal; that spent in the work of love has eternal value, and brings double happiness to ourselves and others.

Think of the Church and its work in this world, of missions at home and abroad, and of the thousand agencies for winning men from sin to God and holiness. Is it indeed true that the coin of this world, by being cast into God's treasury in the right spirit, can receive the stamp of the mint of heaven, and be accepted in exchange for heavenly blessings? It is true. The gifts of faith and love go not only into the Church's treasury, but into God's own treasury, and are paid out again in heavenly goods. And that not according to the earthly standard of value, where the question always is, 'How much?', but according to the standard of heaven, where men's judgements of much and little, great and small are all unknown.

Christ has immortalized a poor widow's farthing. With his approval it shines through the ages brighter than the brightest gold. It has been a blessing to tens of thousands in the lesson it has taught. It tells you that your farthing, if it be your all, your gift, if it be honestly given (as you all ought to give to the Lord), has his approval, his stamp, his eternal blessing.

If we did but take more time in quiet thoughtfulness for the Holy Spirit to show us our Lord Jesus in charge of the Heavenly Mint, stamping every true gift, and then using it for the Kingdom, surely our money would begin to shine with a new lustre. And we should begin to say, The less I can spend on myself, and the more on my Lord, the richer I am. And we shall see how, as the widow was richer in her gift and her grace than the many rich, so he is richest who truly gives all he can.

4. Money giving a continual help on the ladder to heaven

You know how often our Lord Jesus spake of this in his parables. In that of the unjust steward he said, 'Make friends of the mammon of unrighteousness, that they may receive you in the eternal habitations.' In the parable of the talents he said, 'Thou oughtest to have put *my money* to the exchangers.' The man who had not used his talent lost all. In the parable of the sheep and the goats, it is they who have cared for the needy and the wretched in his name who shall hear the word, 'Come, ye blessed of my Father.'

We cannot purchase heaven – as little with money as with works. But in your money giving, heavenly-mindedness and love to Christ, and love to men, and devotion to God's work, are cultivated and proved. The 'Come, ye blessed of my Father, inherit the kingdom' will take count of the money truly spent on Christ and his work. Our money giving must prepare us for heaven.

Oh, how many there are who if heaven and holiness could be bought for a thousand pounds would give it! No money can buy those. But if they only knew, money can wondrously help on the path of holiness and heaven. Money given in the spirit of self-sacrifice, and love, and faith in him who has paid all, brings a rich and eternal reward. Day by day give as God blesses and as he asks – it will help to bring heaven nearer to you, it will help to bring *you* nearer to heaven.

The Christ who sat over against the treasury is my Christ. He watches my gifts. What is given in the spirit of wholehearted devotion and love he accepts. He teaches his disciples to judge as he judges. He will teach me how to give – how much, how lovingly, how truthfully.

Money – this is what I want to learn from him above all – money, the cause of so much temptation and sin, and sorrow and eternal loss; money, as it is received and administered and distributed at the feet of Jesus, the Lord of the Treasury, becomes one of God's choicest channels of grace to myself and to others. In this, too, we are more than conquerors through him who loved us.

Lord, give thy Church, in her poverty – give us all – the spirit of the poor widow.

[From *Thoughts for God's Stewards*]

The Way to Heaven

Not everyone that saith unto me, Lord, Lord, shall enter into the kingdom of heaven; but he that doeth the will of my Father which is in heaven.
(MATTHEW 7:21)

The only way to be fit to enter heaven must be to do the will of God here on earth. Every thought of heaven that does not lead us to do the will of God is a vain imagination.

There are multitudes of Christians who have never seen this. They think that the way to heaven is found in pious desires and religious duties, in trusting Christ for mercy, and seeking to be kept from gross sin. But the thought that Christ puts here – only those who love to do the will of God can enter heaven – has never taken possession of their mind or heart. And yet our Lord makes the difference between the religion of prayer and profession, and the religion of obedience and performance, as plain as words can make it. Not everyone that saith unto me Lord, Lord – that professes to acknowledge and honour me as Saviour – but he that doeth the will of my Father in heaven – he alone – shall enter the kingdom of heaven. It is the Father's presence and the Father's will in heaven that makes heaven what it is: doing the Father's will on earth is the only conceivable way of entering heaven: nothing can give the capacity for enjoying it. There must always be harmony between a life and its environment. To enter the heaven of God's will, without a nature that loves and does God's will, is an impossibility.

[From *Thy Will be Done*]

The Daily Renewal – the Pattern

Seeing that ye have ... put on the new man, which is being renewed unto knowledge after the image of him that created him. (COLOSSIANS 3:9-10)

In every pursuit, it is of consequence to have the goal clearly defined. It is not enough that there be movement and progress, we want to know whether the movement be in the right direction, straight for the mark; and especially when we are acting in partnership with another, on whom we are dependent, do we need to know that our aim and his are in perfect accord. If our daily renewal is to attain its object we need to know clearly, and hold firmly to what its purpose is.

'Ye have put on the new man, which is being renewed unto knowledge.' The divine life, the work of the Holy Spirit within us, is no blind force, as in nature. We are to be workers together with God; our co-operation is to be intelligent and voluntary, 'The new man is being renewed day by day unto knowledge.' There is a knowledge which the natural understanding can draw from the Word, but which is without the life and the power, the real truth and substance, which the spiritual knowledge brings. It is the renewing of the Holy Ghost that gives the true knowledge, which does not consist in thought and conception, but in an inward tasting, a living reception of the very things themselves of which the words and thoughts are but the images. 'The new man is being renewed unto knowledge.' However diligent our Bible study may

118

be there is no true knowledge gained any further than the spiritual renewal is being experienced, the renewal in the spirit of the mind, in its life and inward being, alone brings true divine knowledge.

[From *Prayer's Inner Chamber*]

Today

Wherefore, even as the Holy Ghost saith, 'Today if
ye shall hear his voice, harden not your hearts.'
(HEBREWS 3:7)

The Holy Spirit says, 'Today!', and yet Satan's word is always 'Tomorrow'. It is man's favourite word as well. The child of God who has unbelief in his heart will also say it. He finds God's demand too great for today; God's promise is too high; he hopes it will be easier for him later on. But the same Holy Spirit who says 'Today' to us is also the Mighty Power of God who is himself ready to do in us everything that God wills and asks. Every moment the Spirit is pleading with us to surrender immediately, to trust God right now, and he possesses the power to realize all of God's promises in our lives.

'Today': it is a wonderful word of promise. It says that today, at this very moment, the amazing love of God is for you; at this very moment it is waiting to be poured out into your heart. All that Christ has done and is now doing in heaven, and all that he is able to do in you, is within your reach this very day. Today the Holy Spirit, in whom there is the power for us to claim and enjoy all that the Father and the Son are waiting to bestow – today the Holy Spirit is within you, sufficient for every need, equal to every emergency. With every call to full and entire surrender which we find in our Bibles; with every promise we read of grace for the meeting of earthly and spiritual needs; with every prayer we breathe and with every longing in our hearts, there is the Spirit of Promise whispering, 'Today'.

'Today': it is a word of solemn command. We are not here talking about some higher privilege which you are free to accept or reject. Believer, it is not for you to choose whether or not you will receive the fullness of blessing which the Holy Spirit offers. His 'Today' brings you under the most solemn obligation to respond to God's call and to say, 'Yes, Lord, today I submit completely and immediately to all your will; today I surrender in present and perfect trust in all your grace.'

'Today': it is a word of serious warning. 'The Holy Ghost saith, "Today, if ye shall hear his voice, harden not your hearts."' He has said of those who ignore his 'Today', 'They shall not enter into my rest' (Hebrews 3:11). There is nothing so hardening as delay. When God speaks to us, he asks for a tender heart, open to the whispers of his voice of love. The believer who answers the 'Today' of the Holy Spirit with a 'Tomorrow', hoping for some more convenient time, does not understand how dangerously he is hardening his heart. The delay, instead of making the surrender and obedience and faith easy, makes it more difficult. It closes the heart against the Comforter today and cuts off all hope and power for growth in the future. Believer, when you hear his voice today, open your heart with great tenderness to listen and obey; obedience to the Spirit's 'Today' is your only certainty of power and blessing.

For all Christians whose lives have been characterized by feebleness and failure, who have not yet entered into God's rest, this word 'Today' is the key to all their disappointments and to all their hopes. You waited for strength, to make obedience easier; for feeling, to make the sacrifice less painful. You did not listen to the voice of God, breathing through every word he speaks, even through every word he speaks, even through the Living Word, Jesus Christ, that wonderful note of hope – 'Today'. You thought it referred to the calling of a sinner to repentance; you did not know that it is meant for the believer, that it is a command to immediate, wholehearted submission to all that God says each time the believer hears his voice, a call to immediate, trusting acceptance of all that he gives.

[From *The Promise of the Spirit*]

Strong in Faith

Beloved believer! If you want to be strong in faith, begin at the beginning. Lay a deep foundation. Study what the word says about the God of Creation as a pledge of what the God of Redemption will do (see 2 Kings 19:15-16; Isaiah 40:26-28, 48:11-13; Jeremiah 32:17). Cultivate the habit of bowing in quiet worship and just seeking to understand that behind what is seen there are unseen things. You will then learn to be more occupied with and influenced by the unseen than the seen. You will learn to go through each day in the awareness of the presence and power of the Unseen God. Then your faith will find it easy to trust him for his every promise and for your every need.

[From *The Promise of the Spirit*]

By Faith We Please God

Luther frequently used the expression, 'Let God be God.' He meant by this that we should give him the place which belongs to him as God, and let him do the work which, as God, he can and will do. This is the essence of faith: to let God be God, and so give him the glory. Faith fills the mind with the thought of God who, in the power of his infinite love, works out his purposes in the world, especially in his people, and personally in every believer who yields to him. Faith falls prostrate before this glorious Being and worships him as he orders everything according to his own will. Faith waits and cries and thirsts for God until he makes himself a divine reality to the soul and his Presence becomes nearer and clearer than anything else in existence. And so God reveals himself, and truly becomes God to the soul. He becomes all in all. By faith his glorious Presence rests on the soul.

In Hebrews 11:6 we have a description of God-pleasing faith, and in it the position which this faith must give to God is shown with remarkable clearness. Four times in the same verse God is placed in the foreground as the only object of faith: 'He that cometh to God must believe that he is, and that he is a rewarder of them that diligently seek him.'

'He that cometh to God must believe'

This is the place where faith is born. When a man is drawn by God to himself, when a man turns away from himself and all the world and wishes to meet and know the living God, when he truly wants to draw near to God, then he must believe. It is then that he will learn to believe. It is in such believing that he will really come to God and know that he has found and met him.

'... Must believe that he is'

This is what our faith must first and foremost concentrate upon. This will also be its highest attainment: a sense, a consciousness and an impression – in some measure corresponding to the infinite reality – that God is. What an impression of its presence a magnificent mountain or a great ocean can give us if we just allow ourselves to take in its beauty and grandeur! And what an impression God could make upon us if we only yielded ourselves in adoring silence and let him breathe into us that sense of his Presence which is faith. If you want to be strong in faith, come to God, bow low before him and wait upon him until your soul is filled with the living assurance that he is. This is something infinitely better than believing a promise or believing for a special blessing. This is believing in God.

'... That he is a rewarder'

The verse does not say, '... That there is a reward.' No, our faith must say, '*He* is a rewarder.' It is directly from him, in personal contact with him, that the reward, the blessing, will be received. It is precisely because our faith is mostly more occupied with the reward than with the One who gives it that our efforts at believing are so futile. Oh, that men would learn to have faith in God! How easy faith in the promises would then become.

'... A rewarder of them that diligently seek him'

We hear a great deal about seeking salvation, but there is no such expression anywhere in Scripture. Instead it says, 'Seek the Lord', 'Seek my face', 'Your hearts shall live that seek God'. We should not so much seek blessing or power; rather, we should *seek God*. We need to *come to God*. We need to believe that *God is*, that he is with the Rewarder of those who seek him. 'Acquaint thyself with God, and be at peace.'

Oh, my brother, do you wish to be a true believer, a strong believer? Then have the sort of faith which pleases God. Let the one desire of your soul be to have faith in him. Spend time in holy meditation and silent worship to seek him, to come to him, to learn first of all that he is, and only then that he is the Rewarder. Then you will begin to understand what faith is: the free gift of God, by which he opens up your being so that you may know him and receive all the wonderful reward of grace and strength which he gives to those who please him.

[From *The Promise of the Spirit*]

Power for the Work to Which We Are Called

The preacher will learn to receive his message really from God, through the power of the Holy Spirit, and to deliver it in that power to the congregation. He will know where he can be filled with the love and zeal which will enable him, in his rounds of pastoral visiting, to meet and help each individual in a spirit of tender compassion. He will be able to say with Paul: 'I can do all things through Christ which strengtheneth me' (Philippians 4:13). 'We are more than conquerors through him that loved us' (Romans 8:37). 'We are ambassadors for Christ ... we pray you in Christ's stead, be ye reconciled to God' (2 Corinthians 5:20). These are no vain dreams or pictures of a foolish imagination. God has given us Paul as an illustration, so that, however we may differ from him in gifts of calling, yet in inner experience we may know the all-sufficiency of grace which can do all things for us as it did for him.

[From *The Prayer Life*]

Carnal or Spiritual?

There is a great difference between those two states which is but little understood or pondered. The Christian who 'walks in the Spirit' and has 'crucified the flesh' (Galatians 5:24) is spiritual. The Christian who walks after the flesh and wishes to please the flesh is carnal (see Romans 13:14). The Galatians, who had begun in the Spirit, were ending in the flesh. Yet there were among them some spiritual members who were able to restore the wandering with meekness.

What a difference between the carnal and the spiritual Christian (1 Corinthians 3:1-3)! With the carnal Christian there may be much religion and much zeal for God, and for the service of God. But it is for the most part in human power. With the spiritual, on the other hand, there is a complete subjection to the leading of the Spirit, a deep sense of weakness and entire dependence on the work of Christ – it is a life of abiding fellowship with Christ, wrought out by the Spirit.

How important for me it is to find out and plainly to acknowledge before God whether I am spiritual or carnal! A minister may be very faithful in his orthodoxy, and be most zealous in his service, and yet be so, chiefly, in the power of human wisdom and zeal. And one of the signs of this is that there is little pleasure or perseverance in fellowship with Christ through prayer. Love of prayer is one of the marks of the Spirit.

[From *The Prayer Life*]

Pentecost and the Christian Life

The Daily Renewal – Its Cost

To be filled with heaven, the life must be emptied of earth. We have this truth in Romans 12:2, 'Be ye transformed in the renewing of your mind.' An old house may be renewed, and yet keep very much of its old appearance, or the renewal may be so entire that men exclaim: What a transformation! The renewing by the mind of the Holy Spirit means an entire transformation, an entirely different way of thinking, judging, deciding. The fleshly mind gives place to a 'spiritual understanding' (Colossians 1:9; 1 John 5:20). This transformation is not obtained but at the cost of giving up all that is of nature. 'Be not fashioned according to this world, but be ye transformed.' By nature we are of this world. When renewed by grace we are still in the world, subject to the subtle all-pervading influence from which we cannot withdraw ourselves.

And what is more, the world is still in us, as the leaven of the nature which nothing can purge out but the mighty power of the Holy Spirit, filling us with the life of heaven. Let us allow the truth to take deep hold of us. The divine transformation of the daily renewing of our mind into the image of him who is from above, can proceed in us no faster and no further than our seeking to be freed from every vestige of conformity to this world. The negative, 'Be not fashioned according to this world' needs to be emphasised as strongly as the positive 'Be ye transformed'. The spirit of this world and the Spirit of God contend for the possession of our being. Only as the former is known and renounced and cast out, can the heavenly Spirit enter in, and do his blessed work of renewing and transforming. The whole world and whatever is of the worldly spirit, must be given up. The whole life and whatever is of self must be lost. This daily renewal of the inward man costs much, that is, as long as we are hesitating, or trying to do it in our own strength. When once we really learn that the Holy Spirit does all, and in the faith of the strength of the Lord Jesus have given up all, the renewing becomes the simple, natural, healthy growth of the heavenly life in us.

[From *Prayer's Inner Chamber*]

Being Filled with the Spirit

The Spirit did it all, on the day of Pentecost and afterwards. It was the Spirit who gave the boldness, the Spirit who gave the wisdom, the Spirit who gave the message, and the Spirit who gave the converting power.

And now, to those who feel the need of power, I would say: Is not your whole heart ready to say, 'That is what I want. I see it. Jesus did not send me to the warfare on my own charges; he did not bid me go and preach and teach in my own strength; Jesus meant me to have the fullness of the Holy Spirit. Whether I have a little Sunday School class or a Bible class, or some larger work, the one thing I need is the power of the Holy Spirit, to be filled with the Spirit.'

Are you prepared to receive this from our Jesus? He loves to give it. God delights in nothing so much as to honour his Son, and it is honour to Jesus when souls are filled with the Holy Spirit, because then he proves what he can do for them.

Step one: *I must be filled*

Say it to God in the depth of your heart. God commands it; I cannot live my life as I should live without it.

Step two: *I may be filled*

Then, say as the second step: *I may be filled*. It is possible: the promise is for me. Settle that, and let all doubt vanish. These apostles, once so full of pride and of self-life, were filled with the Holy Spirit because they clave unto Jesus. And, with all your sinfulness, if you will but cling to him, you *may be filled*.

Step three: *I would be filled*

Then, thirdly, say: *I would be filled*. To get the 'pearl of great price' (Matthew 13:46) you must sell all, you must give up everything. You are willing, are you not? Everything, Lord, if I may only have that. Lord, I would have it from you today.

Step four: *I shall be filled*

And then comes the last step: *I shall be filled*. God longs to give it; I shall have it. Never mind whether it comes immediately, as a flood, or in deep silence; or whether it does not come today, because God is preparing you for it tomorrow. But say, *I shall be filled*. If I entrust myself to Jesus he cannot disappoint me. It is his very nature, it is his work in heaven, it is his delight to give souls the Holy Spirit in full measure. Claim it at once; *I shall*. My God, it is so solemn, it is almost awful; it is too blessed and too true – Lord, will you not do it? My trembling heart says, *I shall be filled* with the Holy Spirit. Say to God, '*Father, I shall*, for the name of my Saviour is Jesus, who saves from all sin, and who fills with the Holy Spirit. Glory to his name!'

[From *Absolute Surrender*]

Keeping the Full Blessing of Pentecost

Praying in the Holy Ghost, keep yourselves in the
love of God . . . Now to him that is able to keep you
from falling . . . to the only wise God our Saviour, be
glory . . . now and for ever. Amen.
(JUDE 20-21, 24-25)

Can anyone who has had the full Pentecostal Blessing lose it? Without a doubt he can. God does not give this blessing with such force that people must keep it whether they are willing or unwilling. The blessing is given to the believer like a talent which should be used and looked after and which can bring happiness only by being used. Just as the Lord Jesus, after being baptized with the Holy Spirit, had to be made perfect by obedience and subjection to the guidance of the Spirit, so the Christian who receives the Pentecostal Blessing has to take care that he looks after what has been given to him.

Scripture shows us that we can only keep the blessing we have received by entrusting it to our Lord for safe keeping. Paul wrote to Timothy, 'He is able to keep that which I have committed unto him . . . That good thing which was committed unto thee keep by the Holy Ghost which dwelleth in us' (2 Timothy 1:12, 14). Jude advises his readers, 'Keep yourselves in the love of God . . . [who] is able to keep you from falling.' What we must do is to be humbly dependent upon the Lord who keeps us and through whom alone we are able to retain the blessing. As with the manna in the Old Testament, so too with this blessing: it must be renewed from heaven every day. Just as our bodies must inhale fresh air from outside us every moment, so our spirits must inhale the Holy Spirit. Let us see how this everlasting, uninterrupted keeping of the blessing is achieved.

Jesus maintains the Blessing if we seek communion with him

The only purpose of the Pentecostal Blessing is to manifest Jesus in us as Saviour, in order that he may manifest his saving power in and through us to the world. The Spirit did not come instead of Jesus, but only and wholly in order to make the disciples more intimately and perfectly in relationship with the Lord than they had been when he was on earth. The power from on high did not come as a power which they could consider as their own: that power was bound inseparably to the Lord Jesus and the Spirit. Every action of the power was an immediate action of Jesus in them. All the aspects of the relationship which the disciples had had with Jesus when he was on the earth – following him, receiving his teaching, doing his will, sympathizing with his suffering – were to continue even more powerfully, since through the Spirit the life of Jesus was now inside them. And it is the same with us. The Spirit in us will always glorify Jesus, always show that he alone must be Lord, that everything that is beautiful comes only from him. We must be faithful in seeking his words and his will in Scripture, in sacrificing effort and time we could spend with other people in order to spend time with him, if we are to keep the blessing. Jesus wants us to occupy ourselves wholly with him. Anyone who loves communion with Jesus above everything else will find that Jesus will maintain the Pentecostal Blessing in him.

[From *The Promise of the Spirit*]

The Second Blessing

One illustration of what the Second Blessing or Better Life is appears in the opening words of the Epistle to the Hebrews: 'God, who at sundry times and in divers manners spake in time past unto the fathers by the prophets, hath in these latter days spoken to us by his Son.' Here we see the two stages in God's revelation of himself. God had (and still has) two ways of speaking to men – not one, not

130

three, but two. The first was a preparation for the second, while the second was the fulfilment of the first. The causes of this were not arbitrary, but in the purposes of God there was a need for it. In the first stage God spoke through men – the prophets. Full, direct and immediate revelations of God were not given at that time. Only after the inadequacy of this means of revelation had been felt and a longing for a more direct divine manifestation had been awakened did the full revelation come in. Then *God spoke to us by his Son*.

This does not refer merely to the words which the Son spoke when he was on earth. If that were so, those words could very easily become mere images of divine truth, just like the words of the prophets. The words of God's Son would then occupy our minds without bringing us into direct contact with God. But God speaking through his Son means something infinitely higher than that. Jesus Christ not only has and speaks the Word of God like a prophet, but he is the Word. He is the living expression of the Father's heart, bearing in himself and imparting all the fullness of the Divine life and love. Coming out of God's heart, the Living Word enters our hearts. Out of the depths of God's heart that word comes, and enters into the depths of our hearts. Christ dwells in our hearts as he dwells in the Father's heart. He is our life, our joy and our love, as he is the Father's. So this is what the first verse of Hebrews means when it says that God has not only spoken to us through his servants and their words, through his Book and its words, but also through his Son.

These two stages in God's revelation of himself in his dealings with his people as a whole have their counterpart in the history of the individual soul. After our conversion our religion is very much dependent upon human activities and traditions; to a large extent our faith relies upon our fellow Christians. But as the believer goes on in the spiritual life and grows weary of the failures and disappointments which he frequently meets along the way, he very often begins to long for a more definitely personal fellowship with God, for a more direct experience of his presence and power. A man begins to feel, 'In my dealings with God I have not got beyond words and thoughts and feelings. I have not yet had God speaking through his Son right into my heart.' He discovers that the Saviour has promised to come with his Father to make his abode in the believer's heart – he has promised to manifest himself in the believer's life. He begins to see how, in the Spirit of the glorified Jesus, a beautiful provision has been made for keeping up direct and unbroken communication between the Father in heaven and the child on earth. He understands how God's speaking to us through his Son opens up the possibility of a fellowship surpassing all understanding, and he can now rest content with nothing less. And as he tastes the blessedness of this direct communication of God's presence and love to the soul, he knows that 'God . . . who in divers manners spake in times past by the prophets' has now spoken to him, personally, by his Son.

[From *The Promise of the Spirit*]

Jesus the Mediator and Full Blessing

I do not know that I can find a better case by which to illustrate the place Christ, the Mediator of the covenant, takes in leading into its full blessing than that of the founder of the Keswick Convention, the late Canon Battersby.

It was at the Oxford Convention in 1873 that he witnessed to having 'received a new and distinct blessing to which he had been a stranger before'. For more than twenty-five years he had been most diligent as a minister of the gospel, and, as appears from his journals, most faithful in seeking to maintain a close walk with God. But he was ever disturbed by the consciousness of being overcome by sin. So far back as 1853 he had written, 'I feel again how very far I am from enjoying habitually that peace and love and joy which Christ promises. I must confess that I have it not; and that very ungentle and unchristian tempers often strive within me for the master.' When in 1873 he read what was being published of the

Higher Life, the effect was to render him utterly dissatisfied with himself and his state. There were, indeed, difficulties he could not quite understand in that teaching, but he felt that he must either reach forward to better things, nothing less than redemption from *all* iniquities, or fall back more and more into worldliness and sin. At Oxford he heard an address on the rest of faith. It opened his eyes to the truth that a believer who really longs for deliverance from sinning must simply take Christ at his word, and reckon, without feeling, on him to do his work of cleansing and keeping the soul. 'I thought of the sufficiency of Jesus, and said, I *will rest* in him, and I did rest in him. I was afraid lest it should be a passing emotion; but I found that a presence of Jesus was graciously manifested to me in a way I knew not before, and that *I did abide in him*. I do not want to rest in these emotions, but just to believe, and to cling to Christ as my all.' He was a man of very reserved nature, but he felt it a duty ere the close of the Conference to confess publicly his past shortcoming, and testify openly to his having entered upon a new and definite experience.

In a paper written not long after this he pointed out what the steps are leading to this experience. *First*, a clear view of the possibilities of Christian attainment – a life in word and action, habitually governed by the Spirit, in constant communion with God, and continual victory over sin through abiding in Christ. *Then* the deliberate purpose of the will for a full renunciation of all the idols of the flesh or spirit, and a will-surrender to Christ. And then this last and important step: *We must look up to, and wait upon our ascended Lord for all that we need to enable us to do this.*

A careful perusal of this very brief statement will prove how everything centred here in Christ. The surrender for a life of continual communion and victory is to be to Christ. The strength for that life is to be in him and from him, by faith in him. And *the power* to make the full surrender and rest in him *was to be waited for* from *him alone*.

In June, 1875, the first Keswick Convention was held. In the circular calling it, we read: 'Many are everywhere thirsting that they may be brought to enjoy more of the divine presence in their daily life, and a full manifestation of the Holy Spirit's power, whether in subduing the lusts of the flesh, or in enabling them to offer more effective service to God. It is certainly God's will that his children should be satisfied in regard to these longings, and there are those who can testify that he has satisfied them, and does satisfy them with daily fresh manifestations of his grace and power.' The results of the very first Convention were most blessed, so that after its close he wrote: 'There is a very remarkable resemblance in the testimonies I have since received as to the nature of the blessing obtained, viz., *the ability given* to make a full surrender to the Lord, and the consequent experience of an abiding peace, far exceeding anything previously experienced.' Through all the chief thought was Christ, first drawing and enabling the soul to rest in him, and then meeting it with the fulfilment of its desire, the abiding experience of his power to keep it in victory over sin and in communion with God.

And what was the fruit of this new experience? Eight years later Canon Battersby spoke: 'It is now eight years since that I knew this blessing as my own. I cannot say that I have never for a moment ceased to trust the Lord to keep me. But I can say that so long as I have trusted him, he has kept me; he has been faithful.'

[From *The Two Covenants*]

The Promise of the Holy Spirit

*If ye then, being evil, know how to give good gifts
unto your children: how much more shall your
Heavenly Father give the Holy Spirit to them that
ask him?* (LUKE 11:13)

There are some gifts which God does not give, and some prayers which he does not answer, but there is one prayer he will always

134

answer – and that is a prayer for the Holy Spirit. Let us look up to God. He is willing, waiting, longing and able to give us his Holy Spirit.

What is there in the child of God which corresponds to this great purpose of the Father? In the child there is hunger. And what attitude should each of us have when we pray? We should have a great, longing desire for the Holy Spirit and a willingness to receive him. Is there a longing for the Holy Spirit in our hearts? We need to pray, 'O God, since you are my Father and I, your child, am ready, give me the Holy Spirit.'

We may desire the Holy Spirit and God may be ready to give him to us, and yet there may be a great deal that hinders us from receiving him. This truth is expressed in Ezekiel 36:25-27: 'Then I will sprinkle clean water upon you, and ye shall be clean: from all your filthiness, and from all your idols, will I cleanse you. A new heart also will I give you: and I will take away the stony heart out of your flesh, and I will give you a heart of flesh. And I will put my spirit within you.' How clear that is! How simple! God cleanses away the filthiness and the idols; God takes away the hardness of heart that the world instils in us, and then he gives us the Holy Spirit. So the first thing we need in order to receive him is deliverance from sin.

When the Holy Spirit comes he comes to take complete control: he comes to control the whole of our lives. He does not merely want possession of the minister in the pulpit, or of believers when they are going out to evangelize or do some special task for the Lord. Rather, the Holy Spirit comes to dwell, to stay, to rule, to control. Let us pray, 'Lord God, cleanse me from sin, and accept my total surrender to the control of the Holy Spirit.'

We are looking and longing for the Holy Spirit; our desire may be vague and indefinite or it may be very specific. But somehow we do not receive what we long for. However, when we accept God's claim to the lordship of our lives and submit to it and yield ourselves to the control of the Holy Spirit, then we just need to believe and trust, and we shall receive. Perhaps our faith may be tested by a prolonged wait or by difficulties, but let us believe that

God will satisfy our desire for his Spirit.

I cannot think of anything which I find more wonderful and instructive than the ten days of praying and waiting which preceded the outpouring of the Holy Spirit at Pentecost. It is a mystery, and I cannot understand it. Jesus had died upon earth and had conquered sin; he had been raised from the dead, lifted up to the Father's throne and glorified; he had received the Holy Spirit from the Father so that he could give him to the believers. And yet despite all this there were ten days of waiting in heaven. God was ready, Christ was ready, the Holy Spirit was ready, the Trinity was ready – and yet for ten days the Spirit could not come. Why? Because there had not been enough prayer. Jesus had spent three whole years preparing those disciples and everything was ready in heaven, and yet those ten days of prayer were still needed.

Everything in heaven is ready even now. God is ready – he wants us to receive him as our Father. Christ the Son is ready – his work is finished and he longs to prove to us how complete our redemption and acceptance are. And the Holy Spirit is ready to take possession of us in the name of Jesus, so that he may glorify Christ.

But are we ready? And will our prayers be proof that we are ready? Our prayers should express our desire for more grace in order that we might bring blessing to others. We should long for more of that quiet power of Christ within us which witnesses to people even when we are not talking about him. You know how Peter spoke to the lame man at the temple gate. He did not preach a sermon to him. Instead he told him, 'Such as I have I give thee: in the name of Jesus Christ of Nazareth rise up and walk.' He was saying, 'I know Jesus, and the power of Jesus, and I will give that to you.' Like Peter, we want to say, 'I know Jesus. He has done so much in my life, and he will do it for you.' That is the sort of power we need to have. How do we get this power? By surrender to the Holy Spirit. All our prayers, all our searchings of heart and all our believing must come to this – Jesus Christ by his indwelling Holy Spirit must have complete possession of us. Then we shall be clean, sanctified vessels, ready for the Master's use.

So we are hungry and thirsty. There is only one thing which can satisfy us, and we should be prepared and willing to give everything to obtain it. It is the presence, the rule, the control and the power of the Holy Spirit.

Let us listen to our Redeemer as he speaks to us: 'If ye then, being evil, know how to give good gifts unto your children, how much more shall your heavenly Father give the Holy Spirit to them that ask him?' Let us look up to God upon his throne, expecting the Holy Spirit, and let our hearts have a deep desire, a deep childlike surrender, and a deep, deep trust in God's almighty power.

[From *The Promise of the Spirit*]

How the Blessing is Hindered

Then said Jesus unto his disciples, If any man would come after me, let him deny himself, and take up his cross, and follow me. For whosoever will save his life shall lose it: and whosoever will lose his life for my sake shall find it. (MATTHEW 16:24-25)

There are many who seek the full blessing of Pentecost long and earnestly and yet do not find it. Often the question is put as to what may be the cause of this failure. To this inquiry more than one answer may be given. Sometimes the solution of the problem points in the direction of one or another sin which is still permitted. Worldliness, lovelessness, lack of humility, ignorance of the secret of walking in the way of faith – these, and indeed many more causes, may also be often mentioned with justice. There are, however, many people who think that they have come to the Lord with what of these sources of failure remains in them, and have sincerely confessed them and put them away, and yet complain that the blessing does not come. For all such it is particularly necessary to point out that there remains still one great hindrance – namely, that root from which all other hindrances have their beginning. This root is nothing else than our individual self, the hidden life of self with its varied forms of self-seeking, self-pleasing, self-confidence, and self-satisfaction. The more earnestly anyone strives to obtain the blessing and would fain know what prevents him, the more certainly will he be led to the discovery that it is here the great evil lies. He himself is his worst foe: he must be liberated from himself; and self-life to which he clings must be utterly lost. Only then can the life of God entirely fill him.

That is what is taught us in the words of the Lord Jesus to Peter. Peter had uttered such a glorious confession of his Lord, that Jesus said to him: 'Blessed art thou, Simon Barjonah: for flesh and blood hath not revealed it unto thee, but my Father which is in heaven' (Matthew 16:17). But when the Lord began to speak of his death by crucifixion, the self-same Peter was seduced by Satan to say: 'Be it far from thee, Lord: this shall not be unto thee' (Matthew 16:22). Thereupon the Lord said to him that not only must he himself lay down his life, but that this same sacrifice was to be made by every disciple. Every disciple must deny himself and take up his cross in order that he himself may be crucified and put to death on it. He that would fain save his life will lose it; and he that is prepared to lose his life for Christ's sake will find it.

You see, then, what the Lord here teaches and requires. Peter had learned through the Father to know Christ as the Son of God, but he did not yet know him as the crucified one. Of the absolute necessity of the cross, and death on the cross, he as yet knew nothing. It may be so with the Christian. He knows the Lord Jesus as his Saviour; he desires to know him better, yes, fully; but he does not yet understand that for this end it is necessary that he must have a deeper discernment of the death of the cross as a death which he himself must die; that he must actually deny, and hate, and lose his life – his whole life and being in the world – ere he can receive the full life of God.

The requirement is hard and difficult. And why is this so? Why should a Christian be called upon always to deny himself, his own feeling, and will, and pleasure? Why must he part with his life – that life to maintain which a man is prepared to make any sacrifice? Why should a man hate and lose his life? The answer is very simple. It is because that life is so completely under the power of sin and death that it has to be utterly denied and sacrificed. The self-life must be wholly taken away to make room for the life of God. He that would have the full, the overflowing life of God, must utterly deny and lose his own life.

You see it now, do you not? There is only one great stumbling-block in the way of the full blessing of Pentecost. It lies in the fact that two diverse things cannot at one and the same time occupy the very same place. Your own life and the life of God cannot fill the heart at the same time. Your life hinders the entrance of the life of God. When your own life is cast out, the life of God will fill you. So long as *I myself* am still something, *Jesus himself* cannot be everything. My life must be expelled; then the Spirit of Jesus will flow in. Let every seeker of the full blessing of Pentecost accept this principle and hold it fast.

[From *The Full Blessing of Pentecost*]

How the Full Blessing of Pentecost May Be Increased

He that believeth on me shall never thirst.
(JOHN 6:35)

He that believeth on me ... out of his belly shall flow rivers of living water.
(JOHN 7:38)

Can the full blessing of Pentecost be still further increased? Can anything that is full become still fuller? Yes: undoubtedly. It can

139

become so full that it always overflows. This is especially the characteristic and law of the blessing of Pentecost.

The words of our blessed Lord Jesus which have been quoted, point us to a double blessing. First, Jesus says that he who believes in him shall never thirst: he shall always have life in himself – that is to say, the satisfaction of all his needs. Then he speaks of something that is grander and more glorious: he that believeth in him, out of his heart shall flow rivers of living water to quench the thirst of others. It is the distinction betwixt full and overflowing. A vessel may be full and yet have nothing over for others. When it continues full, and yet has something over for others, there must be in it an over-brimming, ever-flowing supply. This is what our Lord promises to his believing disciples. At the outset, faith in him gives them the blessing that they shall never thirst. But as they advance and become stronger in faith, it makes them a fountain of water out of which streams flow to others. The Spirit who at first only fills us will overflow out of us to souls around us.

It is with the rivers of living water as with many a fountain on earth. When we begin to open them, the stream is weak. The more the water is used, and the more deeply the source is opened up, the more strongly does the water flow. I should like to inquire how far this principle holds good in the realm of the spiritual life and to discover what is necessary to secure that the fullness of the Spirit may constantly flow more abundantly from us. There are several simple directions which may help us in reaching this knowledge.

1. Hold fast that which you have

See to it that you do not misunderstand the blessing which God has given you. Be sure that you do not form any wrong conceptions of what the full blessing is. Do not imagine that the animation, and joy, and power of Pentecost must be felt and seen immediately. No: the Church at present is in a dead-and-alive condition, and the restoration often comes slowly. At first, indeed, one receives the full blessing only as a seed: the full life is wrapt up in a little invisible capsule. The quickened soul has longed for it; he has surrendered himself unreservedly for it; he has believed in silence that God has accepted his consecration and fulfilled his promise. In that faith he goes on his way, silent and happy, saying to himself: 'The blessing of the fullness of the Spirit is for me.' But the actual experiences of the blessing did not come as he had anticipated; or they did come, but lasted only for a short time. The result was that he began to fear that his surrender was not a reality; that he had been rejoicing in what was only a transient emotion; and that the real blessing was something greater and more powerful than he had yet received. The result is that very speedily the blessing becomes less instead of larger, and he moves further back rather than forward through discouragement on account of his disappointment.

The cause of this condition is simply lack of faith. We are bent on judging God and his work in us by sight and feeling. We forget that the whole process is the work of faith. Even in its highest revelations in Christians that have made the greatest progress, faith rests not on what is to be seen of the work of God or on the experiences of it, but on the work of God as spiritual, invisible, deeply hidden, and inconceivable. To you, therefore, my friend, who desires in this time of discouragement to return to the true life according to the promise, my counsel is not to be greatly surprised if it comes to you slowly or if it appears to be involved in darkness. If you know that you have given yourself to God with a perfect heart, and if you know that God, really and with his whole heart, waits to fulfil his promise in you with divine power, then rest in silence before his face and hold fast your integrity. Although the cold of winter appears to bury everything in death, say with the prophet Habakkuk: 'Although the fig tree shall not blossom, neither shall fruit be in the vines ... yet I will rejoice in the Lord, I will joy in the God of my salvation' (Habakkuk 3:17-18). Do this, and you shall know God, and God will know you. If you are sure that you have set yourself before God as an empty, separated, purified vessel, to become full of his Spirit, then continue still to regard yourself so and keep silence before him. If you have believed that God has received you to fill you as a purified vessel – purified through Jesus Christ and by your entire surrender to him – then abide in this attitude day by day, and you may reckon upon it that the blessing will grow and begin to flow. 'He that believeth on him shall not be confounded' (1 Peter 2:6).

2. Regard yourself as living only to make others happy

God is love. His whole being is nothing but a surrender of himself in love to be the life of the creature, to make the creature participate in his holiness and blessedness. He blesses and serves all that lives. His glory as God is that he puts all that he has at the disposal of his creatures.

Jesus Christ is the Son of God's love, the bearer, the bringer, the dispenser of the love. What God is as invisible in heaven, he was as visible on earth. He came, he lived, he suffered and died only to glorify the Father – that is, to let it be seen how glorious the Father in his love is, and to show that in the Godhead there is no other purpose than to bless men and make them happy; to make it manifest that the highest honour and blessedness of any being is to give and to sacrifice.

The Holy Spirit came as the Spirit of the Father and the Son to make us partakers of this divine nature, to shed abroad the love of God in our hearts, to secure the indwelling of the Son and his love in our hearts to such an extent that Christ may verily be formed within us, and that our whole 'inner man' (Ephesians 3:16) shall bear the impress of his disposition and his likeness.

Hence, when any soul seeks and receives the fullness of the Spirit, and desires to have it increased, is it not perfectly evident that he can enjoy this blessing only according as he is prepared to give himself to a life in the service of love? The Spirit came to expel the life of self and self-seeking. The fullness of the Spirit presupposes a willingness to consecrate ourselves to the blessing of others and as the servants of all, and that in a constantly increasing and unreserved measure. The Spirit is the outflowing of the life of God. If we will but yield ourselves to him, he will become rivers of living water, flowing from the depths of our heart.

Christian reader, if you will have the blessing increased, begin to live as a man who is left here on earth only in order that the love of God may work by you. Love all around you with the love of God which is in you through the Spirit. Love the children of God cordially, even the weakest and most perverse. Exercise and exhibit your love in every possible way. Love the unsaved. Present yourself to the Spirit to love him. Then will love constrain you to speak, to work, to give, and to pray. If there is no open door for working, or if you have not the strength for it, the door of prayer is always open, and power can be obtained at the mercy-seat. Embrace the whole world in your love; for Christ, who is in your heart, belongs also to the heathen. The Spirit is the power of Christ for redeeming them. Like God and Jesus and the Spirit, live wholly to bless others. Then the blessing shall stream forth and become overflowing.

[From *The Full Blessing of Pentecost*]

The More Abundant Life

Our Lord spoke about the more abundant life when he said that he had come to give his life for his sheep: 'I am come that they might have life, and that they might have it more abundantly' (John 10:10). A man may have life, and yet, through lack of nourishment, or through illness, there may be no abundance of life or power. This was the distinction between the Old Testament and the New. In the former there was indeed life, under the law, but not the abundance of grace of the New Testament. Christ had given life to his disciples, but they could receive the abundant life only through his resurrection and the gift of the Holy Spirit.

All true Christians have received life from Christ. The greater portion of them, however, know nothing about the more abundant life which he is willing to bestow. Paul speaks constantly of this. He says about himself that the grace of God was 'exceeding abundant' (1 Timothy 1:14). 'I can do all things through Christ which strengtheneth me' (Philippians 4:13). 'Thanks be unto God, which always causeth us to triumph in Christ' (2 Corinthians 2:14). 'We are more than conquerors through him that loved us' (Romans 8:37).

What peculiarly constitutes this abundant life? We cannot too often repeat, or in different ways too often set it forth – the abundant life is nothing less than *the full Jesus having the full mastery over our entire being, through the power of the Holy Spirit*. As the Spirit makes known in us the fullness of Christ, and the abundant life which he gives, it will be chiefly in three aspects:

1. As the crucified one

Not merely as the one who died for us, to atone for our sins; but as he *who has taken us up with himself on the cross to die with him*, and who now works out in us the power of his cross and death. You have the true fellowship with Christ when you can say: 'I have been crucified with Christ – he, the crucified one, lives in me.' *The feelings and the disposition which were in him*, his lowliness and obedience even to the death of the cross – these were what he referred to when he said of the Holy Spirit: 'He shall take of mine, and shall shew it unto you' (John 16:15) – not as an instruction, but as childlike participation of the same life which was in him.

Do you desire that the Holy Spirit should take full possession of you, so as to cause *the crucified Christ to dwell in you?* Understand then, that this is just the end for which he has been given, and this he will surely accomplish in all who yield themselves to him.

2. As the risen one

The Scripture frequently mentions the resurrection in connection with the wonder-working power of God, by which Christ was raised from the dead; and from which comes the assurance of *'the exceeding greatness of his power to usward who believe*, according to the working of his mighty power, which he wrought in Christ, when he raised him from the dead' (Ephesians 1:19, 20). Do not pass hastily from these words. Turn back and read them once more, and learn the great lesson that, however powerless and weak you feel, the omnipotence of God *is working in you*; and, if you only believe, will give you in daily life a share in the resurrection of his Son.

Yes, the Holy Spirit can fill you with the joy and victory of the resurrection of Christ, as the power of your daily life, here in the midst of the trials and temptations of this world. Let the cross humble you to death. God will work out the heavenly life in you through his Spirit. Ah, how little have we understood that it is entirely the work of the Holy Spirit to make us partakers of the crucified and risen Christ, and to conform us to his life and death!

3. *As the glorified one*

The glorified Christ is he who baptizes with the Holy Spirit. When the Lord Jesus himself was baptized with the Spirit, it was because he had humbled himself and offered himself to take part in John's baptism of repentance – a baptism for sinners – in Jordan. Even so, when he took upon himself the work of redemption, he received the Holy Spirit to fit him for his work from that hour till on the cross he 'offered himself without spot to God' (Hebrews 9:14). Do you desire that this glorified Christ should baptize you with the Holy Spirit? Offer yourself then to him for his service, to further his great work of making known to sinners the love of the Father.

God help us to understand what a great thing it is *to receive the Holy Spirit with power from the glorified Jesus!* It means a willingness – a longing of the soul – to work for him, and, if need be, to suffer for him. You have known and loved your Lord, and have worked for him, and have had blessing in that work; but the Lord has more than that to bestow. He can so work in us, and in our brethren around us, and in the ministers of the Church, by the power of the Holy Spirit, as to fill our hearts with adoring wonder.

Have you laid hold of it, my reader? The abundant life is neither more nor less than the full life of Christ as the crucified, the risen, the glorified one, who baptizes with the Holy Ghost and reveals himself in our hearts and lives as Lord of all within us.

I read not long ago an expression – 'Live in what must be.' Do not live in your human imagination of what is possible. *Live in the word – in the love and infinite faithfulness of the Lord Jesus.* Even though it is slow, and with many a stumble, the faith that always thanks him – not for experiences, but for the promises on which it can rely – goes on from strength to strength, still increasing in the blessed assurance that God himself will perfect his work in us.

[From *The Prayer Life*]

Have You Received the Holy Spirit?

Paul said unto them, 'Have ye received the Holy Ghost since ye believed?' (ACTS 19:2)

There was once a professor who discovered that for a long time he had been making a serious mistake in the way he had been teaching his students. He had taken every possible trouble to explain to them the problems which came up in the course of their studies, but he had often found that he could not hold their attention. He asked himself what the reason might be, and he concluded that it was because he had not allowed them to try and solve those problems themselves. They had never clearly recognized the difficulties which existed and which had to be overcome. And so he decided to try another method. He now took great pains to make the problems involved in each exercise plain to them, and then he let them attempt to think them through themselves and seek a solution. The students would usually get stuck, and then the professor's own solution was always welcome and clearly understood.

I find that a similar situation exists with the preaching of God's Word. Preachers tell people about the great redemption of Christ, but if they have never known what it is to be sinners and how deeply they have fallen, the preaching of redemption is almost meaningless to them. It has no interest for them for the simple reason that they have no sense or feeling of the necessity of that redemption. This is the reason why throughout the Church of Christ there is so much profitless preaching.

Just as many of the unsaved are unaware of their need for salvation, so too many Christians are unaware of their need to receive the Holy Spirit. This was the case with the twelve believers whom Paul met at Ephesus. They had been baptized and had professed their faith in Christ. No doubt they were honest, upright, earnest men. But when he talked to them Paul very soon saw that they lacked something, so he asked them, 'Have you received the Holy Spirit?' They answered, 'No, and to tell you the truth, we don't understand what you're talking about. We have not heard about the Holy Spirit.' 'What have you been baptized into, then?' asked Paul. 'John's baptism,' they answered. 'That's very good, as far as it goes,' said Paul. 'You're right to believe that Jesus was the Messiah who was to come, and that he died, but there is a great deal more to it all than that. Jesus rose again after he died, and he has fulfilled his promise that his Holy Spirit would come down.' Once he had told them this, they were ready and willing to be baptized in the name of the Lord Jesus. And yet even this was not enough. Paul then laid his hands upon them and they received the Holy Spirit. And they began to speak in strange tongues, which was one of the manifestations of receiving the Spirit in those days.

The first lesson

This conversation in the book of Acts teaches us some very important lessons. The first is that the most necessary thing in the Christian life is to receive the Holy Spirit. Let us try to understand why this is so. You may say, 'But surely we have received the Holy Spirit. Why do you question that? How can a man be converted without the Holy Spirit?' But I am not here talking about conversion. The expression 'receiving the Holy Spirit' does not refer to

147

that secret working of God's Spirit by which a person is brought to salvation. Receiving the Spirit is something which occurs after conversion. The Holy Spirit does indeed work in the hearts of the unconverted and struggles with them, convincing them of sin and pointing them to Jesus. But the Spirit only works in such hearts – he does not stay in them. The Spirit works in the heart of every man who is converted, but he does not necessarily live there and take up his abode and dwell there. After conversion and baptism into the name of Jesus, believers still have to receive the Holy Spirit. Why is this so? This points us back to what Jesus taught his disciples.

We have the clearest indication of what receiving the Holy Spirit was in the case of the twelve apostles. They were with Jesus for three years. Every day he taught them, and they enjoyed a wonderful personal relationship and fellowship with him. And yet we know how unsanctified they were and how they grieved the Master by the weakness and the lack of love which they displayed. But he said to them, 'The time is coming when everything will be changed. I have promised my Spirit, and when you receive him you will know that I am in my Father, and you are in me, and I am in you, even nearer than I now am upon earth.' So the Holy Spirit came down at Pentecost. And what did that mean? It meant that by the Spirit Jesus could live in them and enable them to live in a new way. Before Pentecost Jesus was outside of them, external to them. During the three years of his earthly ministry, he exercised a great influence over them. But he was not where he wanted to be – in their very hearts. What he wanted to do for them was to make their hearts like his, full of humility, gentleness and love. And so he was always pointing them to a better time, and it began with the day of Pentecost. So an outward Saviour became an inward Saviour. He took possession of the disciples and came and dwelt in their hearts. His character, will and aims became their own.

Why is there so much complaint in the Church of Christ about spiritual feebleness, instability and backsliding? The answer is this: Christ is so often preached about and experienced only as an external Saviour. Preachers talk about Calvary and the Ascension, and yet many believers say, 'Oh yes, I have an almighty Jesus up in heaven, but there seems to be a distance between him and us. We want to feel him nearer.' Why do they feel this way? Because they do not know him as an indwelling Saviour. The Holy Spirit has come to accomplish just that for us. Jesus said, 'He shall glorify me in you,' and by that he did not mean that God was merely going to give us glorious ideas about his Son. The soul cannot feed upon ideas. I want bread. You may tell me about the nature and essence of bread, but that does not feed me. I want the bread within me. And so Christians too often try to feed upon the words of God while forgetting that the living Christ must be an inward Saviour.

In effect Christ said to his disciples, 'You may not dare to preach until you have received the Holy Spirit.' The Holy Spirit was not just an idea, but a reality. And so today no one should dare to speak of the redeeming power of Christ without an inward experience of him in their heart and soul. If we would only live as God would have us live, our work for the Lord would exercise a mighty influence. Our lives, our conversations, our prayers and our whole faith would have a strong power over people and would proclaim that Jesus is not merely an outward Saviour but, through the Holy Spirit, is an inward one.

The second lesson

When Paul met these twelve believers at Ephesus he found them to be honest, earnest men. However, although they were believers in Jesus, they knew only half the truth about him. They had not received the Holy Spirit. So we have seen that the one thing which every Christian needs is to receive the Spirit. This leads us on to our second main point, namely that there may be a great deal of very earnest religion in our lives without our ever having received the Spirit.

A person may even be happy as a Christian for a time without receiving this gift of the Holy Spirit. In Acts chapter 8 we read that Philip went and preached in a city in Samaria. Great numbers of people there believed and were baptized, and there was great joy in the city. News of this came to the Apostles in Jerusalem. They realized that the Samaritans were lacking something, so they sent two of their number to them. When they arrived in the city the very first thing they did was to call the people together to teach them, pray with them and lay hands on them. They received the Spirit, and so enjoyed the full blessing of the Christian dispensation.

The fact that it is possible to be a sincere Christian without having received the Holy Spirit presents us with a great problem in the Church of Christ. If one were to ask the majority of Christians, 'Have you received the Holy Spirit since you believed?' they would almost have their breath taken away by the question. Of course, they would not answer, 'I have never heard about the Holy Spirit,' because he is mentioned quite often. But they might say something like, 'I don't understand what you mean. What does it mean to receive the Holy Spirit? Didn't I receive him when I received Jesus?' Oh, believe me, there is a great difference.

We often hear complaints about the state of the Church. People say that the Church is not what it should be, that there is a widespread spirit of worldliness and a lack of commitment, that there is too much dependence upon tradition or preaching, while in the relationships between Christians there is an absence of the close fellowship of the Spirit which should exist. You may hear about Holiness Conventions or about full salvation and the deeper spiritual life. Some of you may say, 'I can't understand what this is all about.' Really the whole issue boils down to this question: 'Have you received the Holy Spirit?' We need to receive the Spirit so that the life of Christ may enter us and live in us fully.

The third lesson
The third main point which I wish to make is that the greatest aim of the Christian ministry ought to be to bring people to the Holy Spirit. Someone might argue, 'Isn't there a danger here of leading people away from the grace of God in Christ and encouraging them to look into their own hearts too much?' It would certainly be a

grave mistake to preach Christ and the Holy Spirit as two separate Saviours, but a minister is not preaching the full Gospel if he preaches Christ without also stressing the need to receive the Holy Spirit. Receiving the Spirit means that the living, heavenly, glorified Jesus comes and dwells in our hearts. People sometimes wonder if the Spirit is some kind of substitute for Jesus, since Jesus said, 'I will go away, and send the Holy Spirit.' But the Spirit did not come as a replacement for Jesus but rather to bring Jesus closer to us than ever – even closer than he was to the disciples on earth. So the great work of the ministry ought to be to bring the knowledge of the Holy Spirit to believers. Paul asked the Corinthians, 'Know ye not that ye are the temple of the Holy Ghost?' The spiritual life of the whole Corinthian church was feeble because they had no knowledge of the Holy Spirit.

And so we should all pray and wait upon God, and set our hearts and our faith upon this gift that the Father gave to the men of Ephesus, so that we too may be filled with the Holy Spirit. Oh, brother, sister, are you earnestly seeking and crying to him so that you may get filled with the Spirit? The question is often asked, 'How can I receive the Holy Spirit?' You can only receive him through prayer. You must receive him personally from God. God must speak. You may have heard a great deal of good advice on the subject. People may say that in order to receive the Spirit, the believer must search his heart and part with all sin. Others may say that you must have a very simple faith in Christ's promise of the Holy Spirit. All this is very true, but there is something even more important. Quite simply, we must get the Holy Spirit from God himself. We must feel our own powerlessness, and in humility before God, we must let him do his work. There will have to be a personal dealing with God. There must be a very full opening of the heart itself to God. There will have to be prayer, and prayer will have to be the very spirit of our lives. We should constantly be saying, 'I want this one thing, O God: to be filled with the Holy Spirit.'

Are you ready to say, 'O my God, I thirst for you'? . . . But

151

remember, it is a very serious thing to say, 'I am now going to be a vessel set apart for the Holy Spirit to dwell in, to rule and guide me as he pleases.' Perhaps you may think, 'Ah, that is too difficult for me in my circumstances.' Brother, the Holy Spirit is the living God, and he brings the joy of God, the love of God and the Son of God himself into your heart. Don't be afraid. Make the sacrifice.

I plead with you, Christians, even though you may not understand it all very clearly – say to God, 'You have something for me, your child, which I have never before had. There is a blessing I have never before understood or received. I will cry for it. I will wait for it.' Child of God, however ignorant you feel about it, begin by saying trustingly, 'My Father's love for me is greater than my love for him.' You are longing earnestly for the Spirit, but he is knocking at your door even more earnestly. Take him in, in faith and say, 'Blessed Father, are you willing to live in your child and completely fill him with your Spirit? Come into me and rest in me.' Trust God and wait day by day for this change to happen. It may not necessarily be the case that a long wait is needed, but if it is, be patient, depending on your God.

[From *The Promise of the Spirit*]

Walking in the Holy Spirit

Filled with God's Spirit

One thing is needful for the Church – the thing which, above all others, men ought everywhere to seek for with one accord and with their whole heart – to be filled with the Spirit of God.

In order to secure attention to this message and attract the hearts of my readers to the blessing of which it speaks, I have laid particular emphasis on certain main points. These I briefly state here.

1. It is the will of God that every one of his children should live entirely and unceasingly under the control of the Holy Spirit.

2. Without being filled with the Spirit, it is utterly impossible that an individual Christian or a church can ever live or work as God desires.

3. Everywhere and in everything we see the proofs, in the life and experience of Christians, that this blessing is but little enjoyed in the Church, and, alas, is but little sought for.

4. This blessing is prepared for us and God waits to bestow it. Our faith may expect it with the greatest confidence.

5. The great hindrance in the way is that the self-life, and the world, which it uses for its own service and pleasure, usurp the place that Christ ought to occupy.

6. We cannot be filled with the Spirit until we are prepared to yield ourselves to be led by the Lord Jesus to forsake and sacrifice everything for this pearl of great price.

[From *The Full Blessing of Pentecost*]

The Holy Spirit and Money

When the Holy Spirit came down at Pentecost to dwell in men, he assumed the charge and control of their whole life. They were to be or do nothing that was not under his inspiration and leading. In everything they were to move and live and have their being 'in the Spirit', to be wholly spiritual men. Hence it followed as a necessity that their possessions and property, that their money and its appropriations were subjected to his rule too, and that their income and expenditure were animated by new and hitherto unknown principles. In the opening chapters of the Acts we find more than one proof of the all-embracing claim of the Holy Spirit to guide and judge in the disposal of money.

The Holy Spirit takes possession of the money. 'All that believed were together, and had all things common; and they sold their possessions and goods, and parted them to all according as every man had need' (Acts 2:44–45). And again, Acts 4:34: 'As many as were possessors of land or houses, sold them, and brought the prices of the things that were sold, and laid them at the apostles' feet. And Barnabas, having a field, sold it, and brought the money and laid it at the apostles' feet.' Without any command or instruction, in the joy of the Holy Spirit, the joy of the love which he had shed abroad in their heart, the joy of the heavenly treasures that now made them rich, they spontaneously parted with their possessions and placed them at the disposal of the Lord and his servants.

It would have been strange had it been otherwise, and a terrible loss to the Church. Money is the great symbol of the power of happiness of this world, one of its chief idols, drawing men away from God; a never-ceasing temptation to worldliness, to which the Christian is daily exposed. It would not have been a full salvation that did not provide complete deliverance from the power of money. The story of Pentecost assures us that when the Holy Spirit comes in his fullness into the heart, then earthly possessions lose their place in it, and money is valued only as a means of proving our love and doing service to our Lord and our fellow men. The fire from heaven that finds a man upon the altar and consumes the sacrifice, finds his money too, and makes it all *altar gold*, holy to the Lord.

We learn here the true secret of Christian giving, the secret, in fact, of all true Christian living – the joy of the Holy Ghost. How much of our giving, then, has there been in which this element has been too much lacking? Habit, example, human argument and motive, the thought of duty, or the feeling of the need around us, have had more to do with our charities than the power and love of the Spirit. It is not that what has just been mentioned is not needful. The Holy Spirit makes use of all these elements of our nature in stirring us to give. There is a great need for inculcating principles and fixed habits in regard to giving. But what we need to realize is that all this is but the human side, and cannot suffice if we are to give in such measure and spirit as to make every gift a sweet-smelling sacrifice to God and a blessing to our own souls. The secret of true giving is the joy of the Holy Ghost.

[From *Thoughts for God's Stewards*]

The Spirit and the Flesh

The flesh is the name by which Scripture designates our fallen nature – soul and body. The soul at creation was placed between the spiritual or divine and the sensible or worldly, to give each its due, and guide them into that perfect union which would result in man attaining his destiny, a spiritual body. When the soul yielded to the temptation of the sensible, it broke away from the rule of the Spirit and came under the power of the body – it became flesh. And now the flesh is not only without the Spirit, but even hostile to it: 'the flesh lusteth against the Spirit'.

In this antagonism of the flesh to the Spirit there are two sides. On the one hand, the flesh lusts against the Spirit in committing sin and transgressing God's law. On the other hand, its hostility to the Spirit is no less manifested in its seeking to serve God and do his will. In yielding to the flesh, the soul sought itself instead of the God to whom the Spirit linked it; selfishness prevailed over God's will; selfishness became its ruling principle. And now, so subtle and mighty in this spirit of self, that the flesh, not only in sinning against God, but even when the soul learns to serve God, still asserts its power, refuses to let the Spirit alone lead, and, in its efforts to be religious, is still the great enemy that ever hinders and quenches the Spirit. It is owing to this deceitfulness of the flesh that there often takes place what Paul speaks of to the Galatians: 'Having begun in the Spirit, are ye now perfected in the flesh?' Unless the surrender to the Spirit be very entire, and the holy waiting on him be kept up in great dependence and humility, what has been begun in the Spirit very early and very speedily passes over into confidence in the flesh.

And the remarkable thing is what at first sight might appear a paradox, that just where the flesh seeks to serve God, there it becomes the strength of sin. Do we know not how the Pharisees, with their self-righteousness and carnal religion, fell into pride and selfishness, and became the servants of sin? Was it not just among the Galatians, of whom Pauls asks the question about perfecting in the flesh what was begun in the Spirit, and whom he has so to warn against the righteousness of works, that the works of the flesh were so manifest, and that they were in danger of devouring one another? Satan has no more crafty device for keeping souls in bondage than inciting them to a religion in the flesh. He knows that the power of the flesh can never please God or conquer sin, and that in due time the flesh that has gained supremacy over the Spirit in the service of God will assert and maintain that same supremacy in the service of sin. It is only where the Spirit truly and unceasingly has the entire lead and rule in the life of worship that it will have the power to lead and rule in the life of practical obedience. If I am to deny self in communion with men, to conquer selfishness and temper and want of love, I must first learn to deny self in communion with God. *There* the soul, the seat of self, must learn to bow to the Spirit, where God dwells.

[From *The Spirit of Christ*]

The Flesh or the Spirit?

Scripture teaches us that there are but two conditions possible for the Christian. One is a walk according to the Spirit, the other a walk according to 'the flesh'. These two powers are in irreconcilable conflict with each other. So it comes to pass, in the case of the majority of Christians, that, while we thank God that they are born again through the Spirit and have received the life of God – yet their ordinary daily life is not lived according to the Spirit but according to 'the flesh'. Paul writes to the Galatians: 'Are ye so foolish? having begun in the Spirit, are ye now made perfect by the flesh?' (Galatians 3:3). Their service lay in fleshly outward performances. They did not understand that where 'the flesh' is permitted to influence their service of God, it soon results in open sin.

So he mentions not only grave sins as the work of 'the flesh', such as adultery, murder, drunkenness; but also the more ordinary sins of daily life – wrath, strife, variance; and he gives the exhortation: 'Walk in the Spirit, and ye shall not fulfil the lust of the flesh . . . If we live in the Spirit, let us also walk in the Spirit' (Galatians 5:16, 25). The Spirit must be honoured not only as the author of a new life but also as the leader and director of our entire walk. Otherwise we are what the apostle calls 'carnal'.

The majority of Christians have little understanding of this matter. They have no real knowledge of the deep sinfulness and godlessness of that carnal nature which belongs to them and to which unconsciously they yield. 'God . . . condemned sin in the flesh' (Romans 8:3) – in the cross of Christ. 'They that are Christ's have crucified the flesh with the affections and lusts' (Galatians 5:24). 'The flesh' cannot be improved or sanctified. 'The carnal mind is *enmity against God*; for it is not subject to the law of God, *neither indeed can be*' (Romans 8:7). There is no means of dealing with 'the flesh' save as Christ dealt with it, bearing it to the cross. 'Our old man is crucified with him' (Romans 6:6); so we by faith also crucify it, and regard and treat it daily as an accursed thing that finds its rightful place on the accursed cross.

It is saddening to consider how many Christians there are who seldom think or speak earnestly about the deep and immeasurable sinfulness of 'the flesh' – 'In me (that is, in my flesh) dwelleth no good thing' (Romans 7:18). The man who truly believes this may well cry out: 'I see another law in my members . . . bringing me into captivity to the law of sin. . . . O wretched man that I am! who shall deliver me from the body of this death?' (Romans 7:23–24). Happy is he who can go further and say: 'I thank God, through Jesus Christ our Lord . . . *For the law of the Spirit of life in Christ Jesus hath made me free* from the law of sin and death' (Romans 7:25; 8:2).

Would that we might understand God's counsels of grace for us! 'The flesh' on the cross – the Spirit in the heart and controlling the life.

This spiritual life is too little understood or sought after; yet it is literally what God has promised and will accomplish in those who unconditionally surrender themselves to him for this purpose.

[From *The Prayer Life*]

The Holy Spirit and Prayer

The Holy Spirit is 'the Spirit of prayer'. He is definitely called by this name in Zechariah 12:10: 'The spirit of grace and of supplications.' Twice in Paul's epistles there is a remarkable reference to him in the matter of prayer. 'Ye have received the Spirit of adoption, *whereby we cry*, Abba, Father' (Romans 8:15). 'God hath sent forth the Spirit of his Son into your hearts, crying, Abba, Father' (Galatians 4:6). Have you ever meditated on these words: 'Abba, Father'? In that name our Saviour offered his greatest prayer to the Father, accompanied by the entire surrender and sacrifice of his life and love. *The Holy Spirit is given for the express purpose* of teaching us, from the very beginning of our Christian life onward, to utter that word in childlike trust and surrender. In one of these passages we read: 'We cry'; in the other: 'He cries.' What a wonderful blending of the divine and human cooperation in prayer. What a proof that God – if I may say so – has done his utmost to make prayer as natural and effectual as though it were the cry of a child to an earthly Father, as he says: 'Abba, Father.'

Is it not a proof that the Holy Spirit is to a great extent a stranger in the Church, when prayer, for which God has made such provisions, is regarded as a task and a burden? And does not this teach us to seek for the deep root of prayerlessness in our ignorance of, and disobedience to, the divine instructor whom the Father has commissioned to teach us to pray?

If we desire to understand this truth still more clearly we must notice what is written in Romans 8:26, 27: 'Likewise the Spirit also helpeth our infirmities: for we know not what we should pray for as we ought: but the Spirit himself maketh intercession for us with groanings which cannot be uttered. And he that searcheth the hearts knoweth what is the mind of the Spirit, because he maketh intercession for the saints according to the will of God.' Is it not clear from this that the Christian if left to himself does not know how to pray; or how he ought to pray; and that God has stooped to meet us in this helplessness of ours by giving us the Holy Spirit himself to pray for us; and that his operation is deeper than our thought or feeling, but is noticed and answered by God?

Our first work, therefore, ought to be to come into God's presence not with our ignorant prayers, not with many words and thoughts, but in the confidence that the divine work of the Holy Spirit is being carried on within us. This confidence will encourage reverence and quietness, and will also enable us, in dependence on the help which the Spirit gives, to lay our desires and heart-needs before God. The great lesson for every prayer is – see to it, first of all, that you commit yourself to the leading of the Holy Spirit, and with entire dependence on him, give him the first place; for through him your prayer will have a value you cannot imagine, and through him also you will learn to speak out your desires in the name of Christ.

What a protection this faith would be against deadness and despondency in the inner chamber! Only think of it ! In every prayer the triune God takes a part – the Father who hears: the Son in whose name we pray; the Spirit who prays for us and in us. How important it is that we should be in right relationship to the Holy Spirit and understand his work!

[From *The Prayer Life*]

The Spirit and the Cross

Why are there not more men and women who can witness, in the joy of their hearts, that the Spirit of God has taken possession of them and given them new power to witness for him? Yet more urgently arises the heart-searching question to which an answer must be given: what is it that hinders? The Father in heaven is more willing than an earthly father to give bread to his child, and yet the cry arises: 'Is the Spirit straitened? Is this his work?'

Many will acknowledge that the hindrance undoubtedly lies in the fact that the Church is too much under the sway of the flesh and the world. They understand too little of the heart-piercing power of the cross of Christ. So it comes to pass that the Spirit has not the vessels into which he can pour his fullness.

Many complain that the subject is too high or too deep for them. This is a proof of how little we have appropriated and brought into practice the teaching of Paul and Christ about the cross. I bring you a message of joy. The Spirit who is in you, in however limited a measure, is prepared to take you under his teaching, to lead you to the cross, and by his heavenly instruction to make you know something of what the crucified Christ wills to do for you and in you.

But then he wants you to take time, so that he may reveal the heavenly mysteries to you. He wants to make you see how the neglect of the inner chamber has hindered fellowship with Christ, the knowledge of the cross, and the powerful operations of the Spirit. He will teach you what is meant by the denial of self, the taking up of your cross, the losing of your life, and following him.

In spite of all that you have felt of your ignorance, and lack of spiritual insight and fellowship with the cross, he is able and willing to take you under his teaching and to make known to you the secret of the spiritual life above all your expectations.

Begin at the beginning. Be faithful in the inner chamber. Thank him that you can reckon on him to meet you there. Although everything appears cold, and dark, and strained, bow in silence before the loving Lord Jesus, who so longs after you. Thank the Father that he has given you the Spirit. And be assured that all you do not yet know, and still must know – about 'the flesh', and 'the world', and the cross – the Spirit of Christ, who is in you, will surely make known to you. O soul, only believe that this blessing is for you! Christ belongs entirely to you. He longs to obtain full possession of you. He can and will possess you through the Holy Spirit. But for this, time is necessary. Oh, give him time in the inner chamber every day. You can rest assured that he will fulfil his promise in you. 'He that hath my commandments, and keepeth them, he it is that loveth me: and he that loveth me shall be loved of my Father, and I will love him, and *will manifest myself to him*' (John 14:21).

Persevere, in addition to all that you ask for yourself, in prayer for your congregation, your church, your minister; for all believers; for the whole Church of God, that God may strengthen

161

them with power through his Spirit, so that Christ may dwell in your hearts by faith. Blessed time when the answer comes! Continue in prayer. The Spirit will reveal and glorify Christ and his love, Christ and his cross 'as the Lamb slain standing in the midst of the throne'.

[From *The Prayer Life*]

Spiritual Gifts

*Now concerning spiritual gifts, brethren,
I would not have you ignorant.*
(1 CORINTHIANS 12:1)

For a right understanding of the place these gifts held in the Church, and of the teaching of Paul with regard to them, we must first think of their relation to the whole work of the blessed Spirit as that has been set before us in this epistle. We shall then have the right standpoint for answering more than one important question that may arise.

Paul's first mention of the Holy Spirit is where he speaks of him as a Spirit of power. He had preached to them the Gospel in demonstrations of the Spirit and of power. Their conversion had been the proof of the mighty power of God bringing them to the obedience of faith.

The next thought is that he is not only the power but the wisdom of God. As the Spirit of revelation, he unveils the hidden mystery of the cross and shows forth the deep things of God. And that not only in the Apostle himself, but in all believers who yielded themselves fully to become spiritual men with the power of spiritual discernment.

In chapter 3 he is spoken of as the Spirit of holiness; 'the Spirit of God dwelleth in you . . . the temple of God is holy, which temple ye are.' Or, as is put in chapter 6, 'Ye are sanctified, ye are justified in the name of the Lord Jesus, and by the Spirit of God.' The whole life, both of justification and sanctification, depends upon him and his indwelling.

And then we have him as the Spirit of life. 'He that is joined unto the Lord is one spirit'; 'Your body is the temple of the Holy Ghost which is in you.' The indwelling of the Spirit is the indwelling of Christ in us, making us one Spirit with him. In these four words Paul teaches us how the spiritual life has as its essential and indispensable condition the faith and the full surrender to the mastery of the Holy Spirit.

In chapter 12 Paul's teaching concerning spiritual gifts leads us a step further on. There is a diversity of gifts, and yet the body is one. 'By one Spirit are we all baptized into one body . . . and have been all made to drink into one Spirit.' 'Ye are the body of Christ, and members in particular.' In summing up the diversity of gifts, Paul gives a list of some nine workings of the selfsame Spirit. And later on in the chapter he gives another list of eight ministrations with the view of pressing deeply upon them the thought of how the body of Christ needs every member for the full development of its health and the work it has to do in the world.

The great curse of sin is selfishness. Even in the Church of Christ it still prevails. Men think of themselves and their own salvation, and rejoice in the gifts they possess. Many enter the Church without understanding that as members of a body they are to care for each other, to use all their gifts for the help of those who have less. Their first object is to be the building up of the body of Christ in love. The great mark and happiness of their life is to be a love like that of Christ, who gave himself away for others. Gifts, however truly they may come from God, and however indispensable for the welfare of the Church, are nothing without love. It is in the exercise of love that they are to find their true worth and beauty.

In chapter 13 Paul sounds the praises of love. A man may speak with tongues and have the gift of prophecy, and understand all mystery, and have all faith, so that he could remove mountains, and bestow all his goods on the poor, and give his body to be burnt, yet if he have not love, it availeth nothing, he is nothing. Knowledge and gifts tend to puff up; it is only love that seeketh not its own, that never faileth and is the greatest of all. Amid all the contentions and self-exaltation of these carnal Corinthians Paul lifts their thoughts to that one Spirit into which they had been baptized, and that one holy Body of which they are now members, and that divine love in which alone the likeness of God consists. 'Be ye therefore followers of God, as dear children; And walk in love, as Christ also hath loved us.' The spiritual growth of a church depends not only on the preaching, but on the life of fellowship and love, into the healthy exercise of which believers are led.

In chapter 14 Paul descends to particulars, dealing specially with the question of the gift of tongues and of prophecy. The Corinthians had evidently allowed themselves to be drawn away by what appeared miraculous and special. The gift of prophecy, as Paul defines it, 'speaketh edification, and exhortation, and comfort,' was not held in equal honour. Paul says that he would rather speak five words ' with my understanding, that I might teach others also, than ten thousand words in an unknown tongue.' The edification of the Church is to be the highest law; those who can speak in tongues are to remember that the speaking in tongues, unless there be an interpreter, does not bring comfort or instruction to others. And in passing he gives us a picture of what a church meeting could be, and doubtless often was, where the spirit of love was allowed to rule. 'If all prophesy, and there come in one that believeth not, or one unlearned, he is convinced of all, he is judged of all: And thus are the secrets of his heart made manifest; and so falling down on his face he will worship God, and report that God is in you of a truth' – a pledge of what can be true of the church in our time, too, where the Spirit of the Lord is allowed free course.

The passage ends with a reminder that as God is not a God of confusion, but of peace, so those who first prophesy are also to learn to be subject one to another. Then he closes with words that have often been terribly abused, and yet have their divine worth in their own place – In all the churches of the saints 'Let all things be done decently and in order.' The chapters on spiritual gifts, on the supremacy of love, on the sacrifice of everything and everyone to the edification of the body, have been of untold value in the Church of God, and in the full harmony of the truths they contain, are still essential to the building up of the Body of Christ.

[From *The Apostle Paul's Inner Life*]

The Sealing of the Spirit

In whom having also believed, ye were sealed with the Holy Spirit of promise. (EPHESIANS 1:13)

When a king appoints an ambassador or a governor, his commission is sealed with the king's seal, bearing the king's likeness. The Holy Spirit is the seal of our redemption, not in the sense of giving us the assurance of our sonship as something apart from himself: *he himself* by his life in us is the seal of our sonship. His work is to reveal and glorify Christ in us, the image of the Father, and by fixing our heart and our faith on him, to transform us into his likeness. What a wonderful thought. None less than the Spirit of the Father and the Son, the bond of union between them, comes to us as the bond of our union with them, giving us the witness of the divine life within us, and enabling us to live out that life here in the body. *In the Christian life everything depends on knowing the Holy Spirit and his blessed work aright.*

First of all, we need to know that he comes to take the mastery of our whole being – spirit, soul, and body – and through it all to reveal the life and the power of God as it works in our renewed nature. Just as Christ could not be glorified and receive the Spirit from the Father for us until he had died upon the cross, and parted with that life in which he had borne our sin and the weakness of our nature, so the coming of the Holy Spirit into our hearts in power implies that we yield ourselves to the fellowship of the cross, and consent *to die entirely to that life of nature in which self and sin have their power*, that through the Spirit, the new, the heavenly, life may take complete possession of us.

This entire mastery implies on our side complete surrender and obedience. Peter speaks of the 'Holy Ghost, whom God hath given to them that obey him'. Even as Christ came to do God's will alone, and humbled himself to the perfect obedience of the cross, that he might receive the Spirit from the Father and we through him, so the full experience of the Spirit's power rests entirely on our readiness in everything to deny self, in everything to yield ourselves to his teaching and leading. The great reason that believers are so feeble, and so ignorant of the blessings of the Spirit, is this, that at conversion and in their Christian life the question was never faced and settled that by the grace of God they would in everything, in every place, and at every moment, yield themselves to the control of the Spirit. Oh that God's children might accept of God's terms, *the undivided mastery of the Spirit*, the unhesitating surrender of the whole being to his control.

In this connection we need specially to understand that the degree or measure in which the working of the Spirit is experienced may vary greatly. A believer may rejoice in one of the gifts of the Spirit, say peace or joy, zeal or boldness, and yet may be expremely deficient in the other graces which his presence bestows. Our true position towards the blessed Spirit must be that of perfect teachableness, waiting to be led by him in all the will of God, with the consciousness of how much there still is within the heart that needs to be renewed and sanctified, if he is to have the place and the honour that belong to him.

There are specially two great enemies under which man was brought by his fall. These are the world and self. Of the world Christ says, 'The Spirit of truth, whom the world cannot receive because it knoweth him not'. *Worldliness is the great hindrance that keeps believers from living the spiritual life*. Of self Christ said, 'Let a man deny himself', 'Let a man hate his own life'. *Self, in all its forms – self-will, self-pleasing, self-confidence – renders a life in the power of the Spirit impossible.* And from these two great enemies, the power of the world and the power of self, nothing can deliver us but the cross of Christ. Paul boasts in the cross by which he has been crucified to the world. And he tells us: 'They that are Christ's have crucified the flesh,' in which self has its seat and power. To live the spiritual life, nothing less is needed than the entire giving up of the old life to the death, to make room for the blessed Spirit to renew and transform our whole being into the will of God.

Without the Spirit we can do nothing acceptable to God in things great or little. 'No man can say that Jesus is Lord but by the Holy Ghost.' No man can truly say 'Abba, Father,' but by the Spirit of God's Son sent into our hearts. In our fellowship with God, and as much in our fellowship with men, in our religious worship and our daily avocations, in the highest pursuit that life can offer and as much in the daily care of our bodies, everything must bear the seal of the Holy Spirit.

Of the Son we read, 'Him hath God the Father sealed.' It is 'in Christ' that we are sealed. As he, when the Spirit had descended upon him at his baptism, was led by the Spirit to the wilderness, thence by the Spirit to the synagogue in Nazareth, and thence through his whole life to the cross, 'where by the Eternal Spirit he offered himself a sacrifice unto God', so we too are to live our daily life as those who are sealed by the Spirit. As true as it is of Christ, 'Him hath God the Father sealed,' is it true of every believer – the Son, and every son, sealed by the Father. The great mark of the New Testament standard of the Christian life and its devotion is to be that it is all to bear the stamp of the Holy Spirit.

Let us learn the precious lesson that the Holy Spirit cannot inspire our devotions, except as he inspires our daily life. The Spirit of Christ claims and needs the rule of the whole man if he is to perform his blessed work in us. The indwelling of the Holy Spirit in us means nothing less than that in our religious life – and that means our whole life, nothing excluded – nothing is to be thought of, or trusted to, or sought after, but the immediate and continual dependence on his blessed working. The devotion of our public life will be the test of the uprightness of our secret devotion, and at the same time the means of strengthening our confidence in God who works in us through his blessed Spirit. Every thought of faith in the power of the Spirit must find its expression in prayer to God, who will most surely give us his Spirit when we ask him and work in us through the Spirit what we need.

A seal, attached to a document, gives validity to every sentence and every word it contains. Even so the Holy Spirit of promise, with which we are sealed, ratifies every promise that there is in Christ. And this is now one of the great differences between the Bible and the human standard of the Christian life, that while in the former the seal of the Spirit is accepted in his control of every movement and every moment of our life, in the latter we are content with but a very partial surrender to his guidance.

[From *Aids to Devotion*]

Filled with the Spirit

Be not drunken with wine, but be filled with the Spirit, speaking one to another in psalms and hymns and spiritual songs. (EPHESIANS 5:18–19)

To understand the command: 'Be filled with the Spirit,' we need only turn to the Day of Pentecost, where the disciples were all 'filled with the Holy Spirit'. We know what that meant to them. For three years they had lived day and night in closest fellowship with their Lord. His presence had been everything to them. When he spoke of his departure their hearts were sad. He promised that the Spirit would come, not to take his place, but to reveal himself as their Lord, ever present with them as much as when he was upon earth, only far more intimately and more gloriously. He would henceforth not be near them and beside them, without the power of enabling them to do what he had taught them, but would live and work in them, even as the Father had lived and worked in him as man. To be filled with the Spirit would mean to them that Christ on the throne would be to them an ever-present living reality, filling their hearts and life with all his heavenly love and joy. Their fellowship with him on earth would prove to have been but the shadow of that intense and unceasing union with him, which the Spirit would reveal in power.

The command: 'Be filled with the Spirit,' is a pledge that all that the disciples received and enjoyed at Pentecost is indeed for us too. The Church has sunk down from the level of Pentecost to a life in which the spirit of the world and of human wisdom is, alas, far too prevalent. Few believe in the possibility of the unbroken presence of Christ dwelling in the heart, conquering sin by his holy presence, inspiring to devotion and perfect self-sacrifice by the fire of his love, guiding each hour into all his will and work by the leading of his blessed Spirit. The heavenly vision of Christ at the right hand of God, ministering, in the power of his infinite redemption, not only salvation to the penitent, but full salvation to all whom he has sanctified by his one offering, is scarcely known. And, as the result of this, there are but few found to witness to 'the exceeding greatness of his power toward us who believe'.

The condition, too, on which this blessing is to be received cannot be better studied than in the disciples. They had turned their back upon the world, and forsaken all to follow Christ. They had learnt to know and love him, and do his will. As our Saviour said himself: 'If ye love me, ye will keep my commandments, and I will pray the Father, and he will give you another Comforter.' They had continued with him in his temptations; he carried them with him through death and the grave; the joy and the power of the resurrection life filled their hearts with confidence and hope. Their whole being was yielded up and, one might say, lost in the ascended Lord upon the throne – they were indeed ready, fully prepared, to

169

receive the wondrous gift that was to come upon them.

The Church of our day, how sadly it is lacking in that separation from the world, in that intense attachment and obedience to Christ, in that fellowship with his suffering and conformity to his death, in that devotion to Christ on the throne, and in that confident expectation of the never-ceasing flow of the water of life from under the throne, which gives the assurance that the fullness of the Spirit will not be withheld! No wonder that the mighty power of God is so little known and felt in our church life!

Let us turn once again to Pentecost, and think what the great gift was that was bestowed. Though they knew not at once to say in words what it meant, the Spirit woke in them the consciousness that he, in whom the Son and the Father had come to dwell in them, was himself indeed true God, the overflowing fountain, from whom rivers of life flowed through them, and from them on to the world. Coming fresh from the throne of our Lord in heaven, he rested on them as the Spirit of glory and of God, and filled their hearts with the very love and power of Christ in glory. As the mighty power of God dwelling in them, he convinced the world by their boldness, by their love, that God was indeed in their midst.

How different the conception of most Christians of what the Spirit is, and oh, how different their experience of the presence and the power of Christ that he imparts. How much the thought of the Spirit is little more than a mental conception, or a passing emotion, with its sense of power or of happiness. How little there is of the consciousness that fills the soul with deep reverence and quiet rest, with heavenly joy and strength, as the natural and permanent possession of the life of the believer . . .

'Be filled with the Spirit.' This filling has its very great difference in degree, from the first joy of a new but ignorant convert in a revival, through all the experiences by which he is taught what more is needed and is waiting for him, on to being filled with all the fullness of God as that comes through the dwelling of Christ in the heart.

In all filling we know how two things are needed. The one that the vessel be clean and empty and ready, even in its posture, to receive the water that is waiting for it. The other that the water be near and ready to give away itself in full measure to the waiting vessel. In the great transaction between God and man for the filling of the Spirit, man needs first of all to know how complete the surrender is that is needed, and how, even to the death to self and the world, the yielding up of the whole being is indispensable. And then how willing and ready, and oh, so able, the Holy God is to take possession of our being, and to fill it with himself.

When our Lord Jesus said: 'He that believeth on me, out of him shall flow rivers of living water,' he made the one condition of being filled with the Spirit to overflowing, nothing more and nothing less than simple faith in himself. Faith is not an imagination, not an argument or an intellectual conviction; it claims the whole heart, it yields up the whole being; it entrusts itself unreservedly to the power that seeks to take possession of it. *It is in the life of faith, cultivated in secret fellowship and adoring worship, in unceasing dependence and whole-hearted surrender, that the blessing will be found.*

[From *Aids to Devotion*]

The Cross Leads to the Spirit

Jesus of Nazareth . . . being delivered by the determinate counsel and foreknowledge of God, ye have taken, and by wicked hands have crucified and slain: Whom God hath raised up . . . Therefore being by the right hand of God exalted, and having received of the Father the promise of the Holy Ghost, he hath shed forth this, which ye now see and hear . . . Therefore let all the house of Israel know assuredly, that God hath made that same Jesus, whom ye have crucified, both Lord and Christ.

(ACTS 2:22–36)

One of the chief lessons we need to learn in regard to the cross of Christ is its close and inseparable connection with the Spirit of Christ. The right apprehension of this truth is of vital importance, both in the life of the believer and the work of the Church. We may imagine that our trust in the cross and its ever-blessed atonement is clear and full, or we may strive earnestly for its holy imitation and partnership, and yet, unless we yield to the Holy Spirit to teach and strengthen us, and communicate the 'hidden wisdom of God in a mystery' to us, our faith and our practice may stand very largely in the power of men. Or, on the other hand, we may be striving in every possible way for the power of the Spirit in life and work, and wondering why our prayers are so little heard, and the reason may be simply that, with the church around us, we have not understood how the cross, with its testimony against the world that rejected Christ, with its revelation of God's curse on sin, and its confession of the power of sin over all that is nature, with its crucifixion of all that is of self and the flesh and the world – how this is what the Spirit seeks to work, and what we must yield ourselves to, if he is to reign in us. The life of the cross and the life of the Spirit must always grow in equal proportion; they are vitally and inseparably one.

1. The cross leads to the Spirit. See it in our blessed Lord himself
The cross, with its victory over sin, was Christ's path to the Spirit. See how this is the one thought that comes out in Peter's address: it is Jesus, the crucified one, who has been exalted and has received from the Father the Spirit. It is from the crucified one in glory that the Spirit comes. The cross was to him the path and the power through which alone he could receive the Spirit to pour out.

And how then? We can look at it in different aspects. We can speak of the cross as the ransom, the price he paid for our redemption, and his receiving the Spirit from the Father to give us, as what he had purchased and earned. When the curse had been borne, the barrier that prevented God's dwelling in man was removed, and our Mediator could claim the Spirit for us. Or we can regard the

172

cross as the death in which he himself and his obedience were perfected, and he as man was fitted to receive the fullness of the divine Spirit and glory to communicate to us. He became obedient unto death, the death of the cross, therefore God hath highly exalted him. Or we can think of the cross and its death as the only path which he, as our head and forerunner, could open up for us to die out of the old life of nature, and enter into the new life to God. The completeness of his entrance into our death, even unto the very uttermost, was his perfect entrance into a fullness of the Spirit that could overflow unto all his people.

These different aspects have each their unspeakable value. The first, the legal one, points us to that substitution and atonement which is the foundation of the sinner's peace and hope. The second, the personal one, shows us what it was in Christ that gave his suffering such value, and made him our leader and example. The third speaks of the vital connection, in virtue of which the cross shows the very path, the only disposition, through which we can become fully fitted for the Spirit's indwelling.

We need to combine all these, looking now at one and then at another, if we are fully to realize the deep and most needful truth: The cross, the cross alone, the cross borne, and experienced, in its power to slay, is the only path to the throne or the Spirit of God.

2. The cross leads to the Spirit. Look at it in the disciples

It was their fellowship with Christ in the crucifixion that fitted them for the baptism of the Spirit. What was it that separated these hundred and twenty men and women from all the world, and made them the worthy recipients of the pentecostal gift? They had followed Christ, even to the cross; when all had rejected him their heart clung to him. When he had died and their hopes appeared extinguished, they still clung to him, the crucified one. The meaning of the cross they did not yet understand, but he who died upon it was their only life or hope – as far as love could do it they were one with him in his shame and rejection, and he made them one with him in his death and its infinite blessing. All their training for the baptism of the Spirit had led to the cross and been completed there. The cross leads to the fullness of the Spirit.

Let all believers who long and pray to be filled with the Spirit take this to heart. We must be lovers of the cross. We must first trust it, and then share and bear it. What the cross did for Christ, as it gave him through death release from the life of humiliation that now he might 'live unto God', the cross must do for us too. As we yield to the Holy Spirit, as far as we know him, and live the life he gives, of men who have been 'crucified with Christ'; 'who have crucified the flesh'; 'who are crucified to the world', the Spirit in his fullness will come and possess us. The death to self and its will, to the flesh, to the world, which the cross gives is the only path to the Spirit. The more complete the deliverance we get from the old life at the cross, the more entire the death to all that is nature, the more whole-hearted the desire for conformity to Christ's death, the surer and the richer the fullness of the Spirit.

3. The cross leads to the Spirit. This is the path too for the unconverted sinner

It is the cross that works both that conviction of sin and that faith in God's mercy that receives the promise of the Spirit. Read our text over again. See how Peter's preaching all gathers round the two thoughts – how God honoured Christ and how man rejected him. Jesus, whom they had crucified and slain, God had raised from the dead and placed on the throne, and given the Holy Spirit to pour out. In the crucified one they saw their sin and guilt, they saw God's mercy and power to save. It was the cross, with its revelation of man's sin and God's love, that brought them to share with the disciples in the outpouring of the Spirit.

The last words of Peter's address give us the very essence of gospel preaching. 'Know that God hath made that same Jesus, whom ye have crucified, both Lord and Christ.' In the history of the Congo Mission there is a touching narrative of a missionary wondering and mourning over the lack of blessing after five years' preaching. After much thought and prayer he was led to adopt the tone of that verse – to charge the heathen boldly with their rejection of God's Son. The word came with power. When Stanley passed again, some time later, he saw and testified to the extraordinary change. It is the preaching of the cross in this double aspect, as the revelation of man's wickedness, of the very spirit of the world and all who are in it, in rejecting Christ, however ignorantly, as well as of the mercy of God offering pardon and the Holy Spirit, that God will bless.

4. The cross leads to the Spirit. This is the great lesson the preacher needs to learn

See this in the preaching of the Church at Pentecost. Through the man who glories in the cross the Spirit will work. Listen to Peter, not only on the day of Pentecost, but in Solomon's Porch (Acts 3:14–26), or before the Council (4:10; 5:30), or in the house of Cornelius (10:39); it is ever the crucified Lord he preaches, and God owns. And so at all times of revival, when the Spirit of God is poured out, it is in connection with the preaching of the cross in its two-fold aspect – as revealing man's sin and God's mercy.

But that is not all the preacher has to learn. Let him mark well – the blessing of the preaching does not depend only on the matter, but the man. If Peter had not been baptized with the Spirit of the crucified one, he could not have preached him aright in the power of the Spirit. And if Peter had not followed Christ to the cross, and had not, in the midst of failure, held fast to him, even through shame and death, he had not received that Spirit of power. It was what the crucified Lord had done for him in leading him to the cross, that fitted him for what he did from the throne. To be a witness for a crucified Christ needs two things: it needs the very spirit and disposition of the crucified Lord on earth, and then the Spirit of the glorified Lord from heaven. The cross is the dark and dead-looking bud, the Spirit the bright and fragrant flower. The cross is the sour, unripe fruit, the Spirit the ripe grape yielding its living sap, the wine of the kingdom. As in Christ, so with the believer and the penitent sinner, but above all, in the preacher it must ever be, the cross leads to the Spirit.

The Holy Spirit is as much the gift of the Father to his Church as the Son. 'When the fullness of the time was come, God sent forth his Son . . . that we might receive the adoption of sons. And because ye are sons, God hath sent forth the Spirit of his Son into your hearts.' What can it be that both in the personal experience of godly believers, in the life of the church at large, in the work of the Church in the world, the joy and power of the Holy Spirit is so little known? May it not be, is it not possible, that the true cross, not only the cross that is trusted in, but the cross that is borne and experienced in crucifixion power, the cross that is witnessed to by a spirit and life that the world can see, is not known and accepted? It was the real cross, with its suffering and shame, that led Christ to the throne and the fullness of the Spirit. In no other path can we reach what he reached. The cross means for him, and for us, a cross to be borne, a death, in which he and we are crucified together. Let all who pray for revival and the outpouring of the Spirit pray for a revival of the religion of the cross, with all it meant to our Lord; the revival of the Spirit's mighty working will follow soon. It is God's unalterable law in delivering us from sin and the world: the cross leads to the Spirit.

[From *The Cross of Christ*]

A Spirit of Holiness

What Sanctification Is

To understand what the sanctification of the redeemed is, we must first learn what the holiness of God is. He alone is the *Holy One*. Holiness in the creature must be received from him.

God's holiness is often spoken of as though it consisted in his hatred of, and hostility to, sin; but this gives no explanation of what holiness actually is. It is a merely negative statement – that God's holiness cannot bear sin.

Holiness is that attribute of God because of which he always *is*, and *wills*, and *does* what is supremely good; because of which also he desires what is supremely good in his creatures, and bestows it upon them.

God is called 'The Holy One' in Scripture, not only because he punishes sin, but also because he is the *Redeemer* of his people. It is his holiness, which ever wills what is good for all, that moved him to redeem sinners. Both the *wrath* of God which punishes sin, and the *love* of God which redeems the sinner, spring from the same source – his holiness. Holiness is the perfection of God's name.

Holiness in man is a disposition in entire agreement with that of God; which chooses in all things to will as God wills; as it is written: 'As he is holy, so be ye holy' (1 Peter 1:15). Holiness in us is nothing else than oneness with God. The sanctification of God's people is effected by *the communication to them of the holiness of God*. There is no other way of obtaining sanctification, save by the Holy God bestowing what he alone possesses. He alone is the Holy One. He is the Lord who sanctifies.

By the different meanings which Scripture attaches to the words 'sanctification' and 'to sanctify', a certain relationship with God, into which we are brought, is pointed out.

The first and simplest meaning of the word *sanctification* is 'separation'. That which is taken out of its surroundings, by God's command, and is set aside or separated as his own possession and for his service – that is holy. This does not mean separation from sin only, but from all that is in the world, even from what may be permissible. Thus God sanctified the seventh day. The other days were not unclean, for God saw all that he had made and 'beheld it was very good'. But that day alone was holy, which God had taken possession of by his own special act. In the same way God had separated Israel from other nations, and in Israel had separated the priests, to be holy unto him. This separation unto sanctification is always God's own work, and so the electing grace of God is often closely connected with sanctification. 'Ye shall be holy unto me . . . I have separated you . . . that ye should be mine' (Leviticus 20:26). 'The man who the Lord shall choose shall be holy' (Numbers 16:7). 'Thou art an holy people unto the Lord, the Lord thy God hath chosen thee' (Deuteronomy 7:6). God cannot take part with other lords. He must be the sole possessor, and ruler, of those to whom he reveals and imparts his holiness.

But this separation is not all that is included in the word *sanctification*. It is only the indispensable condition of what must follow. When separated, man stands before God in no respect differing from an object without life that has been sanctified to the service of God. If the separation is to be of value, something more must take place. Man must surrender himself willingly, and heartily, to this separation. Sanctification includes *personal consecration* to the Lord to be his.

Sanctification can become ours only when it sends down its roots into, and takes up its abode, in the depths of our personal life; in our will, and in our love. God sanctifies no man against his will, therefore the personal, hearty surrender to God is an indispensable part of sanctification.

It is for this reason that the Scriptures not only speak of *God* sanctifying us, but they say often that *we* must sanctify ourselves.

But even by consecration, true sanctification is not yet complete. *Separation* and *consecration* are together only the preparation for the glorious work that *God will do*, as he imparts his own holiness to the soul. *Partaking of the divine nature* is the blessing which is promised to believers in sanctification. 'That we might be partakers of his holiness' (Hebrews 12:10) – that is the glorious aim of God's work in those whom he separates for himself. But this impartation of his holiness is not a *gift of something that is apart from God himself*; no, it is in personal fellowship with him, and partaking of his divine life, that sanctification can be obtained.

As the Holy One, God dwelt among the people of Israel to sanctify his people (Exodus 29:45–46). As the Holy One, he dwells in us. It is the presence of God alone that can sanctify. But so surely is this our portion, that Scripture does not shrink from speaking of God dwelling in our hearts in such power that we may be 'filled unto all the fullness of God'. True sanctification is fellowship with God and his dwelling in us. So it was necessary that the Holy Spirit should come to dwell in us. This is what sanctification means.

[From *The Power of the Blood of Jesus*]

Entire Sanctification

And the God of peace himself sanctify you wholly;
and may your spirit and soul and body be preserved
entire, without blame at the coming of our Lord Jesus
Christ. Faithful is he that calleth you, who will also
do it. (1 THESSALONIANS 5:23–24)

What a promise! One would expect to see all God's children clinging to it, claiming its fulfilment. Alas, unbelief does not know what to think of it, and but few count it their treasure and joy.

Just listen. God, the God of peace that passeth all understanding, keeping our hearts and thoughts in Christ Jesus – none other but himself can and will do it. This God of peace himself promises to sanctify us wholly, in Christ our sanctification, in the sanctification of the Spirit. It is God who is doing the work. It is in close, personal fellowship with God himself that we become holy.

Ought not each of us to rejoice with exceeding joy at the prospect? But it is as if the promise is too great, and so it is repeated and amplified. May your spirit – the inmost part of our being, created for fellowship with God – and your soul, the seat of the life and all its powers – and body, through which sin entered, in which sin proved its power even unto death, but which has been redeemed in Christ – be preserved.

To prevent the possibility of any misconception, as if it is too great to be literally true, the words are added: 'Faithful is he that calleth you, who will also do it.' Yes, he hath said: 'I the Lord have spoken it; and I in Christ and through the Holy Spirit, will do it.' All that he asks is that we shall come and abide in close fellowship with himself every day.

Child of God, beware of unbelief. It dishonours God; it robs your soul of its heritage. 'All things are possible to him that believeth.' I believe, Lord; help my unbelief.

[From *The Secret of the Faith Life*]

Holiness and Happiness

Let us seek to learn two lessons: Holiness is essential to true happiness; happiness is essential to true holiness. If you would have joy, the fullness of joy, an abiding joy which nothing can take away, be holy as God is holy. Holiness is blessedness. Nothing can darken or interrupt our joy but sin. Whatever be our trial or temptation, the joy of Jesus of which Peter says, 'in whom ye now rejoice with joy unspeakable,' can more than compensate and outweigh. If we lose our joy, it must be sin. It may be an actual transgression, or an unconscious following of self or the world; it may be the stain on conscience of something doubtful, or it may be unbelief that would live by sight, and thinks more of itself and its joy than of the Lord alone: whatever it be, nothing can take away our joy but sin. If we would live lives of joy, assuring God and man and ourselves that our Lord is everything, is more than all to us, oh, let us be holy! Let us glory in him who is our holiness: in his presence is fullness of joy. Let us live in the Kingdom which is joy in the Holy Ghost; the Spirit of holiness is the Spirit of joy, because he is the Spirit of God. It is the saints, God's holy ones, who will shout for joy.

And happiness is essential to true holiness. If you would be a holy Christian, you must be a happy Christian. Jesus was anointed by God with 'the oil of gladness', that he might give us 'the oil of joy'. In all our efforts after holiness the wheels will move heavily if there be not the oil of joy; this alone removes all stain and friction, and makes the onward progress easy and delightful. Study to understand the divine worth of joy. It is the evidence of your being in the Father's presence, and dwelling in his love. It is the proof of your being consciously free from the law and the strain of the spirit of bondage. It is the token of your freedom from care and responsibility, because you are rejoicing in Christ Jesus as your Sanctification, your Keeper, and your Strength. It is the secret of spiritual health and strength, filling all your service with the child-like, happy assurance that the Father asks nothing that he does not give strength for, and that he accepts all that is done, however feebly, in this spirit. True happiness is always self-forgetful: it loses itself in the object of its joy. As the joy of the Holy Ghost fills us, and we rejoice in God the Holy One, through our Lord Jesus Christ, we lose ourselves in the adoration and worship of the Thrice Holy, we become holy. This is, even here in the wilderness, 'the Highway of Holiness: the ransomed of the Lord shall come with singing; the redeemed shall walk there; everlasting joy shall be upon their heads; they shall obtain joy and gladness.'

Do all God's children understand this, that holiness is just another name, the true name, that God gives for happiness; that it is, indeed, unutterable blessedness to know that God does make us holy, that our holiness is in Christ, that Christ's Holy Spirit is within us? There is nothing so attractive as joy: have believers understood that this is the joy of the Lord – to be holy? Or is not the idea of strain, and sacrifice, and sighing, of difficulty and distance so prominent that the thought of being holy has hardly ever made the heart glad? If it has been so, let it be so no longer. 'Thou shalt glory in the Holy One of Israel.' Let us claim this promise. Let the believing assurance that our loving Father, and our beloved Lord Jesus, and the Holy Spirit, who in dovelike gentleness rests within us, have engaged to do the work and are doing it, fill us with gladness. Let us not seek our joy in what we see in ourselves of holiness: let us rejoice in the Holiness of God in Christ as ours; let us rejoice in the Holy One of Israel. So shall our joy be unspeakable and unceasing; so shall we give him the glory.

BE YE HOLY, AS I AM HOLY

[From *Holy in Christ*]

Your Sanctification

For this is the will of God, even your sanctification.
(1 THESSALONIANS 4:3)

What is holiness? God alone is the holy one. There is none holy but the Lord. There is no holiness but his. And nothing can be holy except as he makes it holy. 'Be ye holy for I am holy. I am the Lord which sanctify you.' Holiness is the very nature of God, inseparable from his being, and can only be communicated by his communicating himself and his own life. We are in Christ, who is made of God unto us sanctification. The Spirit of God is the Spirit of holiness. We are God's elect in sanctification of the Spirit, 'chosen to salvation through sanctification of the Spirit.' The three-in-one God is the thrice holy one, and Father, Son and Spirit each share to make us holy. The first step in sanctification is our recognizing how God makes us holy. We have been sanctified in Christ Jesus. The new nature we have derived from him has been created in true holiness. Our part is in the power of the new, divine, holy nature, to act out its impulses and principles. Our justification and our sanctification are equally in Christ, by union with him, and therefore equally of faith. It is as we believe in God through Christ and the Spirit, working in us, that the inflow of the holy life from above is renewed, and that we have the courage and the power to live out the precepts that reveal the way in which that life is to act. Like the whole of salvation, sanctification, or the life of holiness, is the result of man's co-operating with God. That means first of all his entire dependence on and surrender to the divine operation, as the only source of goodness or strength. And then the acting out in life and conduct all that God has worked within us.

And what is now the help we can get from the words, 'This is the will of God, your sanctification'? The first thought is that of the divine obligation of holiness. God wills it. It is not enough to regard it in the other aspects in which it can be presented. It is indeed an essential element of the Christian life, the great proof of our gratitude for our deliverance from the guilt of sin, indispensable to true peace and happiness, our only preparation for heaven. All this is of great importance. But behind all this there is something of still greater force. We need to realize that God wills it. In eternity God predestinated us to be holy; we are 'elect according to the foreknowledge of God in sanctification of the Spirit' (Ephesians 1:4; 1 Peter 1:2). God's whole purpose, as a holy God, was to make us holy as he is holy. The whole of redemption was ordered with a view to this. It is not only one of his commands, among many; it is the command which includes all. The whole being and character of God proclaim it; the whole nature and aim of redemption call for it. Believers, God wills your sanctification. Worship God in his holiness, until every thought of God in his glory and grace is connected with the deep conviction: This blessed God wills my holiness. Rest not until your will has surrendered unconditionally to the will of God, and found its true destiny in receiving that divine will and working it out.

A second thought that suggests itself is that of the divine possibility of holiness. We have learnt in our meditations that the will of God is not only a divine purpose of what is to do, or a divine precept as to what we are to do, but a divine energy that works out its own purpose. All that God wills he works. Not indeed in those who refuse to accept or submit to that will. They have the power to resist it. But in those who yield their consent, who love that will and long that it should be done on earth as in heaven, God himself worketh out all things after the purpose of his will. In every man with a sound strong will, it seeks at once to embody itself in action, and to effect what has been regarded an object of desire. God works in us both to will and to do. When he has worked the will, he delights, if he be waited on and yielded to, to work the doing. When, by his grace, the believer wills as God wills, when he has accepted God's will for sanctification as his own will, he can count upon God's working it. God wills it with all the energy of his divine being. God can as little cease working holiness as he can cease being holy or being God. He wills our sanctification. And if we will but will it too, in the faith of the new nature in which the Holy Spirit works, and yield ourselves to the will of omnipotent love, in the assurance of his working in us, we shall experience how true and blessed the message is: God wills and therefore most certainly works your sanctification.

The third lesson suggested by our text is – the divine means of holiness. The will of God is your sanctification – that is, all that God wills has this one object. Whether it be his will in the eternal counsel, or here in time in providence, whether in mercy or in judgement, whether in precept or promise, all that God wills concerning us is our sanctification. This gives a new meaning, and is our true glory, to every command of Scripture. The commands of God have unspeakable value as marking out for us that path of safety and of life, as guiding us to all that is lovely and of good report. But here is their highest glory: through them the holy one seeks to make us partakers of his own holiness. Do let us learn to regard every indication of God's will, in Scripture or in nature, in things great or little, as the will of the holy one, coming to make us holy. Let every thought of God's will fill us with the longing and the hope to be holy. And let every thought of holiness lead us to the study of, and the delight in, and the faithful doing of God's will. Let every sin that God's Word forbids, such as those Paul mentions, uncleanness and fraud, be put far from us. Let everything that is of the earthly, carnal, selfish nature be put off, that the whole spirit, soul and body may be sanctified: let every command that points to the true Christlike life, humility and love and self-sacrifice, be welcomed as the channel of God's holiness. The desire after and delight and faith in God's holiness and God's will will become inseparably one.

Let all who would experience this remember one thing. It is because it is God's will and God's holiness that there is power and life and blessing in it. Everything depends upon our knowing God and waiting on him, coming under the operation of his holy presence and power. As we know him as the living God, and have

185

communion with him as the holy, living, almighty, ever-present and ever-working One, his will and his holiness will become to us heavenly realities, and we shall know how certainly, how blessedly, his will is actually our sanctification.

[From *Thy Will Be Done*]

Hearing and Doing

Be ye doers of the word, and not hearers only,
deluding your own selves. But . . . being not a hearer
that forgetteth, but a doer that worketh, this man
shall be blessed in his doing. (JAMES 1:22–25)

What a terrible delusion to be content with – to delight in hearing the Word, and yet not doing. And how terribly common, the sight of multitudes of Christians listening to the Word of God most regularly and earnestly, and yet not doing it. If their own servant were to do so, hearing but not doing, how summary the judgement would be. And yet, so complete is the delusion, they never know that they are not living good Christian lives. What can it be that thus deludes us?

There is more than one thing. One is that people mistake the pleasure they have in hearing, for religion and worship. The mind delights in having the truth put clearly before it; the imagination is gratified by its illustration; the feelings are stirred by its application. To an active mind knowledge gives pleasure. A man may study some branch of science – say electricity – without the least intention of applying it practically, for the enjoyment the knowledge gives him. And so people go to church, and enjoy the preaching, and yet do not do what God asks. The unconverted and the converted man alike remain content to go in doing and confessing and still doing the things which they ought not to do . . .

186

It may help us if we take some portion of God's Word and see how we are to deal with it.

Suppose it be the Sermon on the Mount. I begin with the first Beatitude: 'Blessed are the poor in spirit.' I ask – What does this mean? Am I obeying this injunction? Am I at least thoroughly earnest in seeking day by day to maintain this disposition? As I feel how far my proud, self-confident nature is from it, am I willing to wait, and plead with Christ, and believe that he can work it in me? Am I going to do this – to be poor in spirit? Or shall I again be a hearer and not a doer?

And so I may go through the Beatitudes, and through the whole Sermon, with its teaching on meekness and mercy, on love and righteousness, and on doing everything as unto the Father, and in everything trusting him, on doing his will and Christ's words, and verse by verse ask – Do I know what this means? Am I living it out? Am I doing it? Am I what he speaks? And as ever again, the answer comes – I fear not, nay, I see no possibility of living thus, and doing what he says, I shall be led to feel the need of an entire revision of both my creed and conduct. And I shall ask whether the vow, Whatever he says I am going to do, has ever taken the place either in my Bible reading or my life that he demands that it shall have.

Ere I know, such questionings may begin to work in me a poverty of spirit I never knew, and lead me to an entirely new insight into my need of a Christ who will breathe in me his own life, and work in me all he speaks. I will get courage in faith to say: I can do all things in him who strengtheneth me: Whatsoever he saith in his Word, I will do.

[From *Prayer's Inner Chamber*]

Holiness – The Chief Aim of Bible Study

Sanctify them in thy truth: thy word is truth.
(JOHN 17:17)

In his great intercessory prayer our Lord spoke of the words which the Father had given him, of his own giving of them to his disciples, and of their having received and believed them. It was this that had made them disciples. It was their keeping these words that would really enable them to live the life and do the work of true disciples. Receiving the words of God from Christ and keeping them is the mark and power of true discipleship.

In praying the Father to keep them in the world when he had left it, our Lord asks that he would sanctify them in the truth, as it dwells and works in his word. Christ has said of himself, 'I am the truth.' He was the only begotten of the Father, full of grace and truth. His teaching was not like that of the law which came by Moses, giving a knowledge, a promise of good things to come which was but an image or a shadow: the words I speak unto you are spirit and life, giving the very substance and power and divine possession of which they speak. Christ had spoken of the Spirit as the Spirit of truth who would lead into all the truth that there was in himself, not as a matter of knowledge or doctrine, but into its actual experience and enjoyment. And then he prays that in this living truth as it is revealed in him by the Spirit and dwells in the Word, the Father would sanctify them. 'For their sakes', he says, 'I sanctify myself that they themselves may also be sanctified in truth.' And he asks the Father in his power and love to take charge of them, that his object – to sanctify them in the truth through his Word which is truth – may be realized, that they, like himself, may be sanctified in truth. Let us study the wonderful lesson here given us in regard to God's Word.

Sanctify them in thy truth, thy Word is truth. The great object of God's Word is to make us holy. No diligence or success in Bible study will really profit us unless it makes us humbler, holier men. In all our use of holy Scripture it must be definitely our main object. The reason there is often so much Bible reading with so little real result in a Christ-like character, is that 'salvation through sanctification of the Spirit and belief of the truth' is not truly sought. People imagine that if they study the Word and accept its truths this will in some way, of itself, benefit them. But experience tells them that it does not. The fruit of holy character, of consecrated life, of power to bless others does not come, for the simple and most natural reason that we only get what we seek. Christ gave us God's Word to make us holy, it is only when we make this our definite aim in all Bible study that the truth, not the doctrinal truth, but its divine quickening power, imparting the very life of God, that it contains as a seed, can open and impart itself to us.

Sanctify them in thy truth, thy Word is truth. It is God himself who alone can make us holy by his Word. The Word, separate from God and his direct operation cannot prevail. The Word is an instrument: God himself must use it. God is the only holy one. He alone can make holy. The unspeakable value of God's Word is that it is God's means of holiness. The terrible mistake of many is that they forget that God alone can use it or make it effectual. It is not enough that I have access to the dispensary of a physician. I need him to prescribe. Without him my use of his medicines might be fatal. It was so with the scribes. They made their boasts of God's law: they delighted in their study of Scripture and yet remained unsanctified. The Word did not sanctify them because they did not seek for this in the Word, and did not yield to God to do it for them.

Sanctify them in thy truth, thy Word is truth. This holiness through the Word must be sought and waited for from God in prayer. Our Lord not only taught his disciples that they must be holy; he not only sanctified himself for them that they might be sanctified in truth, but he brought his Words and his works to the Father with the prayer that he would sanctify them. It is most needful to set our heart upon being holy, as our first and chief object in studying the Word. But all this is not enough; everything depends upon our following Christ in asking the Father to sanctify us through the Word. It is God, the holy Father, makes us holy, by the Spirit of holiness who dwells in us. He works in us the very mind and disposition of Christ who is our sanctification. And the Father cannot do this except as we tarry before him, and are still, and in deep dependence and full surrender give ourselves up to him. It is in the prayer offered in the name and the fellowship and the faith of the great intercessor – 'Sanctify me through thy truth, thy Word is truth,' that the Father's sanctifying power will be found and our knowledge of God's word truly makes us holy.

How sacred the morning watch! The hour specially devoted to the soul's yielding itself up to God's holiness to be sanctified through the Word. Let us remember, the one aim of God's Word is to make us holy. Let it be our continued prayer, 'Father, sanctify me in thy truth.'

[From *Prayer's Inner Chamber*]

Persevere in Your Surrender

You have heard of Keswick, and the truth for which it stands. It is that *Christ is prepared to take upon himself the care and preservation of our lives every day, and all the day long, if we trust him to do it*. In the testimony given by many, this thought is emphasized. They have told us that they felt themselves called to a new surrender, to an entire consecration of life to Christ, reaching to the smallest things, but they were hindered by the fear of failure. The thirst after holiness, after an unbroken fellowship with Jesus, after a life of persevering childlike obedience, drew them one way. But the question arose: 'Shall I continue faithful?' And to this question there came no answer, till they believed that the surrender must be made, not in their own strength, but *in a power which was bestowed by a glorified Lord*. He would not only keep them for the future, but he must first make possible for them the surrender of faith which expects that future grace. It was in the power of Christ himself that they were able to present themselves to him.

O Christian, only believe that there is a victorious life! Christ, the victor, is your Lord, who will undertake for you in everything and will enable you to do all that the Father expects from you. Be of good courage. Will you not trust him to do this great work for you who has given his life for you and has forgiven your sins? Only dare, in his power, to surrender yourself to the life of those who are kept from sin by the power of God. Along with the deepest conviction that there is no good in you, confess that you see in the Lord Jesus all the goodness of which you have need, for the life of a child of God; and begin literally to live 'by the faith of the Son of God, who loved me, and gave himself for me' (Galatians 2:20).

Let me, for your encouragement, give the testimony of Bishop Moule, a man of deep humility and tender piety. When he first heard of Keswick he was afraid of 'perfectionism' and would have nothing to do with it. Unexpectedly, during a vacation in Scotland, he came in contact with some friends at a small convention. There he heard an address by which he was convinced how entirely the teaching was according to Scripture. There was no word about sinlessness in the flesh or in man. It was a setting forth of how Jesus can keep from sin a man with a sinful nature. The light shone into his heart. He who had always been counted a tender Christian came into touch now with a new experience of what Christ is willing to do for one who gives himself entirely to him.

Listen to what he says on the text: 'I can do all things through Christ which strengtheneth me' (Philippians 4:13). I dare to say that it is possible for those who really are willing to reckon on the power of the Lord, for keeping and victory, to lead a life in which his promises are taken as they stand, and are found to be true. It is possible to cast all our care on him daily, and to enjoy deep peace in doing it. It is possible to have the thoughts and imaginations of our hearts purified in the deepest meaning of the word, through faith. It is possible to see the will of God in everything, and to receive it, not with sighin, but with singing. It is possible, in the inner life of desire and feeling, to lay aside all bitterness and wrath and anger, and evil-speaking, every day and every hour. It is possible, by taking complete refuge in divine power, to become strong through and through; and where previously our greatest weakness lay, to find that the things which formerly upset all our resolves to be patient, or pure, or humble, furnish today an opportunity – through him who loved us, and works in us an agreement with his will, and a blessed sense of his presence and his power – to make sin powerless. These things are divine possibilities, and because they are his work, the true experience of them will always cause us to bow lower at his feet and to learn to thirst and long for more. We cannot possibly be satisfied with anything less than – each day, each hour, each moment, in Christ, through the power of the Holy Spirit – to walk with God.

[From *The Prayer Life*]

Following the Apostle Paul

Paul, Man of Prayer

Behold, he prayeth. (ACTS 9:11)

When our Lord said of Saul to Ananias, 'Behold, he prayeth,' it was meant in the first place very simply as a proof of the reality of his conversion. But to us it may and does mean a great deal more. In the study of his life, in the attempt to discover the secret of his power and his mighty and unceasing influence, in the effort to penetrate into the real depth of his life and work, we shall find this word our surest guide: 'Behold, he prayeth.'

In speaking of Paul's teaching on prayer, we shall at once notice how often and how earnestly he sought to press home the duty on believers. In Romans, 'Continuing instant in prayer'; in Ephesians, 'Praying always with all prayer and supplication and watching thereunto with all perseverance and supplication'; in Philippians, 'In everything by prayer let your requests be made known unto God'; in Colossians, 'Continue in prayer, and watch in the same with thanksgiving'; in 1 Thessalonians, 'Pray without ceasing'; in 1 Timothy, 'I exhort therefore, that first of all, supplications, prayers, intercessions and giving of thanks, be made for all men. I will therefore that men pray everywhere, lifting up holy hands.' He sought to rouse and train the churches to a constant watchful prayerfulness, as absolutely essential to a life in fellowship with God, and in the service of Christ.

What he himself prayed

The study of the different prayers in which he poured out his heart before God in writing to different churches will teach us a lesson of the deepest importance. Our prayers are too often vague, with much repetition of certain well-known expressions. How different it was with Paul. In his prayers we find the deepest needs of the Christian life and the very highest experiences of what the power and the love of God can do. As his theology had its roots in the divine revelation to himself of the fullness that there is in Christ, his heart asked nothing less than that that fullness should become theirs. What a difference it would make in the life of many a minister or missionary if he made Paul's prayers the model of his own intercession. As he took up his high thoughts he would feed the need of first asking for the full experience for himself, and then for his people, and then for grace to preach and live and seek to bring them to nothing less than what he had prayed for. We shall learn from Paul what to pray.

How to pray

The first thought that comes to anyone familiar with Scripture is that of whole-hearted intensity and persistency. He put all his strength into prayer. He speaks of striving, or travail, of a conflict, of an agony. He speaks often of praying without ceasing, of praying day and night. He had learnt the secret of being in Christ so near to God that amid the most difficult circumstances his heart at all times could maintain direct fellowship with God in intercession. The study of how he prayed will give us a glimpse of what our hearts long for – a walk with God in unbroken fellowship and never-ceasing prayer. It was out of his experience that he dared write, 'In nothing be anxious; but in everything let your requests be made known unto God.'

How he asked others to pray for him

Here we shall find one of the most instructive and suggestive lessons. It was not only that the loving remembrance of him in prayer would be a comfort, but he believed in the power of prayer as the actual securing of divine power for his work. How often we pray for ministers or missionaries that God would bless them, without any idea of what they actually are needing of special fitness for being made a blessing. When Paul asked for prayer it was for boldness that he might speak as he ought to speak. They were to feel how entirely dependent upon God he was for the needed grace to do his work aright. He felt that his prayers were not enough, he was one body with the church, and as dependent upon them as they were upon him. How rich the blessing would be if ministers and people thus united with each other in waiting upon God for the power of his Spirit to be given in answer to prayer.

[From *The Inner Chamber and the Inner Life*]

A Monument of Grace

*And the grace of our Lord was exceeding abundant
with faith and love which is in Christ Jesus.*
(1 TIMOTHY 1:14)

In the word 'grace' there are two shades of meaning which need to be carefully distinguished, and then combined. Sometimes Scripture speaks of grace as that gracious disposition which shows itself in favour of the unworthy. In this sense we speak of it specially in connection with the justifying of the ungodly, and praise it as free, sovereign, and unconditional, the only cause of our salvation. At other times the chief thought is that gracious operation of the divine power which works in us effectually, enabling us to do all that God would have us to be in life and service. In this sense we speak of the exceeding abounding, ever active and increasing grace of God, enabling us to abound in every good work, and fitting each one according to his measure for his place in God's kingdom here upon earth. If we would fully understand the mind of the Spirit, we must aim at uniting the two thoughts, and always trust God for the grace that not only pardons and accepts, but works in us each moment with its divine energy to will and to do what is well-pleasing to him.

In both senses Paul was a monument of grace. It was the exceeding abundance of God's grace that chose and saved him as a blasphemer and prosecutor, the chief of sinners, and made him the chief of the Apostles. And it was the exceeding abundance of that grace too that sanctified him, delivered him from the power of sin, and fitted him to live holy and blameless and unreproveable, and strengthened him with divine strength for all the work to which God had called him. 'The grace of our Lord was exceeding abundant with faith and love which is in Christ Jesus.'

In writing to the Corinthians (1 Corinthians 15:9, 10) we see how Paul combines the two aspects, as he first speaks of his utter unworthiness to be an Apostle and then praises the grace that was not in vain, but enabled him to labour more abundantly than they all. 'By the grace of God I am what I am: and his grace which was bestowed upon me was not in vain; but I laboured more abundantly than they all: yet not I, but the grace of God which was with me.' Paul's whole heart was so under the impression that it was all free and sovereign grace that chose and fitted him to be an Apostle, and that enabled him day by day so to labour that he did more than others, that he does not hesitate to speak boldly of what he had done because he felt that there could not be the shadow of a thought of glorying in himself. It was all so markedly the grace of God alone – his alone was the glory. The knowledge of the grace of God is no light matter. Paul tells us what the school was in which he learned. It was during the years of his stay at Tarsus, where he had been favoured with unspeakable visions and revelations of heavenly things, that his Lord saw the danger of him being over-exalted. He sent a thorn in the flesh, an angel of Satan to buffet him. Paul prayed repeatedly for deliverance. He could not understand why the answer was not given, until Jesus appeared to him and said, 'My grace is sufficient for thee: for my strength is made perfect in weakness.' At once he understood it all. He saw that grace takes charge of everything and wards off a danger he had not thought of. That grace comes specially to keep us humble, that God may have all the glory. That grace is strength for whatever work we have to do. That that strength is bestowed in the midst of weakness, that we may learn to be strong in faith and give glory to God. And therefore this was the last lesson which he learned to carry with him through all his weakness and necessities. 'Most gladly will I glory in my infirmities, that the power of Christ may rest upon me . . . when I am weak, then am I strong.' In every difficulty and perplexity he found in the exceeding grace of our Lord the full provision for every need.

It was the intense reality of entire dependence upon grace and an ever growing experience of its sufficiency for every step of his path that enabled Paul to speak with such confidence to Christians. Listen to those wonderful words to the Corinthians (2 Corinthians 9:8): 'And God is able to make all grace abound toward you; that ye, always having all sufficiency in all things, may abound to every good work.' Just think what that means. The almighty power of God, able to make all grace abound in each of his children, so that they at all times in all things having all sufficiency of the grace they need, may abound to all good works. Read the words over again. Note that 'all' is five times repeated. Think of God's omnipotence, able to make grace so abounding that we may, just as God abounds towards us, abound before him in all good works. Can anyone receive a statement more full and all-embracing, covering every possible emergency? For all we need, for cleansing from sin and perfecting holiness, for all we need in the midst of trial and suffering, in the middle of daily labour or spiritual work, we may have the utmost confidence that in Christ's grace there is all-sufficient power to fit us for every good work, that his strength will be made perfect in our weakness. God is in very deed able to make all grace every moment of the day to abound in us, that we may indeed abound to every good work.

If we would learn like Paul to believe and rejoice in this riches of grace, let us learn from him what the secret is of such absolute confidence in the sufficiency of grace for every breath of our spiritual life. At the root of all lies the deep sense of utter unworthiness, impotence and nothingness, a willingness to give up every thought of our own wisdom or strength, and so to live a life of absolute and unceasing dependence on grace alone. To this must be added the confident and joyous assurance that Christ will, if we entrust ourselves to him, take and keep charge of the work of grace down to its minutest details. With this we shall go on to that childlike surrender to an unhesitating obedience which will be the sign that the Father and his child understand and trust each other. And so with each new morning; we shall yield ourselves for God to fulfil his great purpose in us, and show forth the exceeding riches of his grace. And if, at any time, doubt or fear arise, we shall just look at the pattern man Christ gave us in Paul, and believe that he was made a monument of the exceeding grace of God to encourage and strengthen every traveller in the way of life, to praise for what he did for him, and will most certainly do for us too. 'By grace ye are saved through faith'; as boundless as the grace is to work out our salvation each moment let our faith be to claim all that it waits to do for us.

[From *The Apostle Paul's Inner Life*]

Paul a Pattern of Prayer

Go . . . and inquire . . . for one called Saul, of Tarsus:
for, behold, he prayeth. (ACTS 9:11)

. . . For this cause I obtained mercy, that in me first
Jesus Christ might shew forth all longsuffering, for a
pattern to them which should hereafter believe on him
to life everlasting. (1 TIMOTHY 1:16)

God took his own Son, and made him our example and our pattern. It sometimes is as if the power of Christ's example is lost in the thought that he, in whom is no sin, is not man as we are. Our Lord took Paul, a man of like passions with ourselves, and made him a pattern of what he could do for one who was the chief of sinners. And Paul, the man who, more than any other, has set his mark on the Church, has ever been appealed to as a pattern man. In his mastery of divine truth, and his teaching of it; in his devotion to his Lord, and his self-consuming zeal in his service; in his deep experience of the power of the indwelling Christ and the fellowship of his cross; in the sincerity of his humility, and the simplicity and boldness of his faith; in his missionary enthusiasm and endurance – in all this, and so much more, 'the grace of our Lord Jesus was exceeding abundant in him.' Christ gave him, and the Church has accepted him, as a pattern of what Christ would have, of what Christ would work. Seven times Paul speaks of believers following him: 'Wherefore I beseech you, be ye followers of me' (1 Corinthians 4:16), 'Be ye followers of me, even as I also am of Christ' (1 Corinthians 11:1; see also Philippians 3:17, 4:9; 1 Thessalonians 1:6; 2 Thessalonians 3:7–9).

If Paul, as a pattern of prayer, is not as much studied or appealed to as he is in other respects, it is not because he is not in this too as remarkable a proof of what grace can do, or because we do not, in this respect, as much stand in need of the help of his example. A study of Paul as a pattern of prayer will bring a rich reward of instruction and encouragement. The words our Lord used of him at his conversion, 'Behold, he prayeth' (Acts 9:11), may be taken as the keynote of his life. The heavenly vision which brought him to his knees ever after ruled his life. Christ at the right hand of God, in whom we are blessed with all spiritual blessings, was everything to him; to pray and expect the heavenly power in his work and on his work, from heaven direct by prayer, was the simple outcome of his faith in the glorified One. In this, too, Christ meant him to be a pattern, that we might learn that, just in the measure in which heavenliness of Christ and his gifts, the unworldliness of the powers that work for salvation, are known and believed, will prayer become the spontaneous rising of the heart to the only source of its life. Let us see what we know of Paul.

Paul's habits of prayer
These are revealed almost unconsciously. He writes, 'God is my witness . . . that without ceasing I make mention of you *always in my prayers* . . . For I long to see you, that I may impart unto you some spiritual gift, to the end ye may be established' (Romans 1:9, 11). 'My *heart's desire and prayer to God* for Israel is, that they may be saved' (Romans 10:1); 'I have great heaviness and *continual sorrow in my heart* . . . for I could wish that myself were accursed from Christ for my brethren' (Romans 9:2–3); 'I thank my God always on your behalf, for the grace of God which is given you by Jesus Christ' (1 Corinthians 1:4); 'Approving ourselves as the ministers of God, *in watchings, in fastings*' (2 Corinthians 6:4–5); 'My little children, of whom *I travail in birth again* until Christ be formed in you' (Galatians 4:19); '. . . *cease not* to give thanks for you, making mention of you *in my prayers*' (Ephesians 1:16); 'I bow my knees to the Father . . . that he would grant you . . . to be strengthened with might by his Spirit in the inner man' (Ephesians 3:14, 16); 'I thank my God *upon every remembrance of you, always in every prayer of mine for you* making request for with joy . . . For God is my record, how greatly I long after you all in the bowels of Jesus

Christ. And this *I pray*' (Philippians 1:3, 4, 8–9); 'We give thanks to God, . . . *praying always for you*. For this cause also, since the day we heard it, we *do not cease to pray for you*, and to desire' (Colossians 1:3, 9); 'I would that ye knew what *great conflict* I have for you . . . and for as many as have not seen my face in the flesh' (Colossians 2:1); 'We give thanks to God *always* for you all, making mention of you *in our prayers*' (1 Thessalonians 1:2); 'We joy for your sakes before God; *night and day praying exceedingly* that we might perfect that which is lacking in your faith' (1 Thessalonians 3:9); 'We are bound to thank God *always* for you . . . Wherefore also *we pray always* for you' (2 Thessalonians 1:3, 11); 'I thank God . . . that *without ceasing* I have remembrance of thee in my prayers night and day' (2 Timothy 1:3); 'I thank my God, making mention of thee *always in my prayers*' (Philemon 4).

These passages taken together give us the picture of a man whose words, 'Pray without ceasing', were simply an expression of his daily life. He had such a sense of the insufficiency of simple conversion; of the need of the grace and power of heaven being brought down for the young converts in prayer; of the need of much and unceasing prayer, day and night, to bring it down; of the certainty that prayer would bring it down – that his life was continual and most definite prayer. He had such a sense that everything must come from above, and such a faith that it would come in answer to prayer, that prayer was neither a duty nor a burden, but the natural turning of the heart to the only place whence it could possibly obtain what it sought for others.

The contents of Paul's prayers
It is as important to know what Paul prayed, as how frequently and earnestly he did so. Intercession is a spiritual work. Our confidence in it will depend much on our knowing that we ask according to the will of God. The more distinctly we ask heavenly things, which we feel at once God alone can bestow, which we are sure he will bestow, the more direct and urgent will our appeal be to God alone. The more impossible the things are that we seek, the more we will turn

from all human work to prayer and to God alone.

In the Epistles, in addition to expressions in which he speaks of his praying, we have a number of distinct prayers in which Paul gives utterance to his heart's desire for those to whom he writes. In these we see that his first desire was always that they might be 'established' in the Christian life. Much as he praised God when he heard of conversion, he knew how feeble the young converts were, and how for their establishing nothing would avail without the grace of the Spirit prayed down. If we notice some of the principal of these prayers we shall see what he asked and obtained.

Take the two prayers in Ephesians – the one for light, the other for strength. In the former (Ephesians 1:15), he prays for the Spirit of wisdom to enlighten them to know what their calling was, what their inheritance, what the mighty power of God working in them. Spiritual enlightenment and knowledge was their great need, to be obtained for them by prayer. In the latter (Ephesians 3:15), he asks that the power they had been led to see in Christ might work in them, and they be strengthened with divine might, so as to have the indwelling Christ, and the love that passeth knowledge, and the fullness of God actually come on them. These were things that could only come direct from heaven; these were things he asked and expected. If we want to learn Paul's art of intercession, we must ask nothing less for believers in our day.

Look at the prayer in Philippians chapter 1 verses 9–11. There, too, it is first for spiritual knowledge; then comes a blameless life, and then a fruitful life to the glory of God. So also in the beautiful prayer in Colossians chapter 1 verses 9–11. First, spiritual knowledge and understanding of God's will, then the strengthening with all might to all patience and joy.

Or take the two prayers in 1 Thessalonians. One says, 'And the Lord make you to increase in love one toward another, to the end, he may stablish your *hearts unblameable in holiness*' (1 Thessalonians 3:12–13); and the other prayer reads, 'God . . . *sanctify you wholly*, and be preserved blameless' (1 Thessalonians 5:23). The very words are so high that we hardly understand, still less believe, still less experience what they mean. Paul so lived in the heavenly world, he was so at home in the holiness and omnipotence of God and his love, that such prayers were the natural expression of what he knew God could and would do. '. . . The Lord . . . stablish your hearts unblameable in holiness' and, 'God sanctify you wholly' – the man who believes in these things and desires them, will pray for them for others. The prayers are all a proof that he seeks for them the very life of heaven upon earth. No wonder that he is not tempted to trust in any human means, but looks for it from heaven alone. Again, I say, the more we take Paul's prayers as our pattern, and make his desires our own for believers for whom we pray, the more will prayer to the God of heaven become as our daily breath.

[From *The Ministry of Intercession*]

The Example of Paul

Be ye followers of me, even as I also am of Christ.
(1 CORINTHIANS 11:1)

1. Paul was a minister who prayed much for his congregation
Let us read his words prayerfully and calmly so that we may hear the voice of the Spirit.

'*Night and day praying exceedingly* that we . . . might perfect that which is lacking in your faith. . . . The Lord make you to increase . . . to the end he may stablish your hearts unblameable in holiness' (1 Thessalonians 3:10–13).

'The very God of peace sanctify you wholly' (1 Thessalonians 5:23).

What food for meditation!

'Now our Lord Jesus Christ himself . . . comfort your hearts, and stablish you in every good word and work' (2 Thessalonians 2:16–17).

'*Without ceasing, I make mention of you always in my prayers*; Making request . . . that I may impart unto you some spiritual gift, to the end ye may be established' (Romans 1:9–11).

'My heart's desire and prayer to God for Israel is, that they might be saved' (Romans 10:1).

'I . . . *cease not . . . making mention of you in my prayers*; that God . . . may give unto you the spirit of wisdom and revelation in the knowledge of him . . . that ye may know . . . what is the exceeding greatness of his power to us-ward who believe' (Ephesians 1:16–19).

'*For this cause I bow my knees unto the Father* . . . that he would grant you . . . to be strengthened with might by his Spirit in the inner man; that Christ may dwell in your hearts by faith; that ye, being rooted . . . in love . . . might be filled with all the fullness of God' (Ephesians 3:14–19).

'*Always in every prayer of mine for you all making request* with joy . . . I pray, that your love may abound yet more and more . . . that ye may be sincere . . . filled with the fruits of righteousness' (Philippians 1:4, 9–11).

'But my God shall supply all your need according to his riches in glory by Christ Jesus' (Philippians 4:19).

'*We . . . do not cease to pray for you*, and to desire that ye might be filled with the knowledge of his will . . . that ye might walk worthy of the Lord . . . strengthened with all might according to his glorious power' (Colossians 1:9–11).

'I would that ye knew *what great conflict I have for you* . . . as many as have not seen my face in the flesh; that their hearts might be comforted, being knit together in love' (Colossians 2:1–2).

What a study for the inner chamber! These passages teach us that unceasing prayer formed a large part of Paul's service in the Gospel; we see the high spiritual aim which he set before himself, in his work on behalf of believers; and the tender and self-sacrificing love with which he ever continued to think of the Church and its needs. Let us ask God to bring each one of us, and all the ministers of his word, to a life of which such prayer is the healthy and natural outflow. We shall need to turn again and again to these pages if we would really be brought by the Spirit to the apostolic life which God has given us as an example.

2. Paul was a minister who asked his congregation to pray much
Read again with prayerful attention:

'I beseech you, brethren, for the Lord Jesus Christ's sake, and for the love of the Spirit, *that ye strive together with me in your prayers to God for me*; that I may be delivered from them that do not believe in Judea' (Romans 15:30–31).

'We . . . trust . . . in God . . . that he will yet deliver us; *Ye also helping together by prayer for us*' (2 Corinthians 1:9–11).

'*Praying always, with all prayer and supplication* in the Spirit, and watching thereunto with all perseverance and supplication for all saints; *and for me*, that utterance may be given unto me, that I may open my mouth boldly to make known the mystery of the gospel . . . as I ought to speak' (Ephesians 6:18–20).

'For I know that this shall turn to my salvation, *through your prayer*, and the supply of the Spirit of Jesus Christ' (Philippians 1:19).

'*Continue in prayer*, and watch in the same with thanksgiving; *withal praying also for us*, that God would open unto us a door of utterance, to speak . . . as I ought to speak' (Colossians 4:2–4).

'Finally, brethren, *pray for us*, that the word of the Lord may have free course, and be glorified, even as it is with you' (2 Thessalonians 3:1).

What a deep insight Paul had as to the unity of the body of Christ and the relation of the members one to another! It is as we permit the Holy Spirit to work powerfully in us that he will reveal this truth to us, and we too shall have this insight. What a glimpse he gives us of the power of the spiritual life among these Christians, by the way in which he reckoned that at Rome, and Corinth, and Ephesus, and Colossae, and Philippi, there were men and women on whom he could rely for prayer that would reach heaven and have power with God! And what a lesson for all ministers, to lead them to inquire if they truly appreciate the unity of the body at its right value; if they are endeavouring to train up Christians as intercessors; and if they indeed understand that Paul had that confidence because he was himself so strong in prayer for the congregation! Let us learn the lesson and beseech God that ministers and congregations together may grow in the grace of prayer, so that their entire service and Christian life may witness that the Spirit of prayer rules them. Then we may be confident that God will avenge his own elect which cry out day and night unto him.

[From *The Prayer Life*]

Christian Heroes

The Faith of Abel

By faith Abel offered unto God a more excellent
sacrifice than Cain, through which he had witness
borne to him that he was righteous. God bearing
witness in respect of his gifts: and through it he being
dead yet speaketh. (HEBREWS 11:4, RV)

Abel is the first figure to be depicted in this wonderful portrait gallery in Hebrews chapter 11. Since his example of faith is the oldest, it reveals to us the root and beginning and the real secret and very essence of all faith: that is, faith sacrifices. Sacrifice is the fullest expression not only of what faith sometimes does, but also of what it really and always is.

Faith means sacrifice
We are so accustomed to think of faith as the opened hand or heart which receives and takes in what God gives that we forget that faith in its deepest meaning consists of giving as well as receiving. In fact we cannot receive until we give, and we cannot receive more than we give. The reason why our faith so often fails in its attempts to receive is that it wants to do so without the giving. Faith means

sacrifice: the going out of self, the giving up of self, in order to find one's hopes and life in another. The very first element of worship is sacrifice, because it is the simple and complete expression of what God claims, of our relation to him and our hope in him. As the life of faith grows stronger in us and its heavenly significance becomes clearer, we shall see that sacrifice is its strength and value. By faith we offer a sacrifice which is acceptable to God, and this assures us that we are righteous and pleasing in his sight.

Faith finds the lamb for the sacrifice

Why didn't Abel just bow before God and give himself to him as a living sacrifice? Why did he not simply, in an act of consecration and self-dedication, offer himself to the Lord, utterly and entirely? What prompted him to seek a lamb and shed its blood and lay its body before God to be consumed? The reason was this: Abel felt himself to be a sinner. He knew that his sinful life could not be a sacrifice which was acceptable to God.

Sin and death are inseparably connected. The death of the lamb meant confession and vicarious expiation of sin; atonement for and redemption from sin. By substituting the lamb for himself and its death for the death he had deserved, Abel was testifying that for a sinner the only way to God is through death. There is no way to deliverance from sin and its guilt and power, no way into the life of God, except through the death in which sin is atoned for and taken away.

And so our faith centres and rests in Christ, the bleeding Lamb of God. His death is at one and the same time the revelation of what sin is, of how its punishment is borne and of how its power is broken. Faith always presents Christ to God as the sacrifice of perfect obedience and infinite merit. Faith sees something of its divine power and everlasting effectiveness and loses itself in Christ; in presenting him to God the soul presents itself too. The true spirit of self-sacrifice and obedience always finds both its liberty and its power in the sacrifice of the Son of God, since his death to sin was the power behind his death for sin. And so his death for sin, with us and on our behalf, leads to our death to sin with him and on his behalf.

Faith unites itself in death with the lamb in the sacrifice
Abel not only gave up the lamb to death; soon afterwards he yielded up his own life. In a divinely symbolic way the death of the lamb opened up the way and proclaimed the need for his own death, since in a world of sin death is the only path to life. In a far greater way, as we seek to enter into the meaning and power of the death of Christ for us, we hear with ever greater clarity the call to die with him. The more intensely out faith lives on him, the sacrifice for sin, in spirit and in truth, the more the Spirit of Sacrifice takes possession of us. We see that to die with Christ, to be like the One who not only dies for sin but to sin, is the secret of the life of faith.

Faith penetrates through the visible into the invisible; by faith we understand that what is seen comes from what is unseen. Faith enters into the very spirit of the sacrifice of Christ Jesus; it appropriates and assimilates it; it sets its whole being open to its power; it denies self, takes up the cross, and follows Jesus. The blessed truth of Substitution is found to have both its roots and its fruits in that of Identification; the unceasing sprinkling of the heart and of the evil conscience in the precious blood is the guarantee of the unceasing and ever-increasing action in us of the Eternal Spirit through whom Christ offered himself to God. Christ died for us so that we might die with him. The very essence of our full and growing faith is that we forsake everything, we lose our very lives, we become living sacrifices.

'By faith Abel offered unto God a more excellent sacrifice . . . which [faith] he had witness borne to him that he was righteous.'
If we have this faith which lives in the sacrifice of Christ in its completeness as the source and the law of our lives, then we will receive from God the witness or assurance that we are righteous and pleasing to him. It is not possible that a soul should really give

itself utterly to God, *in Christ*, without the Father then giving the soul the deep witness of his pleasure in the soul and his love for it. In Christ the Lamb there is perfect acceptance by God, assurance from God and fellowship with God.

'And through it [Abel], being dead, yet speaketh.'
He not only received witness from God, but also bears witness for God. Although he is dead, he still speaks to us. He speaks not despite his death, but because of it; his death is their power of his witness. In Abel, in Christ, in every believer, it is the faith which sacrifices everything, which gives itself up to God even to the point of death, which speaks with power.

Believer, do you wish to speak for God as Abel does? Remember the lesson: by faith we sacrifice. By faith we enter into fellowship with the Crucified One. By faith we give ourselves to the death, and being dead, we speak. Faith gives up all its life and hope in order to find its life in Christ and his atonement. And then, having found its life in him, it lives like him in the power of his life as a sacrifice to God for men. And as it looks upon the power of sin around it, whether in the more immediate circle or in the wide world which is full of ungodliness and paganism, it casts away all that man would set store by and finds in Jesus Christ and his sacrifice its message and its law, its inspiration and its hope. Because faith lives in him it can speak and work under the impulse of his infinite sympathy for the perishing. The power of his love will win them, because his is a love which gives itself and even dies for them.

So sacrifice, the death of self, makes way for the life of Christ in us. Being dead, we shall speak.

[From *The Promise of the Spirit*]

'Enoch Walked with God'

In Enoch we see how faith manifests itself as a walk with God:

'Enoch walked with God' (Genesis 5:22, 24). These few simple words reveal the deep meaning of the life of faith. Fellowship with God or walking with God is the ruling principle both of the inner life and of its outer expression. God himself is everything to the soul. We will now consider how we can obtain such a life.

Faith seeks the Divine Presence

When a friend invites me to take a walk with him and I call at his house for him, the one thing I want is himself. If he is busy, I wait for him. If he is not at home, and I am told where he can be found, I go and seek him: I want my friend himself. Without his presence, how could I walk with him? This is the great problem in the lives of many Christians: they lack a real, deep sense of the Holy Presence as a spiritual reality to be obtained every day and enjoyed all the day. Do you want to walk with God? Then each morning seek the personal Presence of your God.

Faith enables you to do this — not the faith which only thinks of asking and receiving, working and conquering, but the faith by which, in the death of Christ, the soul has entirely sacrificed itself to God, and now knows that it cannot and need not live one moment without him. In quiet worship and waiting, it looks up to him. It counts upon him to make himself known to his child. It opens its eyes and heart to receive the full reality of the One who is the Mightiest Power, the Most Impressive Object in the universe, and who in infinite love delights in revealing himself to those who seek him. Oh brother, let your faith day by day make this its first aim: to wait for and secure the full sense of the Holy Presence with you. Such faith will make the walk with God a blessed reality.

Faith trusts the Divine Guidance

On one occasion I took a walk with a friend in a strange place on a dark night. I knew neither the turnings which the path might take nor the difficult places where I might be in danger of stumbling. But as I took his arm and he assured me that he knew every step of the way, I dismissed all my fear and walked on with perfect confidence. A walk with God appears to many believers like a walk in the dark. It is true that to our human understanding it is indeed a walk in darkness, but in reality it is a walk in the Light. The person to whom it looks dark, who fears and doubts the daily walk with God, wondering if it might be too high and too difficult for him, should remember that faith trusts in the Divine Guidance. He should cultivate a childlike belief that his Father loves to have his child walk with him, that he has promised to hold his hand and to give him all the strength he needs. Nothing pleases God so much as our unbounded trust that he will enable us to walk with him. Such faith receives the blessing for which it has trusted God.

Faith accepts the Divine Will

Two cannot walk together unless they are agreed about the direction they are to take. When an inferior wishes to walk with a superior, the will of the superior must rule. If I am to walk with God, I must first agree to go in the direction he wants. Faith looks for God's way. Faith studies and discovers his direction in his Word, in his providence and above all in his blessed Son, and it accepts his way and will implicitly. The faith which walks with God implies, in its very nature, the sacrificial, wholehearted and unhesitating acceptance of all his will, and the childlike teachableness which listens and learns in order to know what his will is and how to do it. By such a faith we walk with God.

Faith receives the witness that we are pleasing to God

I cannot enjoy a walk with a friend if I doubt whether my company is agreeable to him or whether my behaviour is acceptable. The real blessing of the child of God is this: not only does God love him with an infinite compassion, even when he is wayward and wrong, but he also loves him in a more positive way, because the attitude of the child's heart and the behaviour which springs from that attitude is pleasing to God. Many Christians think this is an impossible attainment; sadly, it will be unto them according to their faith.

By faith Enoch received the assurance that he was well-pleasing to God. If we ask our Father for it, and tell him that we cannot rest until we know that we are well-pleasing to him, he will give us this assurance. This is just what he wants us to know and rejoice in: the assurance that he sees in us, as we live in Christ and are indwelt and guided by the Spirit, those qualities which make our whole life an acceptable and sweet-smelling sacrifice.

This testimony from God will be given to the heart which has faith, not only because faith is the very thing which is most God-glorifying and God-pleasing, but because it is the spiritual faculty which can recognize God's voice and witness. Faith is the death of the self-life, the silent waiting to allow God in his own hidden, mysterious way to speak to the soul and show himself to it. Faith is the opening of the heart in trust and love to receive what the Everlasting Love so longs to give — the full enjoyment of God's favour and approval. Such faith makes the walk with God what it is meant to be, the highest expression of the joy and the beauty of the Christian life, and the power by which death becomes a translation into the glory of the Presence in which we had already dwelt on earth.

By faith we walk with God. So let it be our one goal to believe and to let God be for us and do for us all that he can as God. Faith is the power by which we yield and give way to God, and allow him as God full freedom to do his utmost for us. If we live in Christ and walk in him, rooted and built up in him, we can and we do walk with God.

[From *The Promise of the Spirit*]

Abraham, a man of Faith

In Abraham's life we see what faith is: the spiritual sense by which man recognizes and accepts the revelation of his God, a spiritual sense called forth and awakened by that revelation. It was because

God had chosen Abraham, and determined to reveal himself, that Abraham became a man of faith. Each new revelation was an act of the divine will; it is the divine will, and the revelation in which it carries out its purpose, that is the cause and the life of faith. The more distinct the revelation or contact with God, the deeper is faith stirred in the soul. Paul speaks of 'trust in the Living God': it is only as the Living One, in the quickening power of the divine life, draws nigh and touches the soul, that living faith will be called forth. Faith is not an independent act, by which in our own strength we take what God says. Nor is it an entirely passive state, in which we suffer God to do to us only what he will. But it is that receptivity of soul in which, as God comes near, and as his living Power speaks to us and touches us, we yield ourselves and accept his Word and his working.

It is thus very evident that faith has two things to deal with: the Presence and the Word of the Lord. It is only the Living Presence that makes the Living Word, so that it comes not in word only but in power. It is on this account that there is so much reading and preaching of the word that bears so little fruit; so much straining and praying for faith with so little result. Men deal with the word more than with the Living God. Faith has very truly been defined as 'taking God at his word'. With many this has meant only 'taking the word as God's'; they did not see the force of the thought, '*taking God* at his word'. A key or a door handle has no value until I use it for the lock and the door I want to open; it is only in direct and living contact with God himself that the word will open the heart to believe. Faith *takes* God at his word; it can do this only when and as he gives himself. I may have in God's book all his precious promises most clear and full; I may have learned perfectly to understand how I have but to trust the promise to have it fulfilled, and yet utterly fail to find the longed-for blessing. The faith that enters on the inheritance is the attitude of soul which waits for God himself, first, to speak his word to me, and then to do the thing he hath spoken. Faith is fellowship with God; faith is surrender to God, the impression made by his drawing nigh, the possession *he takes* of the soul by his word, holding and preparing it for his work. When once it has been awakened, it watches for every appearing of the divine will; it listens for and accepts every indication of the divine presence; it looks for and expects the fulfilment of every divine promise.

Such was the faith through which Abraham inherited the promises. Such is the faith by which the blessing of Abraham comes upon the Gentiles in Christ Jesus, and by which we thus receive the promise of the Spirit. In all our study of the work of the Holy Spirit, and of the way in which he comes, from his first sealing us, to his full indwelling and streaming forth, let us hold fast this word: 'We receive the promise of the Spirit by faith.' Whether the believer be striving for the full consciousness that the Spirit dwells within, for a deeper assurance of his shedding abroad of God's love in the heart, for a larger growth of all his fruits, for the clearer experience of his guiding into all truth, or for the inducement of power to labour and to bless, let him remember that the law of faith, on which the whole economy of grace is grounded, here demands its fullest application: 'According to your faith be it unto you.' 'We receive the promise of the spirit by faith.' Let us seek for Abraham's blessing in Abraham's faith.

[From *The Spirit of Christ*]

Moses, the Man of Prayer

Before Moses was the patriarchal dispensation, with the family life, and the power of fathers, making it. Moses is the first man appointed to be a teacher and a leader of men. In him we find wonderful illustrations of the place and power of intercession in the servant of God.

In Egypt, from the first call, Moses prayed. He asked God what he was to say to the people (Exodus 3:11-13). He told him all their weaknesses, and besought him to be relieved of his mission (4:1–13). When the people reproached him that their burdens were increased, he went and told God (5:22), and he made known to him all his fears (6:12). This was his first training. Out of this was born his power in prayer when, time after time, Pharaoh asked him to entreat the Lord for him, and deliverance came at Moses' request (8:8, 9, 12, 28, 30, 31; 9:28, 29, 33; 10:17, 18). Study these passages until you come under the full impression of how real a factor in Moses' work and God's redemption prayer was.

At the Red Sea, Moses cried to God with the people, and the answer came (14:15). In the wilderness when the people thirsted, and when Amalek attacked them, it was also prayer that brought deliverance (17:4, 11).

At Sinai, when Israel had made the Golden Calf, it was prayer that at once averted the threatened destruction (32:11, 14). It was renewed prayer that gained them restoration (32:31). It was more prayer that secured God's presence to go with them (12:17), and once again prayer that was the revelation of God's glory (18:19). And when that had been given it was fresh prayer that received the renewal of the covenant (34:9-10).

In Deuteronomy we have a wonderful summary of all this (9:18-20, 26; 25:10), in which we see with what intensity he prayed, and how in one case it was for forty days and forty nights that he fell on his face before the Lord (9:25; 10:10).

In Numbers we read of Moses' prayer quenching the fire of the Lord (11:2), and obtaining the supply of meat (11:2, 11), of prayer healing Miriam (12:13), of prayer again saving the nation when they had refused to go up to the land (14:17-20). Prayer brought down judgement on Korah (16:15), and when God would consume the whole congregation, prayer made atonement (verse 46). Prayer brought water out of the rock (20:6), and in answer to prayer the brazen serpent was given (21:7). To prayer God's will was made known in a case of difficulty (27:5), and Joshua given as Moses' successor (verse 16).

Study all this until your whole heart is filled with the thought of the part prayer must play, may play, in the life of a man who would be God's servant to his fellowmen.

[From *Prayer's Inner Chamber*]

Elijah and Prayer

The effectual fervent prayer of a righteous man
availeth much. Elias was a man subject to like
passions as we are. (JAMES 5:16-17)

There is nothing that so much weakens the force of the call to imitate the example of Scripture saints, as the thought that theirs are exceptional cases, and that what we see in them is not to be expected at all. The aim of God in Scripture is the very opposite. He gives us these men for our instruction and encouragement, as a specimen of what his grace can do, as living embodiments of what his will and our nature, at once demand and render possible.

It was just to meet the so common error alluded to, and to give confidence to all of us who aim at a life of effectual prayer, that James wrote: 'Elias was a man subject to like passions as we are.' As there was no difference between his nature and ours, or between the grace that wrought in him and works in us, there is no reason why we should not, like him, pray effectually. If our prayer is to have power, we must seek to have somewhat of Elijah's spirit. The aspiration, Let me seek grace to pray like Elijah, is perfectly legitimate, is most needful. If we honestly seek for the secret of his power in prayer the path in which he trod will open to us. We shall find it in his life with God, his work for God, his trust in God.

Elijah lived with God

Elijah lived with God. Prayer is the voice of our life. As a man lives so he prays. Not the words or thoughts with which he is occupied at set times of prayer, but the bent of his heart as seen in his desires and

217

actions, is regarded by God as his real prayer. The life speaks louder and truer than the lips. To pray well I must live well. He who seeks to live with God, will learn so to know his mind and to please him, that he will be able to pray according to his will. Think how Elijah, at his first message to Ahab, spoke of 'the Lord God, before whom I stand.' Think of his solitude at the brook Cherith, receiving his bread from God through the ravens, and then at Serepta through the ministry of a poor widow. He walked with God, he learned to know God well; when the time came, he knew to pray to a God whom he had proved. It is only out of a life of true fellowship with God that the prayer of faith can be born. Let the link between the life and the prayer be clear and close. As we give ourselves to walk with God, we shall learn to pray.

Elijah worked for God

Elijah worked for God. He went where God sent him. He did what God commanded him. He stood up for God and his service. He witnessed against the people and their sin. All who heard him could say: 'Now I know that thou art a man of God, and that the word of the Lord in thy mouth is true.' His prayers were all in connection with his work for God. He was equally a man of action and a man of prayer. When he prayed down, first the drought and then the rain, it was, as part of his prophetic work, that the people, by judgement and mercy, might be brought back to God. When he prayed down fire from heaven on the sacrifice, it was that God might be known as the true God. All he asked was for the glory of God. How often believers seek power in prayer, that they may be able to get good gifts for themselves. The secret selfishness robs them of the power and the answer. It is when self is lost in the desire for God's glory, and our life is devoted to work for God, that powers to pray can come. God lives to love, and save, and bless men: the believer who gives himself up to God's service in this will find in it new life in prayer. Work for others proves the honesty of our prayer for them. Work for God reveals alike our need and our right to pray boldly. Cultivate the consciousness, and speak it out before God, that you are wholly given up to his service; it will strengthen your confidence in his hearing you.

Elijah trusted in God

Elijah trusted in God. He had learned to trust him for his personal needs in the time of famine; he dared trust him for greater things in answer to prayer for his people. What confidence in God's hearing him we see in his appeal to the God that answers by fire. What confidence in God's doing what he would ask, when he announced to Ahab the abundance of rain that was coming, and then, with his face to the earth, pleaded for it, while his servant, six times over, brought the message, 'There is nothing.' An unwavering confidence in the promise and character of God, and God's personal friendship for himself, acquired in personal intercourse, and proved in work for God, gave power for the effectual prayer of the righteous man.

The inner chamber is the place where this has to be learned. The morning watch is the training school where we are to exercise the grace that can fit us to pray like Elijah. Let us not fear. The God of Elijah still lives; the spirit that was in him dwells in us. Let us cease from the limited and selfish views of prayer, which only aims at grace enough to keep us standing. Let us cultivate the consciousness that Elijah had, of living wholly for God, and we shall learn to pray like him.

[From *Prayer's Inner Chamber*]

Paul Apprehending Christ

They led Paul by the hand, and brought him into Damascus. And he was there three days without sight, and neither did eat nor drink.
(ACTS 9:8, 9)

Christ's apprehending Paul was the act of a moment, complete and immediate. Paul's apprehending of Christ began at the same moment but was continued throughout life, so that in old age he could say, 'Not as though I had already attained . . . but I follow after, if that I may apprehend.'

It is a point of the utmost importance to observe that Paul knows nothing of any progressive stages or gradual progress in his conversion to the Gospel. He looked back to it throughout his life as a sudden overwhelming event, which surprised him in the full tide of his Judaic career, and drove him, in spite of himself, into a new channel. He is a conquered rebel, whom God leads in triumph in the face of the world (2 Corinthians 2:14). If he preaches the Gospel he cannot make any boast of doing so; he was compelled to preach it, under a higher necessity, which he had no power to resist. There he stands — a slave in chains (1 Corinthians 9:15-18).

'His conversion was the fruit of God's grace, manifesting itself in him as a sovereign power which triumphed over his individual will. Paul rose from the ground the captive of that divine grace to which he henceforth was to render himself without reserve or condition.' (Sabatier, pp. 62, 68.)

These words are strong but true. Paul had done his utmost to resist the power of Christ and his truth. The revelation on the way to Damascus overwhelmed and over-mastered him. He was led into the city a prisoner of Jesus Christ. He had surrendered at discretion; during the three following days he could do nothing but bow in speechless amazement at the terrible sin that he had been guilty of, and the inconceivable grace that had been bestowed upon him.

No human thought can conceive or describe what must have passed through his mind as he felt himself face to face with the crucified Jesus on the throne of glory. 'Is this', he must have thought, 'what all my boasted blamelessness in the law has brought me to? I have been found fighting against God himself, crucifying the Son of God afresh.' He had used the law as a pedestal on which to exalt himself and be crowned with the divine favour. And all at once he sees that his righteousness has become his condemnation. He feels that as blasphemer of the name of Jesus Christ, and the persecutor of his Church, he is the chief of sinners. Never man had thus sinned; never man had thus seen his sin in the light of God from heaven.

Saul fell down dead at the feet of Jesus. It is only when we realize the terrible reality of that death to all his hopes and self-confidence, that we can form any idea of the intensity of that new life on which he entered. In him the experience of the prophet Jonah was repeated. Christ has said that no sign should be given to the Jews but that of Jonah. Jonah was the only prophet ever sent on a direct mission to the Gentiles. He had, like all the nation, so little sympathy with God's purpose, that to escape his mission he fled. The experiences he passed through 'in the belly of hell' were to him nothing less than death. As the result he gave himself to fulfil his calling, and yet still proved how little the Spirit of God and his compassion had mastered him. The old covenant could not work anything but an eternal submission. In Jesus Christ the sign of Jonah had its fulfilment. He whom the Father had sent had to spend three days in the grave to prove that it is only through an entire death to the life of nature that the divine glory could enable a man to give his life for the world and the lost, and in the power of heaven to carry out God's purpose of love. Saul had been chosen of God as the Apostle of the Gentiles. In the revelation of Christ, the sign of the prophet Jonah was fulfilled in him too as he was brought into that new world which opened by death and resurrection of our Lord. These three days spent as in the silence of the grave, were his death to the law, to sin, to self, and all its effort. All was summed up in the one word, 'God be merciful to me a sinner.' The proud Pharisee died; the penitent publican rose from his grave, a prepared vessel to carry the message of God's love to the Gentile world.

Amid all the sense of sin and shame, Saul felt that it was infinite grace that Christ had met him as the Saviour of sinners. The vision of the heavenly Christ carried with it the power of his presence as exalted by God to give repentance and remission of sins. The mingled sense of abounding sin and abounding grace, which constituted a chief element of the blessedness of heaven, had come to him.

When Ananias came to him his inmost soul was prepared to receive his message. The work that Christ himself had begun from heaven is continued and completed through a man in the flesh. Saul is to be linked as closely to the body of Jesus on earth as to the head in heaven. Through Ananias he received his sight, a pledge that God who said 'Let there by light,' had shined into his heart the light of the knowledge of the glory of God in the face of Christ Jesus.

Through Ananias he received in baptism the washing away of his sins. Many years later he wrote, 'We were baptized into his death' (Romans 6:3). 'Buried with Christ in baptism, wherein ye are risen with him' (Colossians 2:12). 'For by one Spirit are we all baptized into one body' (1 Corinthians 12:13). Paul wrote to Christians from among the heathen in the confident expectation that the Holy Spirit would teach them to understand the reality of their union with Christ in his death and resurrection. During his three days of darkness, Saul had indeed passed through the pains of death; by faith in the risen Lord, who had manifested himself to him in the power of a divine life, Saul knew the power of his resurrection. It was to him the beginning and the power of the eternal life. Of its meaning he was to learn more in the future, a life in which Christ was put on and he became one with him in the likeness of his death, and in the likeness of his resurrection too. When Jesus the crucified and risen Lord took possession of him he became partaker of the divine reality, for which, in later years, he found the thought and words.

'That thou mayest be filled with the Holy Ghost.' Christ from heaven had opened and prepared the heart; what a deep mystery that his servant on earth should be the instrument for conveying that Holy Spirit which Christ had sent down from his throne of power. It was the very Spirit of Pentecost that was to come upon Saul and make him a member of Christ's body upon earth, dependent upon those to whom he is now united. Saul did not know what Christ had promised the disciples in connection with the gift of the Holy Spirit. 'He shall reveal me'; 'He shall glorify me'; 'He shall guide you into all truth'; 'He shall testify of me'; and 'Ye also shall bear witness'. But all that those words implied became his very own, when in a heart broken and truly opened up by the heavenly vision, he received the Spirit to reveal the Christ who now lived within him. There is no higher expression for the work of the Pentecostal Spirit than this, that he makes Christ such a living reality that a man can truly say, 'Christ liveth in me.'

In the words of our Lord to Ananias with regard to Saul, 'Behold he prayeth,' we find the divine expression for what Saul's conversion really meant. As a Pharisee he had prayed unceasingly; it was part of that blamelessness in the law in which he put his trust. And yet he had never prayed in truth. The heavenly vision brought him for the first time to bow before God in that sense of deep and entire dependence upon him which constitutes the very essence of prayer. And it revealed to him the greatness of the sin in which he had lived, and from which he saw that nothing but divine mercy could free him. How truly that prayer became the spirit and the attitude of his whole future life, his Epistles abundantly testify. In all his understanding of Christ he always found in him the access to the Father in which all that fullness of the divine life could manifest itself in the feebleness of human nature. He that would understand the inner life of St Paul must above all learn to know the place that prayer took in his life.

[From *The Apostle Paul's Inner Life*]

George Müller

God gave George Müller as a proof to his church how literally and wonderfully he still always hears prayer. It is not only that he gave him in his lifetime over a million pounds sterling to support his orphanages, but Mr Müller also stated that he believed that the Lord had given more than thirty thousand souls in answer to prayer. And that not only from among orphans, but also many others for whom he (in some cases for fifty years) had prayed faithfully every day, in the firm faith that they would be saved. When he was asked on what ground he so firmly believed this, his answer was:

1. I have not the least doubt because I am assured that it is the Lord's will to save them, for he willeth that all men should be saved and come to the knowledge of the truth (see 1 Timothy 2:4); and we have the assurance 'that, if we ask anything according to his will, he heareth us' (1 John 5:14).
2. I have never pleaded for this salvation in my own name, but in the blessed name of my precious Lord Jesus, and on his merits alone (see John 14:14).
3. I always firmly believed in the willingness of God to hear my prayers (see Mark 11:24).
4. I am not conscious of having yielded to any sin, for 'if I regard iniquity in my heart, the Lord will not hear me' when I call (Psalm 66:18).
5. I have persevered in believing prayer for more than fifty-two years for some, and shall continue till the answer comes: 'Shall not God avenge his own elect which cry day and night unto him?' (Luke 18:7).

Take these thoughts into your hearts and practise pryaer according to these rules. Let prayer be not only the utterance of your desires, but a fellowship with God, till we know by faith that our prayer is heard. The way George Müller walked is the new and living way to the throne of grace, which is open for us all.

Hudson Taylor

When Hudson Taylor, as a young man, had given himself over unreservedly to the Lord, there came to him a strong conviction that God would send him to China. He had read of George Müller and how God had answered his prayers for his own support and that of his orphans, and he began to ask the Lord to teach him also so to trust him. He felt that if he would go to China with such faith, he must first begin to live by faith in England. He asked the Lord to enable him to do this. He had a position as a doctor's dispenser, and asked God to help him not to ask for his salary, but to leave it to God to move the heart of the doctor to pay him at the right time. The doctor was a good-hearted man, but very irregular in payment. This cost Taylor much trouble and struggle in prayer because he believed, as did George Müller, that the word, 'Owe no man any thing' (Romans 13:8), was to be taken literally, and that debt should not be incurred.

So he learned the great lesson *to move men through God* — a thought of deep meaning, which later on became an unspeakably great blessing to him in his work in China. He relied on that — in the conversion of the Chinese, in the awakening of Christians to give money for the support of the work, and in the finding of suitable missionaries who would hold as faith's rule of conduct that we should make *our desires known to God in prayer and then rely on God to move men to do what he would have done.*

After he had been for some years in China, he prayed that God would give twenty-four missionaries, two for each of the eleven provinces and Mongolia, each with millions of souls and with no missionary. God did it. But there was no society to send them out. He had indeed learned to trust God for his own support, but he dared not take upon himself the responsibility of the twenty-four, if possibly they had not sufficient faith. This cost him severe conflict, and he became very ill under it, till at last he saw that God could as easily care for the twenty-four as for himself. He undertook it in a glad faith. And so God led him, through many severe trials of faith, to trust him fully. Now these twenty-four have increased, in the course of time, to a thousand missionaries who rely wholly on God for support. Other missionary societies have acknowledged how much they have learned from Hudson Taylor, as a man who stated and obeyed this law. *Faith may rely on God to move men to do what his children have asked of him in prayer.*

[From *The Prayer Life*]

George Müller, and the Secret of His Power in Prayer

When God wishes anew to teach his Church a truth that is not being understood or practised, he mostly does so by raising some man to be in word and deed a living witness to its blessedness. And so God raised up in the nineteenth century, among others, George Müller to be his witness that he is indeed the Hearer of prayer. I know of no way in which the principal truths of God's word in regard to prayer can be more effectually illustrated and established than a short review of his life and of what he tells of his prayer-experiences.

He was born in Prussia on 25th September 1805. His early life, even after having entered the University of Halle as a theological student, was wicked in the extreme. Led by a friend one evening, when just twenty years of age, to a prayer meeting, he was deeply impressed, and soon afterwards was brought to know the Saviour. Not long afterwards, he began reading missionary papers, and in course of time offered himself to the London Society for promoting Christianity to the Jews. He was accepted as a student, but soon found that he could not in all things submit to the rules of the Society, as leaving too little liberty for the leading of the Holy Spirit. The connection was dissolved in 1830 by mutual consent, and he became the pastor of a small congregation at Teignmouth. In 1832, he was led to Bristol, and it was as pastor of Bethesda Chapel that he was led to the Orphan Home and other work, in connection with which God has so remarkably led him to trust his word and to experience how God fulfils that word.

A few extracts in regard to his spiritual life will prepare the way for what we specially wish to quote of his experiences in reference to prayer.

> The Lord very graciously gave me, from the very commencement of my divine life, a measure of simplicity and of child-like disposition in spiritual things, so that whilst I was

exceedingly ignorant of the Scriptures, and was still from time to time overcome even by outward sins, yet I was enabled to carry most minute matters to the *Lord in prayer*. And I have found 'godliness profitable unto all things, having promise of the life that now is, and of that which is to come'. Though very weak and ifnorant, yet I had now, by the grace of God, some desire to benefit others, and he who so faithfully had once served Satan, sought now to win souls for Christ.

It was at Teignmouth that he was led to know how to use God's word, and to trust the Holy Spirit as the Teacher given by God to make that word clear. He writes:

God then began to show me that the word of God alone is our standard of judgement in spiritual things; that it can be explained only by the Holy Spirit; and that in our day, as well as in former times, he is the Teacher of his people. The office of the Holy Spirit I had not experimentally understood before that time.

It was my beginning to understand this latter point in particular, which had a great effect on me; for the Lord enabled me to put it to the test of experience, by laying aside commentaries, and almost every other book, and simply reading the word of God and studying it.

The result of this was that the first evening that I shut myself into my room, to give myself to prayer and meditation over the Scriptures, I learned more in a few hours than I had done during a period of several months previously.

But the particular difference was that I received real strength for my soul in so doing. I now began to try by the test of the Scriptures the thing which I had learned and seen, and found that only those principles which stood the test were of real value.

Of obedience to the word of God, he writes as follows, in connection with his being baptized:

It had pleased God, in his abundant mercy, to bring my mind into such a state that I was willing to carry out into my life whatever I should find in the Scriptures. I could say, 'I will do his will,' and it was on that account, I believe, that I saw which '*doctrine is of God*'. . . And I would observe here, by the way, that the passage to which I have just alluded (John 7:17) has been a most remarkable comment to me on many doctrines and precepts of our most holy faith. For instance: 'Resist not evil, but whosoever shall smite thee on thy right cheek, turn to him the other also. And if any man may sue thee at law, and take away thy coat, let him have thy cloak also. And whosoever shall compel thee to go a mile, go with him twain. Give to him that asketh thee, and from him that would borrow of thee, turn not thou away. Love your enemies, bless them that curse you, do good to them that hate you, and pray for them which despitefully use you, and persecute you' (Matthew 5:39-44). 'Sell that ye have, and give alms' (Luke 12:33). 'Owe no man any thing, but to love one another' (Romans 13:8). It may be said, 'Surely these passages cannot be taken literally, for how then would the people of God be able to pass through the world?' The state of mind enjoined in John 7:17 will cause such objections to vanish. *Whosoever is willing to act out* these commandments of the Lord *literally* will, I believe, be led with me to see that to take them *literally* is the will of God . . . Those who do so take them will doubtless often be brought into difficulties, hard to the flesh to bear, but these will have a tendency to make them constantly feel that they are strangers and pilgrims here, that this world is not their home, and thus to throw them more upon God, who will assuredly help us through any difficulty into which we may be brought by seeking to act in obedience to his word.

This implicit surrender to God's word led him to certain views and conduct in regard to money, which mightily influenced his future life. They had their root in the conviction that money was a divine stewardship, and that all money had therefore to be received and dispensed in direct fellowship with God himself. This led him to the adoption of the following four great rules:

1. *Not to receive any fixed salary*, both because in the collecting of it there was often much that was at variance with the freewill offering with which God's service is to be maintained, and in the receiving of it a danger of placing more dependence on human sources of income than in the living God himself.

2. *Never to ask any human being for help*, however great the need might be, but to make his wants known to the God who has promised to care for his servants and to hear their prayer.

3. To take this command (Luke 12:33) literally, '*Sell that thou hast and give alms*,' and never to save up money, but to spend all God entrusted to him on God's poor, on the work of his kingdom.

4. Also to take Romans 13:8, '*Owe no man anything*,' literally, and never to buy on credit, or be in debt for anything, but to trust God to provide.

This mode of living was not easy at first. But Müller testifies that it was most blessed in bringing the soul to rest in God, and drawing it into closer union with himself when inclined to backslide. '*For it will not do, it is not possible, to live in sin, and at the same time, by communion with God, to draw down from heaven everything one needs for the life that now is.*'

[From *With Christ in the School of Prayer*]

A Life of Intercession

A Work of Faith

Intercession is pre-eminently a work of faith. Not just the faith that tries to believe the prayer will be heard, but the faith that is at home amid heavenly realities. A faith that does not trouble about one's own nothingness and feebleness, because it is living in Christ. A faith that does not make its hope depend upon its feelings, but upon the faithfulness of the three-in-one God in what each person has undertaken to do in prayer. A faith that has overcome the world, and sacrifices the visible to be wholly free for the spiritual and heavenly and eternal to take possession of it. A faith that knows that it is heard and receives what it asks, and therefore quietly and deliberately perseveres in its supplication till the answer comes. The true intercessor must be a man of faith.

[From *Prayer's Inner Chamber*]

Power for the Work to Which We Are Called

The preacher will learn to receive his message really from God, through the power of the Holy Spirit, and to deliver it in that power to the congregation. He will know where he can be filled with the love and zeal which will enable him, in his rounds of pastoral visiting, to meet and help each individual in a spirit of tender compassion. He will be able to say with Paul: 'I can do all things through Christ which strengtheneth me' (Philippians 4:13). 'We are more than conquerors through him that loved us' (Romans 8:37). 'We are ambassadors for Christ . . . we pray you in Christ's stead, be ye reconciled to God' (2 Corinthians 5:20). These are no vain dreams or pictures of a foolish imagination. God has given us Paul as an illustration, so that, however we may differ from him in gifts or calling, yet in inner experience we may know the all-sufficiency of grace which can do all things for us as it did for him.

[From *The Prayer Life*]

Wholly Dedicated to God

The true intercessor is a man who knows that God knows of him that his heart and life are wholly given up to God and his glory. This is the only condition on which an officer at the court of an earthly sovereign could expect to exert much influence. Moses and Elijah and Daniel and Paul prove that it is so in the spiritual world. Our blessed Lord is himself the proof of it. He did not save us by intercession, but by self-sacrifice. His power of intercession worked in his sacrifice: it claims and receives what the sacrifice won. As we have it so clearly put in the last words of Isaiah 53: 'He poured out his soul unto death, and was numbered with the transgressors, and he bare the sins of many' and — study this in connection with the whole chapter of which it is the crown — 'and made intercession for the transgressors.' He first gave himself up to the will of God. There he won the power to influence and guide that will. He gave himself for sinners in all-consuming love, and so he won the power to intercede for them. There is no other path for us.

It is the man who seeks to enter personally into death with Christ, and gives himself wholly for God and men, who will dare to be bold like Moses or Elijah, who will persevere like Daniel or Paul. Whole-hearted devotion and obedience to God are the first marks of an intercessor.

[From *Prayer's Inner Chamber*]

God's Omnipresence

God fills the world and every moment is present in everything. Just as it is with the Father, so now our Lord Jesus is everywhere present, above all with each of his redeemed ones. This is one of the greatest and most important lessons which our faith must learn. We can clearly understand this from the example of our Lord's disciples. What was the special privilege of the disciples, who were always in fellowship with him? It was *uninterrupted enjoyment of the presence of the Lord Jesus*. It was because of this they were so sorrowful at the thought of his death. They would be deprived of that presence. He would be no longer with them. How, under these circumstances, did the Lord Jesus comfort them? He promised that the Holy Spirit from heaven should so work in them a sense of the fullness of his life and of his personal presence that he would be even more intimately near and have more unbroken fellowship with them than ever they experienced while he was upon earth.

This great promise is now the inheritance of every believer, although so many of them know little about it. Jesus Christ, in his divine personality, in that eternal love which led him to the cross, longs to have fellowship with us every moment of the day and to keep us in the enjoyment of that fellowship. This ought to be explained to every new convert: 'The Lord loves you so that he would have you near him without a break, that you may have experience of his love.' This is what every believer must learn who has felt his powerlessness for a life of prayer, of obedience, and of holiness. This alone will give us power as intercessors to conquer the world and to win souls out of it for our Lord.

[From *The Prayer Life*]

The Spirit of Prayer

*With all prayer and supplication, praying at
all seasons in the Spirit, and watching
thereunto in all perseverance and
supplication for all the saints, and on my
behalf.* (EPHESIANS 6:18)

Praying always in the Spirit for all saints will be the secret of true revival in God's children. *And on my behalf!* The minister who is pleading as intercessor for the saints whom he watches over *has equal need of their prayers in return.* As the life-blood which is ever purified by the fresh air we breathe circulates through the whole body and maintains its unity in vital power, even so the Spirit of prayer, breathing in the air of heaven, and breathing out and up to heaven the unceasing supplication of love on behalf of the whole body and every member, is essential to the health of the body of Christ. The work of the ministry depends upon it. The minister is to train believers to this as one of their highest privileges. The work of the missionary who, like Paul, carries the Gospel to the heathen depends upon it. Oh that we believed in the new power that could come upon our missions if believers answered the call 'praying at all seasons in the Spirit, and watching thereunto in all perseverance and supplication on my behalf'. What grace would come in answer! 'To make known with boldness the mystery of the Gospel,' and to preach, whether to the wise or to the ignorant, to the Greek or the Jew, to the follower of Muhammed or of dumb idols, Christ a stumbling-block to the Jew and foolishness to the Gentiles

233

— Christ, the power of God and the wisdom of God.

[From *Aids to Devotion*]

Paul's Request for Prayer

I beseech you, brethren, that ye strive together
with me in your prayers to God for me; that
I may be delivered from them that do not
believe in Judaea; and may come to you with
joy by the will of God. (ROMANS 15:30-32)

Paul had in the first chapter of Romans told them how he made mention always of them in his prayers, making request that he might have a prosperous journey by the will of God to come to them. He knew that he would see Rome, but as yet had no idea how he would get there. He intended first to visit Jerusalem, but knew not how he would be delivered from the dangers to which he might be exposed through his adversaries among the Jews. He asks them to strive together with him in prayer that he might be delivered from them who do not believe in Judaea. We know from the Acts through what dangers he had to pass. Men had vowed not to eat until they had killed him. Was it owing to the prayers of the saints in Rome to whom he writes that that deliverance came? Paul evidently felt that their prayers would not be in vain.

Baumgarten, in his Commentary on the Acts, has some most suggestive thoughts on this subject. He points out how the Roman Empire was utterly hostile to the Kingdom of Christ. We see it in our Lord's crucifixion, and later on in the death of James. We see signs of it in Paul's treatment at Philippi, and in Felix, willing to show the Jews a pleasure, leaving Paul bound for two years. Festus himself, willing to do the Jews a pleasure, offered to send Paul to Jerusalem. And all at once he allows Paul's appeals to Caesar, and the Roman Empire becomes responsible for Paul's deliverance from the Jews and his safe conduct to Rome.

'The question arises, has anything new happened that the world empire becomes the servant of Christ's Kingdom in bringing the Apostle to preach the Gospel in Rome itself! Something new has taken place. The conversion of the Gentiles has gathered large companies in many cities, and even in Rome itself. Of these communities we know with what devotion and love they regarded Paul, and accompanied him in wrestling prayer on his journey. This prayer of the saints, rendered effective by the Great High Priest in Heaven, is the power which has conquered the world power. The prayer of the saints, in close and living fellowship with their Head in Heaven, is the new power working on the earth. By the power of the Holy Spirit the saints knew that they had to battle with the powers of darkness, and yet were assured that in their living fellowship with the Lord in Heaven its power had been broken and overcome.'

Such thoughts give us an insight into what a reality there was in Paul's request for intercession, as a striving together with him in prayer, what actual power there was for effectual, much-availing prayer in the hearts of the saints, and what the victory was that had been won in heaven, and manifested on earth in God's servant. The lesson comes to us as from heaven that, if the Missionary would train his converts in the art of fervent prayer, he would have in them a mighty power to wield against the forces of darkness. The mighty power of Rome had to yield to the power of prayer.

See how Paul applies this faith in other circumstances. Just before writing the second epistle to the Corinthians he had in Asia 'been pressed out of measure, above strength, insomuch that we despaired even of life; But we had the sentence of death in ourselves. But God delivered us: in whom we trust that he will yet deliver us; ye also helping together by prayer for us.' Paul had such a vision of the spiritual unity of the body of Christ through all its members that he felt himself actually dependent upon the prayer of the churches. Where he stood alone he knew God as a God of prayer, and had power with him. But where he had believers to whom he was linked, he felt their prayer to be indispensable for his experience of God's power.

It is only when this sense of unity binds minister and people, binds all believers together, that the full power of the Holy Spirit can be expected to work. 'For the gift bestowed upon us by the means of many persons thanks may be given by many on our behalf,' an unceasing sacrifice of prayer and praise.

Just one more passage: In writing to the Philippians from Rome, he tells of 'Some indeed preach Christ even of envy and strife supposing to add affliction to my bonds.' He was content, he rejoiced and would rejoice because Christ was preached. 'For I know that this shall turn to my salvation through your prayer, and the supply of the Spirit of Jesus Christ.' Rome and Philippi were far asunder. But Paul lived so in prayer for the churches, and had taught them so to pray for him and his work, that he felt assured that every seeming evil would work out for his salvation, through their prayer and the consequent supply of the Spirit of Jesus Christ.

Let us pray for ministers and missionaries and workers, that the Holy Spirit may give us a new vision of the inconceivable power that prayer can exert.

[From *The Apostle Paul's Inner Life*]

The Model Prayer

'*Our Father which art in heaven!*' To appreciate this word of adoration aright, I must remember that none of the saints had in Scripture ever ventured to address God as their Father. The invocation places us at once in the centre of the wonderful revelation the Son came to make of his Father as our Father too. It comprehends the mystery of redemption — Christ delivering us from the curse that we might become the children of God. The mystery of regeneration — the Spirit in the new birth giving us the new life. And the mystery of faith — before the redemption is accomplished or understood, the word is given on the lips of the disciples to prepare them for the blessed experience still to come. The words are the key to the whole prayer, to all prayer. It takes time, it takes life to study them; it will take eternity to understand them fully. The knowledge of God's Father-love is the first and simplest, but also the last and highest lesson in the school of prayer. It is in the personal relation to the living God, and the personal conscious fellowship of love with himself, that prayer begins. It is in the knowledge of God's Fatherliness, revealed by the Holy Spirit, that the power of prayer will be found to root and grow. In the infinite tenderness and pity and patience of the infinite Father, in his loving readiness to hear and to help, the life of prayer has its joy. O let us take time, until the Spirit has made these words to us spirit and truth, filling heart and life: 'Our father which art in heaven.' Then we are indeed within the veil, in the secret place of power where prayer always prevails.

'*Hallowed be thy name.*' There is something here that strikes us at once. While we ordinarily first bring our own needs to God in prayer, and then think of what belongs to God and his interests, the Master reverses the order. First, *thy* name, *thy* kingdom, *thy* will; then, give *us*, forgive *us*, lead *us*, deliver *us*. The lesson is of more importance than we think. In true worship the Father must be first, must be all. The sooner I learn to forget myself in the desire that *he* may be glorified, the richer will the blessing be that prayer will bring to myself. No one ever loses by what he sacrifices for the Father.

This must influence all our prayer. There are two sorts of prayer: personal and intercessory. The latter ordinarily occupies the lesser part of our time and energy. This may not be. Christ has opened the school of prayer specially to train intercessors for the great work of bringing down, by their faith and prayer, the blessings of his work and love on the world around. There can be no deep growth in prayer unless this be made our aim. The little child may ask of the father only what it needs for itself; and yet it soon learns to say, 'Give some for my sister too.' But the grown-up son, who only lives for the father's interest and takes charge of the father's business, asks more largely, and gets all that is asked. And Jesus would train us to the blessed life of consecration and service, in which our interests are all subordinate to the Father's name, and kingdom, and will. Let us live for this. Each time we adore *our Father*, let there follow in the same breath, *thy* name, *thy* kingdom, *thy* will; for this we look up and long.

'*Hallowed be thy name*.' What name? This new name of Father. The word *Holy* is the central word of the Old Testament; the *name* Father is the central word of the New Testament. In this name of love, all the holiness and glory of God are now to be revealed. And how is the name to be hallowed? By God himself: '*I will hallow* my great name which ye have profaned.' Our prayer must be that in ourselves, in all God's children, in presence of the world, God himself would reveal the holiness, the divine power, the hidden glory of the name of Father. The Spirit of the Father is the *Holy* Spirit: it is only when we yield ourselves to be led *of him* that the name will be *hallowed* in our prayers and our lives. Let us learn the prayer: 'Our Father, hallowed be thy name.'

'*Thy kingdom come*.' The Father is a King and has a kingdom. The son and heir of a king has no higher ambition than the glory of his father's kingdom. In time of war or danger this becomes his passion; he can think of nothing else. The children of the Father are here in the enemy's territory, where the kingdom, which is in heaven, is not yet fully manifested. What more natural than that, when they learn to hallow the Father-name, they should long and cry with deep enthusiasm: 'Thy kingdom come.' The coming of the kingdom is the one great event on which the revelation of the Father's glory, the blessedness of his children, the salvation of the world depends. On our prayers too the coming of the kingdom waits. Shall we not join in the deep longing cry of the redeemed: 'Thy kingdom come'? Let us learn it in the school of Jesus.

'*Thy will be done, as in heaven, so on earth*.' This petition is too frequently applied alone to the *suffering* of the will of God. In heaven God's will is *done*, and the Master teaches the child to ask that the will may be done on earth just as in heaven: in the spirit of adoring submission and ready obedience. Because the will of God is the glory of heaven, the doing of it is the blessedness of heaven. As the will is done, the kingdom of heaven comes into the heart. And wherever faith has accepted the Father's love, obedience accepts the Father's will. The surrender to, and the prayer for a life of heaven-like obedience, is the spirit of childlike prayer.

'*Give us this day our daily bread.*' When first the child has yielded himself to the Father in the care for his name, his kingdom, and his will, he has full liberty to ask for his daily bread. A master cares for the food of his servant, a general of his soldiers, a father of his child. And will not the Father in heaven care for the child who has in prayer given himself up to his Father's interests? We may indeed in full confidence say: 'Father, I live for my honour and thy work; I know thou carest for me.' Consecration to God and his will gives wonderful liberty in prayer for temporal things: the whole earthly life is given to the Father's loving care.

'*And forgive us our debts, as we also have forgiven our debtors.*' As bread is the first need of the body, so forgiveness is the first need of the soul. And the provision for the one is as sure as for the other. We are children, but sinners too; our right of access to the Father's presence we owe to the precious blood and the forgiveness it has won for us. Let us beware of the prayer for forgiveness becoming a formality: only what is really confessed is really forgiven. Let us in faith accept the forgiveness as promised: as a spiritual reality, an actual transaction between God and us, it is the entrance into all the Father's love and all the privileges of children. Such forgiveness, as a living experience, is impossible without a forgiving spirit to others: as *forgiven* expresses the heavenward relation of God's child, so *forgiving* expresses the earthward relation. In each prayer to the Father I must be able to say that I know of no one whom I do not heartily love.

'*And lead us not into temptation, but deliver us from the evil one.*' Our daily bread, the pardon of our sins, and then our being kept

239

from all sin and the power of the evil one, in these three petitions all our personal need is comprehended. The prayer for bread and pardon must be accompanied by the surrender to live in all things in holy obedience to the Father's will, and the believing prayer in everything to be kept by the power of the indwelling Spirit from the power of the evil one.

[From *With Christ in the School of Prayer*]

Praying like Christ

*And in the morning, rising up a great while
before day, he went out, and departed into a
desert place, and there prayed.* (MARK 1:35)

*And he saith unto them, Come ye yourselves
apart into a desert place, and rest a while.*
(MARK 6:31)

In his life of secret prayer, my Saviour is my example. He could not maintain the heavenly life in his soul without continually separating himself from man, and communing with his Father. With the heavenly life in me it is not otherwise: it has the same need of entire separation from man, the need not only of single moments, but of time enough for communion with the Fountain of Life, the Father in heaven.

It was at the commencement of his public ministry that the event happened which so attracted the attention of his disciples that they wrote it down. After a day full of wonders and of work at Capernaum (Mark 1:21-32), the press in the evening became still greater. The whole town is before the door; sick are healed, and devils are cast out. It is late before they get to sleep; in the throng there is little time for quiet or for secret prayer. And, lo, as they rise early in the morning, they find him gone. In the silence of the night

240

he has gone out to seek a place of solitude in the wilderness; when they find him there, he is still praying.

And why did my Saviour need these hours of prayer? Did he not know the blessedness of silently lifting up his soul to God in the midst of the most pressing business? Did not the Father dwell in him? And did he not in the depth of his heart enjoy unbroken communion with his Father? Yes, that hidden life was indeed his portion. But that life, as subject to the law of humanity, had need of continual refreshing and renewing from the fountain. It was a life of dependence; just because it was strong and true, it could not bear the loss of direct and constant communion with the Father, with whom and in whom it had its being and its blessedness.

What a lesson for every Christian! Many dealings with men are dissipating, and dangerous to our spiritual life: they bring us under the influence of the visible and temporal. Nothing can atone for the loss of secret and direct communion with God. Even work in the service of God and of love is exhausting: we cannot bless others without power going out from us; this must be renewed from above. The law of the manna, that what is heavenly cannot remain good long on earth, but must day by day be renewed afresh from heaven, still holds good. Jesus Christ teaches it us: Every day I need time to have communion with my Father in secret. My life is like his, a life hid in heaven, in God; it needs time day by day to be fed from heaven. It is *from heaven* alone that the power to lead *a heavenly life* on earth can come.

And what may have been the prayers that occupied our Lord there so long? If I could hear him pray, how I might learn how I, too, must pray! God be praised, of his prayers we have more than one recorded, that in them too we might learn to follow his holy example. In the deep high-priestly prayer (John 17) we hear him speak, as in the deep calm of heaven, to his Father; in his Gethsemane prayer, a few hours later, we see him call out of the depths of trouble and darkness unto God. In these two prayers we have all: the highest and the deepest that there is to be found in the communion of prayer between Father and Son.

In both these prayers we see how he addresses God. Each time it is *Father! O my Father!* In that word lies the secret of all prayer. The Lord knew that he was a Son, and that the Father loved him: with that word he placed himself in the full light of the Father's countenance. This was to him the greatest need and greatest blessing of prayer, to enter into the full enjoyment of the Father's love. Let it be thus with me too. Let the principal part of my prayer be the holy silence and adoration of faith in which I wait upon God until he reveals himself to me, and gives me, through his Spirit, the loving assurance that he looks down on me as Father, that I am well-pleasing to him. He who in prayer has not time in quietness of soul, and in full consciousness of its meaning, to say 'Abba, Father,' has missed the best part of prayer. It is in prayer that the witness of the Spirit, that we are children of God, and that the Father draws night and delights in us, must be exercised and strengthened. 'If our heart condemn us not, we have confidence towards God; and whatsoever we ask, we receive of him, because we obey his commandments, and do the things that are pleasing in his sight.'

In both these prayers I also see what he desired: *that the Father may be glorified*. He speaks: 'I have glorified thee; glorify thy Son, that thy Son *also may glorify thee*.' That will assuredly have been the spirit of every prayer; the entire surrender of himself to live only for the Father's will and glory. All that he asked had but one object, 'That God might be glorified.' In this, too, he is my example. I must seek to have the spirit of each prayer I offer: Father bless thy child, and glorify thy grace in me, only that thy child may glorify thee. Everything in the universe must show forth God's glory. The Christian who is inspired with this thought, and avails himself of prayer to express it, until he is thoroughly imbued with it, will have power in prayer. Even of his work in heaven our Lord says: 'Whatsoever ye shall ask in my name, that will I do, *that the Father may be glorified in the Son*.' O my soul, learn from thy Saviour, ere ever thou pourest out thy desires in prayer, first to yield thyself as a whole burnt-offering with the one object that God may be glorified in thee.

Then thou hast sure ground on which to pray. Thou wilt feel the strong desire, as well as the full liberty, to ask the Father that in each part of Christ's example, in each feature of Christ's image, thou mayest be made like him, that so God may be glorified; Thou wilt understand how that only in continually renewed prayer can the soul surrender itself to wait that God may from heaven work in it what will be to his glory. Because Jesus surrendered himself so entirely to the glory of his Father, he was worthy to be our Mediator, and could in his high-priestly prayer ask such great blessings for his people. Learn like Jesus to seek only God's glory in prayer, and thou shalt become a true intercessor, who can approach the throne of grace not only with his own needs, but also can pray for others the effectual fervent prayer of a righteous man that availeth much. The words which the Saviour himself put into our mouths in the Lord's Prayer: 'Thy will be done,' because he was made like unto his brethren in all things, he took from our lips again and made his own in Gethsemane, that from him we might receive them back again in the power of his atonement and inter- cession, and so be able to pray them even as he had done. Thou, too, shalt become Christlike in that priestly intercession on which the unity and prosperity of the Church and the salvation of sinners so much depend.

And he who in every prayer makes God's glory the chief object will also, if God calls him to it, have strength for the prayer of Gethsemane. Every prayer of Christ was intercession, because he had given himself for us; all he asked and received was in our interest; every prayer he prayed was in the spirit of self-sacrifice. Give thyself, too, wholly to God for man, and as with Jesus so with us, the entire sacrifice of ourselves to God in every prayer of daily life is the only preparation for those single hours of soul-struggle in which we may be called to some special act of the surrender of the will that costs us tears and anguish. But he who has learned the former will surely receive strength for the latter.

O my brother, if thou and I would be like Jesus we must espe- cially contemplate Jesus praying alone in the wilderness. *There is the secret of his wonderful life.* What he did and spoke to man *was first spoken and lived through with the Father.* In communion with him, the anointing with the Holy Spirit was each day renewed. He who would be like him in his walk and conversation must simply begin here, that he follow Jesus into solitude. Even though it cost the sacrifice of night rest, of business, of intercourse with friends, *the time must be found to be alone with the Father.* Besides the ordinary hour of prayer, he will feel at times irresistibly drawn to enter into the holy place, and not to come thence until it has been revealed anew to him that God is his portion. In his secret chamber, with closed door, or in the solitude of the wilderness, God must be found every day, and our fellowship with him renewed. If Christ needed it, how much more we! What it was to him it will be for us.

[From *Like Christ*]

The Spirit of Supplication

And I will pour upon the house of David . . .
the spirit of grace and of supplications.
(ZECHARIAH 12:10)

Likewise the Spirit also helpeth our infirmities: for
we know not what we should pray for as we ought:
but the Spirit itself maketh intercession for us with
groanings which cannot be uttered. And he that
searcheth the hearts knoweth what is the mind of the
Spirit, because he maketh intercession for the saints
according to God. (ROMANS 8:26-27)

Praying always with all prayer and supplication in
the Spirit, and watching thereunto with all
perseverance and supplication for all the saints.
(EPHESIANS 6:18)

The Holy Spirit has been given to every child of God to be his life. He dwells in him, not as a separate Being in one part of his nature, but as his very life. He is the divine power or energy by which his life is maintained and strengthened. All that a believer is called to be or to do, the Holy Spirit can and will work in him. If he does not know or yield to the Holy Guest, the Blessed Spirit cannot work, and his life is a sickly one, full of failure and of sin. As he yields, and waits, and obeys the leading of the Spirit, God works in him all that is pleasing in his sight.

This Holy Spirit is, in the first place, a Spirit of prayer. He was promised as a 'Spirit of grace and supplications', the grace for supplication. He was sent forth into our hearts as 'the Spirit of adoption, whereby we cry, Abba, Father' (Romans 8:15). He enables us to say, in true faith and growing apprehension of its meaning, Our Father which art in heaven. 'He maketh intercession for the saints according to God' (Romans 8:27). And as we pray in the Spirit, our worship is as God seeks it to be, 'in spirit and in truth' (John 4:24). Prayer is just the breathing of the Spirit in us; power in prayer comes from the power of the Spirit in us, waited on and trusted in. Failure in prayer comes from feebleness of the Spirit's work in us. Our prayer is the index of the measure of the Spirit's work in us. To pray aright, the life of the Spirit must be right in us. For praying the effectual, much-availing prayer of the righteous man everything depends on being full of the Spirit.

1. Believe that the Spirit dwells in you (see Ephesians 1:13)

Deep in the inmost recesses of his being, hidden and unfelt, every child of God has the Holy, Mighty Spirit of God dwelling in him. He knows it by faith, the faith that, accepting God's word, realizes that of which he sees as yet no sign. 'We . . . receive the promise of the Spirit by faith' (Galatians 3:14). As long as we measure our power for praying aright and perseveringly by what we feel, or think we can accomplish, we shall be discouraged when we hear of how much we ought to pray. But when we quietly believe that, in the midst of all our conscious weakness, the Holy Spirit as a Spirit of supplication is dwelling within us, *for the very purpose of enabling us to pray in such manner and measure as God would have us*, our hearts will be filled with hope. We shall be strengthened in the assurance which lies at the very root of a happy and fruitful Christian life, that *God has made an abundant provision for our being what he wants us to be*. We shall begin to lose our sense of burden and fear and discouragement about our ever praying sufficiently, because we see that the Holy Spirit himself will pray, is praying, in us.

2. Beware above everything of grieving the Holy Spirit (see Ephesians 4:30)

If you do, how can he work in you the quiet, trustful, and blessed sense of that union with Christ which makes your prayers well pleasing to the Father? Beware of grieving him by sin, by unbelief, by selfishness, by unfaithfulness to his voice in conscience. Do not think grieving him a necessity: that cuts away the very sinews of your strength. Do not consider it impossible to obey the command, 'Grieve not the holy Spirit' (Ephesians 4:30). He himself is the very power of God to make you obedient. The sin that comes up in you against your will, the tendency to sloth, or pride, or self-will, or passion that rises in the flesh, your will can, in the power of the Spirit, at once reject, and cast upon Christ and his blood, and your communion with God is immediately restored. Accept each day the Holy Spirit as your leader and life and strength; you can count upon him to do in your heart all that ought to be done there. He, the unseen and unfelt one, but known by faith, gives there, unseen and unfelt, the love and the faith and the power of obedience you need, because he reveals Christ unseen within you, as actually your life and strength. Grieve not the Holy Spirit by distrusting him, because you do not feel his presence in you.

Especially in the matter of prayer grieve him not. Do not expect, when you trust Christ to bring you into a new, healthy prayer-life, that you will be able all at once to pray as easily and powerfully and joyfully as you fain would. No; it may not come at once. But just bow quietly before God in your ignorance and weakness. That is the best and truest prayer, to put yourself before God just as you are, and to count on the hidden Spirit praying in you. 'We know now what we should pray for as we ought' (Romans 8:26); ignorance, difficulty, struggle, marks our prayer all along. But, 'the Spirit . . . helpeth our infirmities'. How? 'The Spirit itself,' deeper down than our thoughts or feelings, 'maketh intercession for us with groanings which cannot be uttered' (Romans 8:26). When you cannot find words, when your words appear cold and feeble, just believe: The Holy Spirit is praying in me. Be quiet before God, and give him time and opportunity; in due season you will learn to pray. Beware of grieving the Spirit of prayer, by not honouring him in patient, trustful surrender to his intercession in you . . .

3. Praying . . . in the Spirit . . . for all saints (Ephesians 6:18)
The Spirit, who is called 'the Spirit of supplication' (Zechariah 12:10), is also and very specially the Spirit of intercession. It is said of him, 'the Spirit itself maketh intercession for us with groanings which cannot be uttered' (Romans 8:26). 'Praying always . . . for all the saints' (Ephesians 6:18). It is the same word as is used of Christ, who 'ever liveth to make intercession for us' (Hebrews 7:25). The thought is essentially that of mediation — one pleading for another. When the Spirit of intercession takes full possession of us, all selfishness, as if we wanted him separate from his intercession from others, and have him for ourselves alone, is banished, and we begin to avail ourselves of our wonderful privilege to plead for others. We long to live the Christ-life of self-consuming sacrifice for others, as our heart unceasingly yields itself to God to obtain his blessing for those around us. Intercession then becomes, not an incident or an occasional part of our prayers, but their one great object. Prayer for ouselves then takes its true place, simply as a means for fitting us better for exercising our ministry of intercession more effectually.

May I be allowed to speak a very personal word to each of my readers? I have humbly besought God to give me what I may give them — divine light and help truly to forsake the life of failure in prayer, and to enter, even now, and at once, upon the life of intercession which the Holy Spirit can enable them to lead. It can be done by a simple act of faith, claiming the fullness of the Spirit, that is, the full measure of the Spirit which you are capable in God's sight of receiving, and he is therefore willing to bestow. Will you not, even now, accept of this by faith?

Let me remind you of what takes place at conversion. Most of us, you probably too, for a time sought peace in efforts and struggles to give up sin and please God. But you did not find it thus. The peace of God's pardon came by faith, trusting God's word concerning Christ and his salvation. You had heard of Christ as the gift of his love, you knew that he was for you too, you had felt the movings and drawings of his grace; but never till in faith in God's word you accepted him as God's gift to you, did you know the peace and joy that he can give. Believing in him and his saving love made all the difference and changed your relation from one who had ever grieved him, to one who loved and served him. And yet, after a time, you have a thousand times wondered you love and serve him so ill.

At the time of your conversion you knew little about the Holy Spirit. Later on you heard of his dwelling in you, and his being the power of God in you for all the Father intends you to be, and yet his indwelling and inworking have been something vague and indefinite, and hardly a source of joy or strength. At conversion you did not yet know your need of him and still less what you might expect of him. But your failures have taught it you. And now you begin to see how you have been grieving him, by not allowing him to work in you all God's pleasure.

All this can be changed. Just as you, after seeking Christ, and praying to him, and trying without success to serve him, found rest in accepting him by faith, just so you may even now yield yourself to the full guidance of the Holy Spirit, and claim and accept him to work in you what God would have. Will you not do it? Just accept him in faith as Christ's gift, to be the Spirit of your whole life, of your prayer-life too, and you can then begin, however feeble you feel, and unable to pray aright, to bow before God in silence, with the assurance that he will teach you to pray.

My dear brother, as you consciously by faith accepted Christ, to pardon, you can consciously now in the like faith accept of Christ who gives the Holy Spirit to do his work in you. Christ redeemed us that we might receive the promise of the Spirit by faith. Kneel down, and simply believe that the Lord Christ, who baptizes with the Holy Spirit, does now, in response to your faith, begin in you the blessed life of a full experience of the power of the indwelling Spirit. Depend most confidently upon him, apart from all feeling or experience, as the Spirit of supplication and intercession to do his work. Renew that act of faith each morning, each time you pray; trust him, against all appearances, to work in you — be sure he is working — and he will give you to know what the joy of the Holy Spirit is as the power of your life.

'I will pour [out] . . . the spirit of supplication' (Zechariah 12:10). Do you not begin to see that the mystery of prayer is the mystery of the divine indwelling? God in heaven gives his Spirit in our hearts to be there the divine power praying in us, and drawing us upward to our God. God is a spirit, and nothing but a like life and Spirit within us can hold communion with him. It was for this man was created, that God might dwell and work in him, and be the life of his life. It was this that Christ came to exhibit in his life, to win back for us in his death, and then to impart to us by coming again from heaven in the Spirit to live in his disciples. It is this, the indwelling of God through the Spirit, that alone can explain and enable us to appropriate the wonderful promises given to prayer. God gives the Spirit as a Spirit of supplication, too, to maintain his divine life within us as a holy life out of which prayer ever rises upward.

Without the Holy Spirit no man can call Jesus Lord, or cry, Abba, Father; no man can worship in spirit and truth, or pray without ceasing. The Holy Spirit is given the believer to be and do in him all that God wants him to be or do. He is given him especially as the Spirit of prayer and supplication. Is it not clear that everything in prayer depends upon our trusting the Holy Spirit to do his work in us; yielding ourselves to his leading, depending only and wholly on him?

We read, 'Stephen [was] a man full of faith and the Holy Ghost.' The two ever go together, in exact proportion to each other. As our faith sees and trusts the Spirit in us to pray, and waits on him, he will do his work; and it is the longing desire, and the earnest supplication, and the definite faith the Father seeks. Do let us know him, and in the faith of Christ who unceasingly gives him, cultivate the assured confidence, we can learn to pray as the Father would have us.

[From *The Ministry of Intercession*]

Personal Prayer Life

Meeting the Holy God

I beseech you, think not little of the grace that you have a holy God who longs to make you holy. Think not little of the voice of God which calls you to give time to him in the stillness of the inner chamber, so that he may cause his holiness to rest on you. Let it be your business every day, in the secrecy of the inner chamber, to meet the Holy God. You will be repaid for the trouble it may cost you. The reward will be sure and rich. You will learn to hate sin, and to regard it as accursed and conquered. The new nature will give you a horror of sin. The living Jesus, the holy God, will, as conqueror, be your power and strength; and you will begin to believe the great promise contained in 1 Thessalonians 5:23-24: 'The very God of peace sanctify you wholly . . Faithful is he that calleth you, who also will do it.'

[From *The Prayer Life*]

How To Be Delivered from Prayerlessness

Brethren, have we not seriously forgotten this truth? From a defective spiritual life nothing better can be expected than a defective prayer life. It is vain for us, with our defective spiritual life, to endeavour to pray more or better. *It is an impossibility*. Nothing less is necessary than that we should experience that he who 'is in Christ Jesus is a new creature: old things have passed away; behold, all things are become new.' This is literally true for the man who understands and experiences what it is to be in Jesus Christ.

Our whole relationship to the Lord Jesus must be a new thing. I must believe in his infinite love, which really longs to have communion with me every moment and to keep me in the enjoyment of his fellowship. I must believe in his divine power, which has conquered sin and will truly keep me from it. I must believe in him who, as the great intercessor, through the Spirit, will inspire each member of his body with joy and power for communion with God in prayer. My prayer life must be brought entirely under the control of Christ and his love. Then, for the first time, will prayer become what it really is, the natural and joyous breathing of the spiritual life, by which the heavenly atmosphere is inhaled and then exhaled in prayer.

[From *The Prayer Life*]

Alone with God

When thou prayest, enter into thine inner chamber,
and having shut thy door, pray to thy Father, which
is in secret. (MATTHEW 6:6)

Man was created for fellowship with God. God made him in his own image and likeness, that he might be fit for this, capable of understanding and enjoying God, entering into his will and delighting in his glory. Because God is the everywhere present and all-pervading one, he could have lived in the enjoyment of an unbroken fellowship amidst whatever work he had to do. Of this fellowship sin robbed us.

Nothing but this fellowship can satisfy the heart of either man or God. It was this Christ came to restore: to bring back to God his lost creature, and bring back man to all he was created for. Fellowship with God is the consummation of all blessedness on earth as in heaven. It comes when the promise so often given becomes a full expression: I will be with thee, I will never leave thee nor forsake thee, and when we can say: thy Father is always with me.

This fellowship with God is meant to be ours all the day, whatever our condition or the circumstances that surround us. But its enjoyment depends upon the reality of the fellowship in the inner chamber. The power of maintaining close and glad fellowship with God all the day will depend entirely upon the intensity with which we seek to secure it in the hour of secret prayer. The one essential thing in the Morning Watch or the Quiet Hour is *fellowship with God*.

It is this our Lord teaches is to be the inner secret of secret prayer: 'Shut thy door, and pray to thy Father which seeth in secret.' The first and chief thing is, see that there in secret you have the Father's presence and attention. Know that he sees and hears you. Of more importance than all your requests, however urgent, of more importance than all your earnestness and effort to pray aright, is this one thing — the childlike, living assurance that *your* Father sees you, that you have now met him, and that with his eye on you and yours on him, you are now enjoying actual fellowship with him.

[From *Prayer's Inner Chamber*]

The God of Our Salvation

My soul waiteth only upon God [marg: is silent unto God]; from him cometh my salvation.
(PSALM 62:1, RV)

If salvation indeed comes from God, and is entirely his work, just as our creation was, it follows, as a matter of course, that our first and highest duty is to wait on him to do that work as pleases him. Waiting becomes then the only way to the experience of full salvation, the only way, truly, to know God as the God of our salvation. All the difficulties that are brought forward as keeping us back from full salvation, have their cause in this one thing: the defective knowledge and practice of waiting upon God. All that the Church and its members need for the manifestation of the mighty power of God in the world, is the return to our true place, the place that belongs to us, both in creation and redemption, the place of absolute and unceasing dependence upon God. Let us strive to see what the elements are that make up this most blessed and needful waiting upon God: it may help us to discover the reasons why this grace is so little cultivated, and to feel how infinitely desirable it is that the Church, that we ourselves, should at any price learn its blessed secret.

The deep need for this waiting on God lies equally in the nature of man and the nature of God. God, as Creator, formed man, to be a vessel in which he could show forth his power and goodness. Man was not to have in himself a fountain of life, or strength, or happiness: the ever-living and only living One was each moment to be the communicator to him of all that he needed. Man's glory and blessedness was not to be independent, or dependent upon himself, but dependent on a God of such infinite riches and love. Man was to have the joy receiving every moment out of the fullness of God. This was his blessedness as an unfallen creature.

When he fell from God, he was still more absolutely dependent on him. There was not the slightest hope of his recovery out of his state of death, but in God, his power and mercy. It is God alone who began the work of redemption; it is God alone who continues and carries it on each moment in each individual believer. Even in the regenerate man there is no power of goodness in himself: he has and can have nothing that he does not each moment receive; and waiting on God is just as indispensable, and must be just as continuous and unbroken, as the breathing that maintains his natural life.

254

It is, then, because Christians do not know their relation to God of absolute poverty and helplessness, that they have no sense of the need of absolute and unceasing dependence, or the unspeakable blessedness of continual waiting on God. But when once a believer begins to see it, and consent to it, that he by the Holy Spirit must each moment receive what God each moment works, waiting on God becomes his highest hope and joy. As he apprehends how God, as God, as infinite love, delights to impart his own nature to his child as fully as he can, how God is not weary of each moment keeping charge of his life and strength, he wonders that he ever thought otherwise of God than as a God to be waited on all the day. God unceasingly giving and working; his child unceasingly waiting and receiving: this is the blessed life.

'Truly my soul waiteth upon God; from him cometh my salvation.' First we wait on God for salvation. Then we learn that salvation is only to bring us to God, and teach us to wait on him. Then we find what is better still, that waiting on God is itself the highest salvation. It is ascribing to him the glory of being All to us. May God teach us the blessedness of waiting on him.

'*My soul, wait thou only upon God*' (Psalm 62:5).

[From *Waiting on God*]

In Everything Give Thanks

In everything give thanks: for this is the will of God
in Christ Jesus concerning you.
(1 THESSALONIANS 5:18)

'In everything give thanks' — that means a life of unceasing joy. The bestowment of a gift makes me glad. Giving thanks is the expression of that gladness to the giver. For what in the gift he has bestowed, for what he has proved himself to be as a friend, my happiness offers him all it has to give, all he desires — the acknowledgement of

255

indebtedness and obligation and grateful love. Every father does his utmost to make his children happy; he loves not only to see them happy, but to see them connect their happiness with himself and his love. It is the will of God that in everything, in every circumstance and condition, the whole life of his child should be one of unceasing praise and thanksgiving. If it be not always so with us, let us set ourselves to learn the lesson: In everything give thanks: for this is the will of God in Jesus Christ concerning you.

In everything give thanks: there is good reason for it. God is not a hard master, who reaps where he has not sown. He never commands joy without giving abundant cause for it. He does not expect thanks where there is nothing to thank for. He would have us remember that, in the most trying circumstances and the deepest sorrow, there is cause for thanksgiving infinitely outweighing any reason for mourning. Whatever we lose, God and his love are still left us. The very loss is meant to make the love more precious: the trial is love seeking to give itself more completely to us. Whatever we lose, there is always the unspeakable gift — God's own Son to be our portion and our friend. Whatever we lose, there is always a peace that passeth understanding, a joy that is unspeakable, a riches of glory that will supply every need, an abounding grace that perfects Christ's strength in our weakness. There are always the exceeding great and precious promises, and the heavenly treasures that cannot pass away. God is educating us through loss and trial, into the full enjoyment of our heavenly heritage and the perfect fitness for his own fellowship. So let us believe that the command is most reasonable, and say that this will of God, in everything give thanks, is ours too.

In everything we give thanks — this is both the mark and the means of a vigorous Christian life. It draws us off from ourselves, and fixes the heart upon God. It lifts us above the world, and makes us more than conquerors through him who loved us. It places our peace, our happiness, our life, beyond the reach of circumstances. So far from rendering us indifferent to the suffering of our fellowmen, it fills us with hope in seeking to relieve them, it teaches us what joy there is in the kindness and love of God, and makes that the keynote of our life. It gives wings to our prayer, our faith, our love, to live the true heavenly life in God's presence and worship. It ennobles in torment every temptation with the hallelujah of victory.

In everything give thanks. God himself will work it in you. This is the will of God in Christ Jesus concerning you. We have seen more than once that the will of God is a loving, almighty power, working out its own purpose with our intelligent consent. We are co-workers with God — that means, not that he does part and we do part, but that he does all in us and we do all through him. It means that he works in us to will and to do, and that we, through faith in his working, in the power that worketh in us, work out his will. Just because it is the will of God, the believing soul is sure that it can be. It is the will of God in Christ. The expression is so frequent that its meaning is passed over. All that God is and does to us, he is and does through our Lord Jesus. The Father does nothing in us but through the Son. The Son does nothing but as the Father does it through him. It means that he works in us to will and to do, and that we, through faith in his working, in the power that worketh in us, work out his will. Just because it is the will of God, the believing soul is sure that it can be. It is the will of God in Christ. The expression is so frequent that its meaning is passed over. All that God is and does to us, he is and does through our Lord Jesus. The Father does nothing in us but through him. Our experience of God's work in us depends upon our abiding in Christ, our drawing and remaining near to God in and through Christ. To a soul seeing its life in Christ alone, the will of God ensures a life of unceasing praise and thanks.

In everything give thanks — it needs a life of entire consecration. Many of God's commands become an unbearable burden, an impossible strain, because we look to the feeble, sickly life to do what only the strength of vigorous health can perform. We cannot take up one part of God's will, and do it when we please. A life of undivided and absolute surrender to all God's will is the condition of being able to perform any part of it effectively. Every command to perform some special part of God's will is a call to enquire whether we have accepted all his will as the law of our life. The soul that has done this, that is learning the lesson of daily guidance for daily duty, and is prepared to meet every new demand, with the question as to its implicit submission to that will, and its unquestioning confidence in the provision of sufficient strength, all settled, has found the secret of obedience to this command too. When God is known as our exceeding joy, when a walk in the light of his countenance all the day is counted equally a privilege and an indispensable necessity, the giving of thanks in everything is not looked upon as a hopeless attainment. Because it is the will of a loving and almighty Father, that will can be done.

In everything give thanks! These are indeed the Christians the world stands in need of. It is the happy Christian — not the happy man who happens also to be a Christian, but — the Christian who proves that happiness is in God, and who lives the life of joy and praise because he lives in God's presence, who will find the joy of the Lord his strength in God's service, and who will be the best witness to what the grace of God can do to give true joy and blessing. It is the will of God in Christ to us. Let us rest content with nothing less.

[From *Thy Will Be Done*]

The Fight Against Prayerlessness

I once received a letter from a minister, well known for his ability and devotion, in which he writes, 'As far as I am concerned, it does not seem to help me to hear too much about the life of prayer, about the strenuous exertion for which we must prepare ourselves, and about all the time and trouble and endless effort it will cost us. These things discourage me — I have so often heard them. I have time after time put them to the test, and the result has always been sadly disappointing. It does not help me to be told: "You must pray more, and hold a closer watch over yourself, and become altogether a more earnest Christian." '

My reply to him was as follows: 'I think in all I spoke at the conference or elsewhere, I have never mentioned exertion or struggle, because I am so entirely convinced that our efforts are futile unless we first learn how to abide in Christ by a simple faith.'

My correspondent said further: 'The message I need is this: "See that your relationship to your living Saviour is what it ought to be. Live in his presence, rejoice in his love, rest in him." ' A better message could not be given, if it is only rightly understood. 'See that your relationship to the living Saviour is what it ought to be.' But this is just what will certainly make it possible for one to live the life of prayer.

We must not comfort ourselves with the thought of standing in a right relationship to the Lord Jesus while the sin of prayerlessness has power over us, and while we, along with the whole Church, have to complain about our feeble life which makes us unfit to pray for ourselves, for the Church, or for missions, as we ought. But if we recognize, in the first place, that a right relationship to the Lord Jesus, above all else, includes prayer, with both the desire and power to pray according to God's will, then we have something which gives us the right to rejoice in him and to rest in him.

I have related this incident to point out how naturally discouragement will be the result of self-effort and will so shut out all hope of improvement or victory. And this indeed is the condition of many Christians when called on to persevere in prayer as intercessors. They feel it is certainly something entirely beyond their reach — they have not the power for the self-sacrifice and consecration necessary for such prayer; they shrink from the effort and struggle which will, as they suppose, make them unhappy. They have tried in the power of the flesh to conquer the flesh — a wholly impossible thing. They have endeavoured by Beelzebub to cast out Beelzebub — and this can never happen. It is Jesus alone who can subdue the flesh and the devil.

We have spoken of a struggle which will certainly result in disappointment and discouragement. This is the effort made in our own strength. But there is another struggle which will certainly lead to victory. The Scripture speaks of 'the good fight of faith', that is to say, a fight which springs from and is carried on by faith. We must get right conceptions about faith and stand fast in our faith. Jesus Christ is ever the author and the finisher of faith. It is when we come into right relationship with him that we can be sure of the help and power he bestows. Just, then, as earnestly as we must, in the first place, say: 'Do not strive in your own strength; cast yourself at the feet of the Lord Jesus, and wait upon him in the sure confidence that he is with you, and works in you'; so do we, in the second place, say: 'Strive in prayer; let faith fill your heart — so will you be strong in the Lord, and in the power of his might.'

An illustration will help us to understand this. A devoted Christian woman who conducted a large Bible class with zeal and success once came in trouble to her minister. In her earlier years she had enjoyed much blessing in the inner chamber, in fellowship with the Lord and his word. But this had gradually been lost and, do what she would, she could not get right. The Lord had blessed her work, but the joy had gone out of her life. The minister asked what she had done to regain the lost blessedness, 'I have done everything,' said she, 'that I can think of, but all in vain.'

He then questioned her about her experience in connection with her conversion. She gave an immediate and clear answer: 'At first I spared no pains in my attempt to become better, and to free myself from sin, but it was all useless. At last I began to understand that I must lay aside all my efforts, and simply trust the Lord Jesus to bestow on me his life and peace, and he did it.'

'Why then,' said the minister, 'do you not try this again? As you go to your inner chamber, however cold and dark your heart may be, do not try in your own might to force yourself into the right attitude. Bow before him, and tell him that he sees in what a sad state you are that your only hope is in him. Trust him with a childlike trust to have mercy upon you, and wait upon him. In such a trust you are in a right relationship to him. You have nothing — he has everything.' Some time later she told the minister that his advice had helped her; she had learned that faith in the love of the Lord Jesus is the only method of getting into fellowship with God in prayer.

Do you not begin to see, my reader, that there are two kinds of warfare — the first when we seek to conquer prayerlessness in our own strength. In that case, my advice to you is: 'Give over your restlessness and effort; fall helpless at the feet of the Lord Jesus; he will speak the word, and your soul will live.' If you have done this, then, second, comes the message: 'This is but the beginning of everything. It will require deep earnestness, and the exercise of all your power, and a watchfulness of the entire heart — eager to detect the least backsliding. Above all, it will require a surrender to a life of self-sacrifice that God really desires to see in us and that he will work out for us.'

[From *The Prayer Life*]

So Will You Have Power in Prayer

If ye abide in me, and my words abide in you, ye shall
ask what ye will, and it shall be done unto you.
(JOHN 15:7)

Prayer is both one of the means and one of the fruits of union to Christ. As a means it is of unspeakable importance. All the things of faith, all the pleadings of desire, all the yearning after a fuller surrender, all the confessions of shortcoming and of sin, all the exercises in which the soul gives up self and clings to Christ, find their utterance in prayer. In each meditation on abiding in Christ, as some new feature of what Scripture teaches concerning this blessed life is apprehended, the first impulse of the believer is at once to look up to the Father and pour out the heart into his, and ask

261

from him the full understanding and the full possession of what he has been shown in the Word. And it is the believer, who is not content with this spontaneous expression of hope, but who takes time in secret prayer to wait until he was received and laid hold of what he has seen, who will really grow strong in Christ. However feeble the soul's first abiding, its prayer will be heard, and it will find prayer one of the great means of abiding more abundantly.

But it is not so much as a means, but as a fruit of the abiding, that the Saviour mentions it in the parable of the Vine. He does not think so much of prayer — as we, alas, too exclusively do! — as a means of getting blessing for ourselves, but as one of the chief channels of influence by which, through us as fellow-workers with God, the blessings of Christ's redemption are to be dispensed to the world. He sets before himself and us the glory of the Father, in the extension of his kingdom, as the object for which we have been made branches; and he assures us that if we but abide in him, we shall be Israels, having power with God and man. Ours shall be the effectual, fervent prayer of the righteous man, availing much, like Elijah's for ungodly Israel. Such prayer will be the fruit of our abiding in him, and the means of bringing forth much fruit.

To the Christian who is not abiding wholly in Jesus, the difficulties connected with prayer are often so great as to rob him of the comfort and the strength it could bring. Under the guise of humility, he asks how one so unworthy could expect to have influence with the Holy One. He thinks of God's sovereignty, his perfect wisdom and love, and cannot see how his prayer can really have any distinct effect. He prays, but it is more because he cannot rest without prayer than from a loving faith that the prayer will be heard. But what a blessed release from such questions and perplexitites is given to the soul who is truly abiding in Christ! He realizes increasingly how it is in the real spiritual unity with Christ that we are accepted and heard. The union with the Son of God is a life union: we are in very deed one with him — our prayer ascends as his prayer. It is because we abide in him that we can ask what we will, and it is given to us.

There are many reasons why this must be so. One is that abiding in Christ, and having his words abiding in us, teach us to pray *in accordance with the will of God*. With the abiding in Christ our self-will is kept down, the thoughts and wishes of our nature are brought into captivity to the thoughts and wishes of Christ; like-mindedness to Christ grows upon us — all our working and willing become transformed into harmony with his. There is deep and oft-renewed heart-searching to see whether the surrender has indeed been entire; fervent prayer to the heart-searching Spirit that nothing may be kept back. Everything is yielded to the power of his life in us, that it may exercise its sanctifying influence even on ordinary wishes and desires. His Holy Spirit breathes through our whole being; and without our being conscious how, our desires, as the breathings of the divine life, are in conformity with the divine will, and are fulfilled. Abiding in Christ renews and sanctifies the will: we ask *what we will,* and it is given to us.

In close connection with this is the thought that abiding in Christ teaches the believer in prayer *only to seek the glory of God*. In promising to answer prayer, Christ's one thought (see John 14:13) is this, '*that the Father may be glorified in the Son*'. In his intercession on earth (John 17), this was his one desire and plea; in his intercession in heaven, it is still his great object. As the believer abides in Christ, the Saviour breathes this desire into him. The thought, *Only the glory of God,* becomes more and more the keynote of the life hid in Christ. At first this subdues, and quiets, and makes the soul almost afraid to dare to entertain a wish, lest it should not be to the Father's glory. But when once its supremecy has been accepted, and everything yielded to it, it comes with mighty power to elevate and enlarge the heart, and open it to the vast field open to the glory of God. Abiding in Christ, the soul learns not only to desire, but spiritually to discern what will be for God's glory; and one of the first conditions of acceptable prayer is fulfilled in it when, as the fruit of its union with Christ, the whole mind is brought into harmony with that of the Son as he said: 'Father, glorify thy name.'

Once more: Abiding in Christ, we can fully avail ourselves *of the name of the Christ*. Asking in the name of another means that that other authorized me and sent me to ask, and wants to be considered as asking himself: he wants the favour done to him. Believers often try to think of the name of Jesus and his merits, and to argue themselves into the faith that they will be heard, while they painfully feel how little they have of the faith of his name. They are not living wholly in Jesus' name; it is only when they begin to pray that they want to talke up that name and use it. This cannot be. The promise '*Whatsoever ye ask in my name*' may not be severed from the command, 'Whatsoever ye do, *do all in the name* of the Lord Jesus.' If the name of Christ is to be wholly at my disposal, so that I may have the full command of it for all I will, it must be because I first put myself wholly at his disposal, so that he has free and full command of me. It is the abiding in Christ that gives the right and power to use his name with confidence. To Christ the Father refuses nothing. Abiding in Christ, I come to the Father as one with him. His righteousness is in me, his Spirit is in me; the Father sees the Son in me, and gives me my petition. It is not — as so many think — by a sort of imputation that the Father looks upon us as if we were in Christ, though we are not in him. No; the Father wants to see us living in him: thus shall our prayer really have power to prevail. Abiding in Christ not only renews the will to pray aright, but secures the full power of his merits to us.

Again: Abiding in Christ also works in us *the faith that alone can obtain an answer*. 'According to your faith be it unto you': this is one of the laws of the kingdom. 'Believe that ye receive, and ye shall have.' This faith rests upon, and is rooted in the Word, but is something infinitely higher than the mere logical conclusion: God has promised, I shall obtain. No; faith, as a spiritual act, depends upon the words abiding in us as living powers, and so upon the state of the whole inner life. Without fasting and prayer (Mark 9:29), without humility and a spiritual mind (John 5:44), without a wholehearted obedience (1 John 3:22), there cannot be this living faith. But as the soul abides in Christ, and grows into the consciousness of its union with him, and sees how entirely it is he who makes it and its petition acceptable, it dares to claim an answer because it knows itself one with him. It was by faith it learnt to abide in him; as the fruit of that faith, it rises to a larger faith in all that God has promised to be and to do. It learns to breathe its prayers in the deep, quiet, confident assurance: We know we have the petition we ask of him.

Abiding in Christ, further, keeps us in the place where *the answer can be bestowed*. Some believers pray earnestly for blessing; but when God comes and looks for them to bless them, they are not to be found. They never thought that the blessing must not only be asked, but waited for, and received in prayer. Abiding in Christ is the place for receiving answers. Out of him the answer would be dangerous — we should consume it on our lusts (James 4:3). Many of the richest answers — say for spiritual grace, or for power to work and to bless — can only come in the shape of a larger experience of what God makes Christ to us. The fullness is *in him*; abiding in him is the condition of power in prayer, because the answer is treasured up and bestowed in him.

Believer, abide in Christ, for there is the school of prayer — mighty, effectual, answer-bringing prayer. Abide in him, and you shall learn what to so many is a mystery: *That the secret of the prayer of faith is the life of faith* — the life that abides in Christ alone.

[From *Abide in Christ*]

True Humility

Humility

Humility is the root virtue of the Christian life. The law is absolute in God's kingdom — 'He that humbleth himself shall be exalted.' Our disappointment in striving after higher degrees of grace, faith, spiritual knowledge, love to souls and power to bless, is all owing to this. We have not accepted the humility of Christ as the beginning and the perfection of his salvation. 'God giveth grace to the humble' has a far wider and deeper application than we think.

Docility is one form of humility. In the morning watch we place ourselves as learners in Christ's school; let docility, let humility be the distinguishing mark of the learner, and, if we feel how little we have of it, let us listen to the voice that says 'Take my yoke upon you, and you learn of me; for I am meek and lowly of heart: and ye shall find rest unto your souls.'

[From *Prayer's Inner Chamber*]

The Root of Every Virtue

Humility, the place of entire dependence of God, is, from the very nature of things, the first duty and the highest virtue of the creature, and the root of every virtue . . .

Humility is the only soil in which the graces root; the lack of humility is the sufficient explanation of every defect and failure. Humility is not so much a grace or virtue along with others; it is the root of all, because it alone takes the right attitude before God, and allows him as God to do all . . .

In the life of earnest Christians, of those who pursue and profess holiness, humility ought to be the chief mark of their uprightness.

[From *Humility: the Beauty of Holiness*]

Humility in the Life of Jesus

I am among you as he that serveth. (LUKE 22:27)

Listen to the words in which our Lord speaks of his relation to the Father, and see how unceasingly he uses the words *not*, and *nothing*, of himself. The *not I*, in which Paul expresses his relation to Christ, is the very spirit of what Christ says of his relation to the Father.

'The Son can do *nothing* of himself' (John 5:19)

'I can of mine own self do *nothing*; my judgement is just; because I seek *not* mine own will' (John 5:30),

'I receive *not* honour from men' (John 5:41).

'I am come . . . *not* to do mine own will' (John 6:38).

'My doctrine is *not* mine' (John 7:16).

'I am *not* come of myself' (John 7:28).

'I do *nothing* of myself' (John 8:28).

'I . . . came from God; *neither* came I of myself, but he sent me' (John 8:42).

'I seek *not* mine own glory' (John 8:50).

'The words that I speak . . . I speak *not* from myself' (John 14:10).

'The word which ye hear is *not* mine' (John 14:24)

267

These words open to us the deepest roots of Christ's life and work. They tell us how it was that the Almighty God was able to work his mighty redemption work through him. They show what Christ counted the state of heart which became him as the Son of the Father. They teach us what the essential nature and life is of that redemption which Christ accomplished and now communicates. It is this: he was nothing, that God might be all. He resigned himself with his will and his powers entirely for the Father to work in him. Of his own power, his own will, and his own glory, of his whole mission with all his works and his teaching — of all this he said, It is not I; I am nothing; the Father is all.

This life of entire self-abnegation, of absolute submission and dependence upon the Father's will, Christ found to be one of perfect peace and joy. He lost nothing by giving all to God. God honoured his trust, and did all for him, and then exalted him to his own right hand in glory. And because Christ had thus humbled himself before God, and God was ever before him, he found it possible to humble himself before men too, and to be the servant of all. His humility was simply the surrender of himself to God, to allow him to do in him what he pleased, whatever men around might say of him, or do to him . . .

Humility was not only a temporary sentiment, wakened up and brought into exercise when he thought of God, but the very spirit of his whole life, that Jesus was just as humble in his communion with men as with God. He felt himself the servant of God for the men whom God made and loved; as a natural consequence, he counted himself the servant of men, that through him God might do his work of love. He never for a moment thought of seeking his honour, or asserting his power to vindicate himself. His whole spirit was that of a life yielded to God to work in. It is not until Christians study the humility of Jesus as the very essence of his redemption, as the very blessedness of the life of the Son of God, as the only true relation to the Father, and therefore as that which Jesus must give us if we are to have any part with him, that the terrible lack of actual, heavenly, manifest humility will become a burden and a sorrow, and our ordinary religion be set aside to secure this, the first and the chief of the marks of the Christ within us.

[From *Humility: the Beauty of Holiness*]

Humility in the Teaching of Jesus

Learn of me; for I am meek and lowly in heart.
(MATTHEW 11:29)

And whosoever will be chief among you, let him be your servant: Even as the Son of man came . . . to minister. (MATTHEW 20:27-28)

Let us listen to Jesus' teaching, where we shall hear how he speaks about humility, and how far he expects people, and specially his disciples, to be humble as he was.

1. Look at the commencement of his ministry. In the Beatitudes with which the Sermon on the Mount opens, he speaks: 'Blessed are the poor in spirit: for theirs is the kingdom of heaven . . . Blessed are the meek: for they shall inherit the earth' (Matthew 5:3, 5). The very first words of his proclamation of the kingdom of heaven reveal the open gate through which alone we enter. The poor, who have nothing in themselves, to them the kingdom comes. The meek, who seek nothing in themselves, theirs the earth shall be. The blessings of heaven and earth are for the lowly. For the heavenly and the earthly life, humility is the secret of blessing.

2. 'Learn of me, for I am meek and lowly in heart: and ye shall find rest unto your souls' (Matthew 11:29). Jesus offers himself as teacher. He tells us what the spirit both is, which we shall find in him as a teacher, and which we can learn and receive from him. Meekness and lowliness is the one thing he offers us; in it we shall find perfect rest of soul. Humility is to be our salvation.

3. . . . 'Whosoever will be chief among you, let him be your servant: Even as the Son of man came . . . to minister' (Matthew 20:27-28). Humility, as it is the mark of Christ the heavenly, will be the one standard of glory in heaven: the lowliest is the nearest to God. The primacy in the Church is promised to the humblest.

4. Speaking to the multitude and the disciples, of the Pharisees and their love of the chief seats, Christ said once again, 'He that is greatest among you shall be your servant' (Matthew 23:11). Humiliation is the only ladder to honour in God's kingdom.

5. After the parable of the Pharisee and the Publican, Christ spake again, 'Every one that exalteth himself shall be abased; and he that humbleth himself shall be exalted' (Luke 18:14). In the temple and presence and worship of God, everything is worthless that is not pervaded by deep, true humility towards God and men . . .

6. After washing the disciples' feet, Jesus said, 'If I then, your Lord and Master, have washed your feet; ye also ought to wash one another's feet' (John 13:14). The authority of command, and example, every thought, either of obedience or conformity, make humility the first and most essential element of discipleship.

7. At the Holy Supper table, the disciples still disputed who should be greatest. Jesus said, 'he that is greatest among you, let him be the younger; and he that is chief, as he that doth serve . . . I am among you as he that serveth' (Luke 22:26-27). The path in which Jesus walked, and which he opened up for us, the power and spirit in which he wrought out salvation, and to which he saves us, is ever the humility that makes me the servant of all.

[From *Humility: the Beauty of Holiness*]

Quietly

It is good that a man should both hope and quietly
wait for the salvation of the Lord.
(LAMENTATIONS 3:26)

'Take heed, and be quiet; fear not, neither be fainthearted' (Isaiah 7:4). 'In quietness and in confidence shall be your strength' (Isaiah 30:15). Such words reveal to us the close connection between quietness and faith, and show us what a deep need there is of quietness, as an element of true waiting upon God. If we are to have our whole heart turned towards God, we must have it turned away from the creature, from all that occupies and interests, whether of joy or sorrow.

God is a being of such infinite greatness and glory, and our nature has become so estranged from him, that it needs our whole heart and desires set upon him if we are even in some little measure to know and receive him. Everything that is not God, that excites our fears, or stirs our efforts, or awakens our hopes, or makes us glad hinders us in our perfect waiting on him. The message is one of deep meaning: 'Take heed and be quiet'; 'In quietness shall be your strength'; 'It is good that a man should quietly wait.'

That the very thought of God in his majesty and holiness should silence us, Scripture abundantly testifies.

'The Lord is in his holy temple: let all the earth keep silence before him' (Habakkuk 2:20).

'Hold thy peace at the presence of the Lord God' (Zephaniah 1:7).

'Be silent, O all flesh, before the Lord: for he is raised up out of his holy habitation' (Zechariah 2:13).

As long as the waiting on God is chiefly regarded as an end towards more effectual prayer and the obtaining of our petitions, this spirit of perfect quietness will not be obtained. But when it is seen that the waiting on God is itself an unspeakable blessedness, one of the highest forms of fellowship with the Holy One, the adoration of him in his glory will of necessity humble the soul into a holy stillness, making way for God to speak and reveal himself. Then it comes to the fulfilment of the precious promise, that all of self and self-effort shall be humbled: 'The haughtiness of men shall be made low, and the Lord alone shall be exalted in that day' (Isaiah 2:17).

Let everyone who would learn the art of waiting on God

remember the lesson: 'Take heed, and be quiet'; 'It is good that a man quietly wait.' Take time to separate from all friends and all duties, all cares and all joys; time to be still and quiet before God. Take time not only to secure stillness from man and the world, but from self and its energy. Let the word and prayer be very precious; but remember, even these may hinder the quiet waiting. The activity of the mind in studying the word, or giving expression to its thoughts in prayer, the activities of the heart, with its desires and hopes and fears, may so engage us that we do not come to the still waiting on the All-Glorious One; our whole being prostrate in silence before him. Though at first it may appear difficult to know how thus quietly to wait, with the activities of mind and heart for a time subdued, every effort after it will be rewarded; we shall find that it grows upon us, and the little season of silent worship will bring a peace and a rest that give a blessing not only in prayer, but all the day.

'*It is good* that a man should quietly wait for the salvation of the Lord.' Yes, it is good. The quietness is the confession of our impotence. That with all our willing and running, with all our thinking and praying, it will not be done: we must receive it from God. It is the confession of our trust that our God will in his time come to our help — the quiet resting in him alone. It is the confession of our desire to sink into our nothingness, and to let him work and reveal himself. Do let us wait quietly. In daily life let there be in the soul that is waiting for the great God to do his wondrous work a quiet reverence, an abiding watching against too deep engrossment with the world, and the whole character will come to bear the beautiful stamp: quietly waiting for the salvation of God.

[From *Waiting on God*]

'All Lowliness and Meekness'

*I beseech you to walk worthily of the calling
wherewith ye were called, with all lowliness and
meekness, forbearing one another in love, giving
diligence to keep the unity of the Spirit in the bond of
peace.* (EPHESIANS 4:1-3)

Here are the very roots of the Christian life: 'Walk worthy of your high calling, with *all lowliness and meekness*, giving diligence to keep the unity of the Spirit in the bond of peace.' The great mark of the high calling is a Christ-like humility. The first mark of true devotion, a life wholly devoted and given up to God, is this, 'Walk with *all lowliness and meekness*.'

The one mark that you are truly a partaker of God's grace will be *a deep and never-ceasing* humility, as the proof that God has come to you and revealed himself, and brought everything like self and its pride down into the very dust.

And if you would enter still more deeply into the meaning of the words, just think that this lowliness and meekness do not comprise your disposition and attitude only towards God, but specially towards man. 'In all *lowliness and meekness*, with long-suffering, forbearing one another in love.' You can have no surer proof that God's spiritual blessings in Christ Jesus have reached and mastered a man than his *lowliness and meekness* in his dealings with his fellow men. The exceeding greatness of God's power in us who believe, raising us out of the death to self and sin with Christ Jesus to the throne, 'seated with him in the heavenly places', makes us like Christ, willing to wear the servant's garb and do the servant's work. What is impossible with men is possible with God.

How surely this is the true Christlike disposition we see from Paul's words to the Philippians: 'Do nothing through vain glory but in *lowliness of mind*, each counting the other better than himself.' As the Master himself, the meek and lowly Lamb of God, had spoken, 'Learn of me, for I am meek and lowly of heart,' so Paul enforces

273

what he has written, by adding, 'Have this mind in you which was also in Christ Jesus,' who emptied himself, taking the form of a servant, becoming obedient even unto death, yea, the death of the cross. The self-emptying in the heavenly glory, the form of a servant during all his earthly life, and then the humbling of himself to the death of the cross — such was the mind of Christ. It is in this that our salvation is rooted; it is in the participation in this that salvation consists; it is in the spirit and practice of a life like this — with all lowliness and meekness, with long-suffering, forbearing one another in love — that Christ will be magnified and our hearts sanctified, and the true witness be given that we have been with Jesus.

And it is thus alone that we give diligence to keep the 'unity of the Spirit in the bond of peace'. It is not what we know, or think, or speak of the beauty of love, and the unity of the body, and the power of the Holy Spirit, that proves the true Christian life. It is in the meekness and lowliness of Christ, in daily dealings with our fellow Christians, even when they tempt and try us, that we are to show that we will sacrifice anything to maintain the unity of the Spirit and the bond of love unbroken. It is he that is servant of all to whom Jesus gives the name of chief. It may not be easy; but Christ came from heaven to bring humility back to this earth, and to work it out in our hearts.

Let us ask whether, in the teaching and preaching of the Church, this lowliness and meekness of Christ has the place it holds in the Will and the Word of God. Whether in the fellowship of Christians, as far as we know them, there is the endeavour to maintain this standard of Christian living, and to keep the unity of the Spirit from being disturbed by aught of pride or self. And whether in our own life, and our search after the deepening of the spiritual life, this meekness and lowliness, so pleasing to God, so glorious as seen in Christ Jesus, so beautiful as a grace in a believer, is in very deed our heart's desire and our confident hope. Oh, let it be in every act of devotion the first thing we ask of God, a heart humbled and brought low by his infinite love, and yielded to his Holy Spirit to work out in us, and in his Body around us, the blessed likeness of Jesus our

Lord. By the Spirit's aid it can become the undertone and the habit of a life devoted to God.

[From *Aids to Devotion*]

Humility, the Glory of the Creature

They shall cast their crowns before the throne, saying, 'Worthy art thou, our Lord and our God, to receive the glory and the honour and the power: for thou didst create all things, and because of thy will they were, and were created. (REVELATION 4:11)

When God created the universe it was with the one object of making his creations partakers of his perfection and blessedness, and of displaying in them the glory of love and wisdom and power. God wished to reveal himself in and through created beings by communicating to them as much of his own goodness and glory as they were capable of receiving. But this was not a giving to the creature of something which it could possess by itself, a certain life or goodness of which it had charge and control. By no means. Because God is the ever-living, ever-active One, who upholds all things by the word of his power and in whom all things exist, the relation of the creature to God could only be one of unceasing, absolute, universal dependence. Just as God by his power once created, so by that same power God must at every moment maintain. The life which God bestows is imparted now once for all, but every moment by the constant activity of his mighty power. The creature has not only to look back to the origin and first beginning of existence, and acknowledge that it owes everything to God but it must also now, at every moment, present itself as an empty vessel in which God can dwell and manifest his power and goodness. This attitude of humility, of entire dependence upon God, is from the very nature of things the first duty and the only happiness of the creature. It is its highest virtue — indeed, it is the root of its every virtue.

So it follows that pride, or loss of this humility, is the root of every sin and evil. It was when the now-fallen angels began to look upon themselves with complacency that they were led to disobedience, and so were cast down from the light of heaven into outer darkness. The same thing happened when the serpent breathed the poison of his pride, the desire to be like God, into the hearts of our first parents, so that they too fell from their high estate into all the wretchedness in which man is now sunk. In heaven and earth pride or self-exaltation is the gate and the birth of hell.

So it follows that we can only be redeemed by the restoration of the lost humility, of the original and only true attitude of the creature to its God. And so Jesus came to bring humility back to earth, to make us partakers of it, and through it to save us. He humbled himself in becoming a man. The humility which we see in him first possessed him in heaven; it brought him from there to here, and he brought it. Here on earth 'he humbled himself, becoming obedient even unto death' (Philippians 2:8). His humility gave his death its value, and so became our redemption. And now the salvation which he gives to us is nothing less and nothing other than a sharing of his own life and death, his own character and spirit, his own humility, which is the ground and root of his relation to God and of his redeeming work. Jesus Christ took and filled the place and destiny of the creature, man, by his life of perfect humility. His humility is our salvation; his salvation is our humility.

And so the lives of the saints or saved ones must bear the stamp of deliverance from sin and full restoration to the original state of man: their relation to God and to their fellow men must be marked by an all-pervading humility. Without this they cannot have a lasting, consistent experience of God's presence and favour and of the power of his Spirit. Without humility there can be no abiding faith, love, joy or strength. Humility is the only soil in which the graces take root; a lack of humility is a sure explanation of every defect and failure in the Christian's life. Humility is not a grace or virtue like all the others; rather, it is the foundation for all of them, because it alone ensures a right attitude to God and allows him to do his will.

God has created us as intelligent beings in such a way that the clearer our understanding of the real nature or the absolute need of a command is, the more ready and full will be our obedience to that command. God's call to humility has been so neglected in the Church because the true nature of humility has been too little understood. It is not something which we bring to God or which he bestows upon us. Rather, it is simply the sense of nothingness which comes to us when we truly see that God is all, and which causes us to make way for God to be in all our lives. We then consent to be the vessel in which the life and the glory of God are to work and manifest themselves, and surrender our whole selves — will, mind, body and emotions — to the Lord. Humility is our true nobility as God's creatures. It is simply an acknowledgement of the truth that we are creatures, and a yielding to God so that he may take his rightful place in us.

Humility ought to be the chief mark of the uprightness of earnest Christians, of those who pursue and profess holiness. It is often said that this humility is lacking. One reason for this lack may be that in the teaching of the Church humility has never had the position of supreme importance which rightly belongs to it. And again, this oversight may be due to neglect of the truth that, although sin is indeed a strong motivation to humility, there is one of even wider and mightier influence. It makes even Jesus, the angels and the holiest saints in heaven humble. It is the knowledge that the first and chief mark of the relation of the creature to the Creator and the secret of his blessedness is the humility and nothingness which leaves God free to be all.

[From *Consecrated to God*]

Books by Andrew Murray

This is a list of Andrew Murray's books in English, with the publisher and date of the earliest edition traced in Britain or the United States of America.

Abide in Christ: thoughts on the blessed life of fellowship with the Son of God. Nisbet, 1882

Absolute surrender: addresses delivered in England and Scotland. Marshall, 1895.

Aids to devotion: thoughts on the Holy Spirit in the epistle to the Ephesians. Nisbet, 1910.

Back to Pentecost: the fulfilment of 'The Promise of the father' (Acts 1:4). Oliphants, 1918.

Be perfect! a message from the Father in heaven to his children on earth: meditations for a month. Nisbet, 1893.

The blood of the cross . . . a continuation of The power of the blood of Jesus. Marshall, Morgan and Scott, 1935.

Carnal and spiritual. Marshall, 1896. An address on 1 Corinthians 3:1-4.

The children for Christ: thoughts for Christian parents on the consecration of the home life. Nisbet, 1887.

The cleansed heart. Marshall, 1896.

The dearth of conversions. Marshall, 1897.

The deeper Christian life: an aid to its attainment. Chicago: Revell, 1896.

Divine healing: a series of addresses. New York: Christian Alliance, 1900?

Eagle wings. 1896. Sermons.

Faith that stands in the power of God. Marshall, 1896.

Foreign missions and the Week of Prayer. Jan. 5-12, 1902. Marshall, 1901.

The fruit of the vine. Marshall, 1898.

The full blessing of Pentecost: the one thing needful. Nisbet, 1908.

God's best secrets. Los Angeles: Biola, 1923.

Have faith in God. Philadelphia: Altemus, 1896.

Have mercy upon me: the prayer of the penitent in the fifty-first psalm explained and applied. Nisbet, 1895. Reprinted from the *South African Pioneer.*

The holiest of all: an exposition of the epistle to the Hebrews. New York: Revell, 1894?

Holy in Christ: thoughts on the calling of God's children to be holy as he is holy. New York: Randolph, 1888.

Humility: the beauty of holiness. Nisbet, 1895? Reprinted from the *South African Pioneer.*

In defence of the Boers. Oberlin, 1899?

In my name . . . Philadelphia, 1896.

The inner chamber and the inner life. Hodder and Stoughton, 1905.

Jesus himself. (Two . . . addresses.) Marshall, 1893.

A key to the missionary problem: thoughts suggested by the report of the Ecumenical Missionary Conference held in New York, April 1900. Nisbet, 1901.

The kingdom of God in South Africa: a survey of missions to the heathen, south of the Zambesi. Nisbet, 1906?

Let us draw nigh: the way to a life abiding continually in the secret of God's presence: meditations on Hebrews 10:19-25. Chicago: Revell, 1894.

Like Christ: thoughts on the blessed life of conformity to the Son of God: a sequel to Abide in Christ. Nisbet, 1884.

Lord, teach us to pray: a pocket book on prayer. Philadelphia: Altemus, 1896.

The Lord's table: a help to the right observance of the Holy Supper. Nisbet, 1897.

'Love delights to give.' Marshall, 1896.

'Love made perfect.' Marshall, 1894. Two addresses delivered at the South African Keswick Mission, 1893; also known as 'Perfect love'

'Made exceeding glad.' Nisbet, 1897. Memoir of William James Neethling.

The Master's indwelling. New York: Revell, 1896.

The ministry of intercession: a plea for more prayer. Nisbet, 1898.

Money: thoughts for God's stewards. Marshall, 1896.

The mystery of the true vine: meditations for a month. Nisbet, 1898.

The new life: words of God for young disciples of Christ. Nisbet, 1891.

Out of his fulness: addresses delivered in America. Nisbet, 1897.

Out of the grave a new life. Marshall, 1896. Address on Luke 23:29–43.

The pocket companion series. Morgan and Scott, 1914–27. Daily texts with commentary.

The power of the blood of Jesus. Marshall, Morgan and Scott, 1935. Translated from the Dutch edition of 1895.

The prayer life: the inner chamber and the deepest secret of Pentecost. Morgan and Scott, 1914.

The school of obedience: addresses at the students' convention at Stellenbosch, 28th to 31st July, 1898. Nisbet, 1898.

The Spirit of Christ: thoughts on the indwelling of the Holy Spirit in the believer and the Church. Nisbet, 1888.

The spiritual life: lectures delivered before the students of the Moody Bible Institute, Chicago. New York: Revell, 1895.

The state of the Church: a plea for more prayer. Nisbet, 1911.

The supreme need: in response to a call to the Church, in Mrs. Head's booklet, 'The forgotten friend.' Oliphants, 1918.

Three things the Christian needs to know. Marshall, 1896.

Thy will be done: the blessedness of a life in the will of God: meditations for a month. Nisbet, 1901.

The two covenants and the second blessing. New York: Revell, 1898.

Waiting on God! Nisbet, 1896.

'We can love all the day.' Marshall, 1896. Address on Galatians 5:22.

Why do you not believe?: words of instruction. Nisbet, 1894.

With Christ in the school of prayer: thoughts on our training for the ministry of intercession. Nisbet, 1886.

Within, or, The kingdom of God is within you. Service and Paton, 1897.

Working for God! a sequel to Waiting on God! Nisbet, 1901.

'Ye are the branches.' Marshall, 1896. Address on John 15:5.

Dates in Andrew Murray's Life

1828   Born in Graaff-Reinet, South Africa
1838   Family moves to Scotland
1845   Graduates from Aberdeen University
        Moves to Holland. Converted.
1848   Ordained minister of the Dutch Reformed Church
        Returns to South Africa
1850   Begins ministry in Bloemfontein
1856   Marries Emma Rutherfoord
1858   Publishes first book, a Life of Christ for children
1860   Begins ministry in Worcester
1864   Begins ministry in Cape Town
1871   Begins ministry in Wellington
1873   Founds the Huguenot Seminary
1877   Founds Mission Training Institute at Wellington
1880   Keswick Convention: receives fresh spiritual power
1882   Published first English book, *Abide in Christ*
1895   Addresses Keswick and Northfield Conventions
1906   Retires from active ministry
1917   Dies

HANDBOOKS OF PASTORAL CARE SERIES

General Editor: Marlene Cohen

This series is an aid for all involved in the pastoral ministry.
Informed by biblical theology, the series offers practical
resources for counselling while emphasizing the importance
of a wider context of care in which the Christian community,
prayer, preaching and nurture are essential to wellbeing and
growth. Details of the first volumes are given on the
following pages.

Growing Through Loss and Grief
Althea Pearson

All of life involves loss. Whether great or small, reactions to loss frequently follow a common pattern. From even minor experiences of loss, counsellors can gain valuable insight into major traumas such as redundancy, sexual abuse, marriage failure, declining health or bereavement.

From her extensive experience as a counsellor and trainer, Dr Althea Pearson also demonstrates that loss, however traumatic, always brings some measure of gain in its wake. Therefore, though tackling a subject which requires the greatest sensitivity on the part of the counsellor, *Growing Through Loss and Grief* helps to show the way to new understandings, fresh hope and new beginnings.

Setting Captives Free
Bruce A. Stevens

Setting Captives Free is based on the assumption that all truth is God's truth, and freely draws on the insights and therapy techniques from counselling theories, clinical psychology and psychiatry to inform and equip all who are involved in the pastoral ministry of the Church. Differentiating between individual, marital and group counselling, and the skills appropriate to each, Dr Stevens demonstrates the many opportunities for healing and growth that these varying styles offer.

Illustrated throughout with case studies on grief, depression, incest, marital conflict and self-esteem, and including a supplement on the complementary role of psychiatric medicine by Dr Ian Harrison, this highly practical guide will prove an invaluable resource.

HANDBOOKS OF PASTORAL CARE SERIES

Free To Love

Margaret Gill

Sexuality lies at the heart of our deepest human needs for companionship, intimacy and acceptance, yet through fear, ignorance and emotional hurts, it is often regarded as a sleeping snake, best left untouched. Many counsellors and pastoral carers are not sufficiently at ease with their own sexuality to help those experiencing sexual difficulties to the place of healing and freedom to which a full recognition of the God-givenness of sexuality can lead.

Free To Love brings together Margaret Gill's extensive experience as a medical doctor working in psychosexual medicine and as a Christian counsellor. Her deeply sensitive, wise and professional approach will be an invaluable guide to all aspects of sexual identity and experience encountered in pastoral care today.

DECEMBER 1994

Happy Families?

John and Olive Drane

The Christian Church's lofty teaching on family life all too often imposes unrealistic ideals, which tend to magnify the normal stresses felt by any family. A sense of guilt for failing to achieve perceived Christian standards often compounds other problems. When those problems are serious, denial is commonplace and yet another family is well on the way to being screwed up.

John and Olive Drane first question the evangelical definition of a family, looking beyond the Western nuclear family for a better model. Biblical characters who are often held up as shining examples are honestly appraised, and the stereotypic advice sometimes given by clergy is brought under critical review.

Sweeping these unhelpful, burdensome attitudes aside, the authors suggest a more realistic and compassionate way that the Church can affirm and support families.

John Drane is Director of the Centre for Christian Spirituality and Contemporary Society at the University of Stirling. The place of the family in the Church has long been a concern of John and his wife Olive, and they have co-authored several published articles on the subject.

SPRING 1995

For Better, For Worse
Mary and Bruce Reddrop

An extremely wise, sensitive and informed guide for Christian councelling dealing with marriage problems. Emphasis is given to the counsellors' own categories of thinking, Christian belief about marriage, appropriate and inappropriate psychological strategies, etc., with the goal of increasing counsellors' competence and self-understanding. Practical chapters deal with identifying root problems and their origins, biblical anthropology (and its various interpretations), the nature of marital breakdown, feelings and behaviour, causes of conflict, sexual difficulties, separation and divorce, counselling for change, and much more.

The Reddrops are a highly experienced team. Mary trained as a teacher and social worker and was Director of Family Life Education for the Marriage Guidance Council of Victoria before establishing her own private practice as a psychotherapist. She is also supervisor and trainer for the Anglican Marriage Guidance Council in Melbourne, of which her husband, Bruce, was Director for almost thirty years. He is also Founding President of the Australian Association of Marriage and Family Counsellors.

SPRING 1995